★ ★ ★ ★ ★ ★

THE AMERICAN COMPROMISE

George Bancroft, from an unretouched Brady photograph. Courtesy Library of Congress.

Francis Parkman. Courtesy Massachusetts Historical Society.

Henry Adams. Courtesy Harvard University Archives.

THE
AMERICAN
COMPROMISE

Theme and Method in the Histories of
Bancroft, Parkman, and Adams

★ ★ ★ ★ ★ ★

by Richard C. Vitzthum

UNIVERSITY OF OKLAHOMA PRESS : NORMAN

Library of Congress Cataloging in Publication Data

Vitzthum, Richard C.   1936–
    The American compromise.
    Bibliography: p.
    1. United States—Historiography. 2. Bancroft, George,
1800–1891. 3. Parkman, Francis, 1823–1893. 4. Adams, Henry,
1838–1918. I. Title.
E175.7.V57   973'.07'2024   73–7429
ISBN 0–8061–1142–9

for
MARCELLA

★ ★ ★ ★ ★ ★

Preface

To THOSE of us who would like to see the writing of history
regain the place it once held as one of the major forms of literary art, the lack of in-depth literary studies of the historical
classics poses an intriguing challenge. Close analysis of such
classics is next to nonexistent. During the past century historians have developed an awesome methodology with which to
test all kinds of historical evidence and the history written
from it, a methodology explained and scrutinized in scores of
handbooks, articles, and monographs. In contrast, criticism
of history as literature consists of a handful of essays. Designed to help redress the balance, this study explores the
major works of three nineteenth-century American historians
who saw the writing of history as high art.

What follows is at core literary criticism. Though I examine
Bancroft, Parkman, and Adams in critically conventional
ways and in ways no historian has yet, I believe, been ex-
amined, I focus throughout on explicating the texts of their
books. Of how many shortcomings such an approach to historiography can be guilty I think I am aware, though probably every reader of this book will discover new ones that
escaped me. To the colleagues, students, librarians, and
friends, too numerous to mention individually, who have in

one way or another helped me, most of the book's good points are due; its shortcomings are my responsibility alone.

I owe special thanks to the Maryland Research Board. Twice—once in the summer of 1968 and again in the summer of 1972—the board funded this project generously, for which I am deeply grateful.

Davidsonville, Maryland   RICHARD C. VITZTHUM

★ ★ ★ ★ ★ ★

Contents

★ ★ ★ ★ ★ ★

THE AMERICAN COMPROMISE

CHAPTER ONE

★ ★ ★ ★ ★ ★

The
E Pluribus Unum
Approach

As the nineteenth century slips farther and farther into the past, three of the American historians it produced loom increasingly large among their nineteenth-century co-workers.[1] Between 1834 and 1892, George Bancroft, Francis Parkman, and Henry Adams published some thirty volumes of American history that constitute perhaps the finest historical narrative yet written in America and, as a whole, one of the most interesting interpretations of the meaning of American civilization that we have. Although they have all received a fair amount of critical attention in recent years, the three have never been systematically studied in relation to each other.[2]

[1] Some indication of the weeding that has gone on during the past thirty-five years among nineteenth-century historians of America can be gained by comparing *Marcus W. Jernegan Essays in American Historiography* (ed. by William T. Hutchinson), first published in 1937, with *Pastmasters: Some Essays on American Historians* (ed. by Marcus Cunliffe and Robin W. Winks), published in 1969. Twelve of the twenty-one *Jernegan* essays deal with nineteenth-century historians, including ones on Bancroft, Parkman, and Adams. Only two of the thirteen *Pastmaster* essays, one on Parkman and one on Adams, do. I, of course, would argue that Bancroft deserved to be included in the *Pastmasters* collection.

[2] David Levin's *History as Romantic Art* has been the only serious effort to link the historians in any way, and of course Levin not only excludes Adams from his study but combines his analysis of Bancroft and Parkman with two writers, Prescott and Motley, who concentrated on non–North American subjects.

Yet I believe their histories form, within the canon of nine-teenth-century American historiography, a distinct tradition whose basic theme and method is suggested by the motto *e pluribus unum*.

From the many, one. Bancroft, in his ten-volume *History of the United States from the Discovery of the American Continent*, published between 1834 and 1874, traces the gradual centralization and unification of the colonies between their various foundings and their independence in 1782. Parkman, focusing first on the exploration and colonization of New France and then on the conflict between France and England for control of North America, shows how the centrifugal tendencies of the British colonies were halted enough during the French and Indian War to allow England to beat the centripetally organized colony of France to the north. The sprawling, powerful English colonies, so argues Parkman's nine-volume *France and England in North America*, published between 1865 and 1892, combined to overcome their far weaker morally and physically yet far more centralized antagonist. Adams' nine-volume *History of the United States During the Administrations of Jefferson and Madison* (1889–91) develops the thesis that the United States, committed by Jefferson in 1801 to a policy of national decentralization, was forced by domestic as well as foreign affairs more and more to unify and to assert its sovereignty until in the War of 1812 it defeated England's challenge to its national existence. All three see America's history as basically a conflict between separatist, decentralizing, anarchic forces on the one hand and unifying forces of central authority and sovereignty on the other.

They use the ability to wage successful war as the ultimate yardstick of political and social cohesion. Each takes one of the three major wars fought on North American soil before the Civil War and presents it as the culmination of his narrative. Thus Bancroft devotes the last four of his ten volumes to the War of Independence; Parkman ends his series with his big book, *Montcalm and Wolfe*, which recounts the French and Indian War; and Adams leads us up to the War of 1812 in his first five volumes, which then dominates the last four. Each of these wars, all of course won by the American side, serves not only as the climax of the story but as the conclusion of the theme of successful unification in the face of dissent and separatism. From the individualistic, at times almost inchoate, diversity of American society comes enough unity to save the society from collapse, a theme that so interests the three historians that they each write their histories in large part to account for it. Undoubtedly, the Union victory in the Civil War gave fresh personal meaning to the theme for all of them. With the three earlier wars they are able to give their own interpretations of the meaning of *e pluribus unum* impressive force.

Their interpretations differ; yet each writer clearly prefers the orderliness and efficiency of "oneness" to the potentially chaotic individualism of "manyness." They all interpret freedom as the chance to serve one's fellow man and one's country rather than one's self. Even Bancroft, sympathetic as he was to popular Jacksonian democracy, makes it clear again and again in the *History* that personal freedom must be interpreted as the reverse of selfishness. His last word, literally at the end of the last chapter of his last volume, is that "for success the liberty of the individual must know how to set itself bounds; and the states, displaying the highest quality of greatness, must learn to temper their rule of themselves by their own moderation."[3] Despite their devotion to American democracy, the historians are more interested in the men and institutions that govern it than they are in its grass-roots give and take: they concentrate on those who hold authority and who lead, not on the masses from which the authority and

---

[3] George Bancroft, *History of the United States from the Discovery of the American Continent*, X, 593. All subsequent references to the work will be to this, the first, edition.

leadership arises. It is the coming together in focal men and ideas of the power lying in the citizenry at large that dominates their narratives.

As a result, they tend to measure American history in terms of moral character. Invariably, the leaders who devote themselves to unifying and centralizing America and to asserting its sovereignty at one stage or another of its development are praised, while those who in any way encourage its disunity or decentralization are damned. As a rule, the success or failure of leaders in this sense is explained in terms of strength or weakness of moral fiber, with loyalty and sacrifice of self to the goal of united action the clearest sign of strength and private ambition the clearest sign of weakness. Yet Bancroft's, Parkman's, and Adams' interest in character goes beyond the individual to the character of Americans as a whole, and the historians' generalizations about the national character conform to their views of the proper relationship between unity and diversity in America. Insofar as Americans as a nation eschew private ambition, political disloyalty, or social anarchy, they are good; insofar as they fail to achieve moral or intellectual self-discipline, love of country, and dedication to the common good, they are bad. Portrayal of character, whether individual or national, is the historians' chief means of giving the theme of unity and diversity human significance.

Yet Bancroft, Parkman, and Adams are not ideologues trying to prove a thesis but historians trying to explain the actual events of early American history. Even Bancroft, with his notorious penchant for reading cosmic meaning into history, is, his philosophizing notwithstanding, surprisingly commonsensical and wary in his handling of much of his narrative. He shares with the others a powerful feeling for the untidiness of American history, and although he, unlike Parkman and Adams, finds the reason for America's achievement of nationhood in a benevolent overruling Providence, he makes it plain that on the human level, at least, it was a touch-and-go business, particularly during the Revolution. The works of all three hum with the conviction that America drifted, almost unconsciously, into nationality: the pressures that forced it to unify are often shown as being external rather than internal, providing barely enough momentum, usually in the nick of time, to nudge it out of danger. Yet this shapeless, lethargic, undisciplined civilization managed not merely to survive but to help revolutionize the world's political and social ideals. The fact intrigues the historians, who return to it again and again in their work. They explain it, finally, in terms of what they see as a peculiarly American genius for compromise.

Although the phrase *e pluribus unum* implies compromise, it connotes a pulling together of parts into unity which does not fully describe the kind of compromise Bancroft, Parkman, and Adams dramatize in their histories. Rather than following the circle pattern suggested by *e pluribus unum*, with the separate points on the circle's circumference radiating inward to a common center, they tend to conceptualize American compromise linearly, with polar, undesirable extremes at opposite ends of straight-line scales and a desirable balance between the extremes somewhere in the middle. Abstruse as it may sound, the distinction between the circular and linear concepts of compromise is important to an understanding of their histories. The *e pluribus unum*, circular idea connotes a certain inevitability about the unifying process, as though the many somehow gravitate automatically and without conscious effort into oneness. The linear concept, on the other hand, implies not only relentless conflict between the poles themselves but the possibility of dramatic lurches from the middle toward the extremes. All three historians interpret American history as an intensely dramatic journey along a narrow path of moderation between abysses of excess yawning on either side. Though they establish many polarities in their works, the one they all see as fundamental consists of anarchy, or complete diffusion and decentralization, at one extreme and tyranny—complete subordination and centralization—at the other. Between anarchy and tyranny, they argue, America has charted and must continue to chart a wary middle course.

Their faith in compromise gives their works an empirical, practical flavor which is also due in part to their thoroughness as scholars. All did an enormous amount of spadework in published and unpublished source material, with the result that their books are exhaustive and well informed enough to be valuable as basic narratives today. Yet there is more to their work with sources than a residue of scholarly common sense in the tone of their books. The thought, form, and phrasing of source material saturates their pages to an extent unknown in twentieth-century historiography. R. G. Collingwood, one of the handful of modern commentators to concern themselves at all with pre-twentieth-century techniques of assimilating sources, has called the nineteenth-century method "scissors and paste" history.[4] Bancroft, Parkman, and Adams were certainly all scissors-and-paste historians. But within that general historiographical tradition they were direct heirs to the eighteenth- and early nineteenth-century American annalist-plagiarist school that George H. Callcott has recently analyzed.[5] Callcott shows that virtually all American historians in Bancroft's day regarded verbatim copying of sentences, paragraphs, and even whole chapters from prior histories without acknowledgement and the rewriting of quoted material as completely legitimate practices. The histories of Bancroft, Parkman, and Adams constitute a unique methodological phase between this earlier, analist-plagiarist approach and the monographic, analytical, anti-scissors-and-paste approach that has dominated American historiography in the twentieth-century.

[4] *The Idea of History*, 257–61.
[5] *History in the United States 1800–1860*, 128–38.

If its political connotations are set aside, the *e pluribus unum* label can be used to describe their method as well as their theme. The "many" in this case are the hundreds of documents, letters, narratives and other pieces of evidence from which each historian drew his narrative. The "one" is the unified, idiosyncratic narrative he himself created. In this sense, the consistency between historical theme and historiographical method in their works is remarkable. Just as it is their basic aim to recount and to applaud the gradual crystallization of the diffuse particles of American society into a unified nation, so is it their method to discipline the veritable babel of voices speaking to them from their sources into a single, characteristic authorial voice. What is most intriguing in all this from a literary point of view is the persistence with which, page after page, chapter after chapter, volume after volume, they incorporate the very language of their sources into their prose even as they obliterate its tone and conform it to their own. Some preliminary comments on the technique, which I call paraphrasing, may forestall later misunderstandings.

Although the term "paraphrasing" normally refers to passages that merely restate a source's ideas or information in different words, I have broadened it for the purposes of this study to include passages in which verbal and syntactical echoes of source material can be heard. In the works of the three historians, paraphrases are often very similar to their originals, and to some it may seem that much of what I call paraphrasing in their histories is pure and simple plagiarism. I take that chance because it seems to me that paraphrasing, as Bancroft, Parkman, and Adams use it, does not deserve the reprimand conveyed by the terms "plagiarism" or "scissors and paste history." Paraphrasing was one of their most useful and artistically interesting methods, allowing them freedom to maneuver yet at the same time to follow their evidence closely. To disqualify paraphrasing on the grounds that it is unimaginative or even immoral is not only to underrate its

9

literary potential but to place a needless burden on the narrative historian who may want to use it. If he is denied the paraphrase, as for instance Collingwood would seem to wish, he is forced into the awkward and unnatural position of having to erase all signs of individual documents, aside from quotations, from his work, like a thief covering his tracks. Bancroft, Parkman, and Adams felt no such pressure. For them, the most telling advantage of the paraphrase seems to have been that it gave them an excellent means for compromising between the old annalist-plagiarist tradition of adhering closely to the best historical "authorities" available and their own nineteenth-century ambition to be original literary artists. Here again the key idea is compromise. Between total adherence to and total dismissal of the documents each historian pursues a methodological middle way. For us, their paraphrasing provides a window, as it were, into the line-by-line and page-by-page composition of much of their histories, allowing us an unusual view of how three masters of the craft actually wrote their narratives.

Bancroft's, Parkman's, and Adams' histories constitute, thus, a tradition characterized by what might be roughly termed an *e pluribus unum* approach both in theme and in method. Yet any tradition, historiographical or otherwise, always reveals disagreement, change, and development as much as it does uniformity, and the factors separating the three historians are no less important than those connecting them. To be sure, the lives the three led were at least in some ways similar. All were acquainted as adults; all were New Englanders, educated at Harvard; all were deeply influenced by their Puritan heritage; and all chose to write history about the American past. Yet Adams and Parkman were by birth independently wealthy, while Bancroft had to make his fortune; Bancroft and Adams left New England as relatively young men and centered much of their lives in Washington, while Parkman lived in or near Boston to his death; Adams was the great-grandson and grandson of U.S. presidents, yet of the three Bancroft alone aspired to and gained high political office; Parkman and Adams were agnostics, while Bancroft was a deeply committed, if hard to define, Christian; Adams did his work in American history in a twenty-year span in the middle of his life and went on to other kinds of literary enterprise afterwards, while Bancroft and Parkman concentrated on history throughout their adult lives. More important, though Adams studied Bancroft's and Parkman's histories and Bancroft not only praised both Parkman and Adams as historians but in the 1880's read and commented on Adams' *History* before it was published commercially, none of the three was the disciple or master of either of the others. So unlike are their histories, in fact, that it is understandable why no study firmly linking them has yet been undertaken. It is the aim of this one to present the evidence for such a linkage from a source that is, after all is said and done, the most interesting and reliable we have: the histories themselves.

11

CHAPTER TWO

★ ★ ★ ★ ★ ★

Freedom, Union, and Providence

THE TRADITION began in 1832 or 1833 at the moment when George Bancroft finally decided to write a history of the United States from the beginnings to his own day. He had been looking for a life's work from the time he set sail from Boston in 1818, at the age of seventeen, to study at Göttingen. By New Year's Day, 1822, six months before he returned to America, he seems to have made up his mind to follow the usual career pattern of bright but poor Harvard scholars and become a minister,[1] but a few months back in Boston convinced him not only that he was not to take the pulpit by storm but that teaching Greek at Harvard was not to his taste. During the same period he wrote and published a book of poems that he himself sensed were poor: later he tried to buy up and destroy all the copies. So with Joseph Cogswell he set out to found the Round Hill School in Northampton, Massachusetts, along the lines of the Prussian *Gymnasium*, only to lose interest in the project and by 1830 to sell his share in the school to Cogswell. Since returning from Europe he had been writing essays and reviews for Jared Sparks and the *North Atlantic Review* and translating German grammars and scholarly works, but none of this foreshadowed his approaching dedi-

[1] Russell B. Nye, *George Bancroft: Brahmin Rebel*, 55.

12

cation to American history. For reasons that will probably never be completely clear,[2] he made up his mind in the early 1830's to become a historian, and in 1834 the first volume of his *History of the United States from the Discovery of the American Continent* came off the press.

His commitment to the *History* was for life. Though the progress of the work was uneven, interrupted as it was in the 1840's and again in the 1860's and 1870's by Bancroft's appointments to cabinet and ambassadorial posts, it was steady. By 1874, forty years after he began, he had the tenth volume finished in time for a centenary edition of the whole work in 1876. Two additional volumes, *History of the Formation of the Constitution of the United States of America*, appeared in 1882, and until he died in 1891 he was working on historical projects. His political adventures, beginning with his plunge into the Massachusetts Democratic party in the thirties, continuing with his appointment by Polk as secretary of the navy and then ambassador to England in the forties, and ending in the sixties and seventies with his appointment by Andrew Johnson as ambassador to Prussia, seem to have had little effect on the coherence and continuity of the work as a whole. They did, of course, play a part in forcing him to reduce his goal of bringing the narrative up to the present to the more realistic one of ending it with the Revolutionary War. He simply lacked the time to finish his initial plan. Yet as they stand the ten volumes present a unified story of America's colonization by, conflict with, and ultimate separation from England. Together with the two-volume *History of the Constitution*, they chronicle the growth of the United States from an atomistic collection of colonies to a sovereign nation.

In some ways, the political interruptions helped Bancroft in writing the *History*. In the forties and again in the sixties his jobs in high office opened for him countless doors to manu-

2 *Ibid.*, 94; John Spencer Bassett, *The Middle Group of American Historians*, 177 f.

13

script materials in both America and Europe. Although John Spencer Bassett may have been right in saying that "Bancroft did not make the best use of the material at his disposal,"[3] Bancroft at least had opportunities, enjoyed by no other American historian of his generation, to look the material over. Primary documents of all kinds flooded into his study after 1845, giving him a knowledgeableness about his subject that helps explain why a basically unsympathetic critic has recently called him "a formidable historian."[4] Then, too, the interruptions seemed to have whetted his appetite for writing. He was very impatient, for example, to start work on Volume IV in 1849 when he got back from London, and within five years he finished three volumes, the most concentrated output of his career.

Whether in the broader sense of political creed his career in politics influenced his history is a harder question to answer. If it did, the influence was complete before he wrote Volume I, for there is no evidence of change in the political orientation of the volumes thereafter. That the *History* shows a Jacksonian, "common man" bias from beginning to end has been plain to most of its readers, but whether the bias—it is of course more than that, in fact a reasonably complete philosophical system—was on the one hand the cause or on the other the result of Bancroft's involvement with the Democratic party during the early thirties is an arguable point. Those best qualified to judge have approached the problem cautiously.[5] We are perhaps safest in assuming that no clear cause-and-effect relationship existed and that Bancroft's Democratic politics and the Jacksonian flavor of the *History* flowed together from a common source of conviction that crystallized sometime in the 1820's and early 1830's.

[3] *Middle Group*, 206.
[4] Richard Hofstadter, *The Progressive Historians: Turner, Beard, Parrington*, 16.
[5] See Bassett, *Middle Group*, 166–73, and Nye, *Brahmin Rebel*, 83–100.

At the heart of that conviction and the interpretation of early American history to which it led in the *History* lie the themes of freedom and union.[6] In his introduction to the first volume, Bancroft remarks that an "immense concourse of emigrants of the most various lineage is perpetually crowding to our shores; and the principles of liberty, uniting all interests by the operation of equal laws, blend the discordant elements into harmonious union."[7] The idea here implied that, far from contradicting each other, the centrifugal drive toward freedom and the centripetal drive toward union in America somehow harmonize is voiced throughout the *History*. In his preface to Volume IX, for example, published thirty-two years later in 1866, Bancroft offers the book "reverently on the altar of freedom and union,"[8] again suggesting that freedom and union are complementary. Whenever he uses the terms in this way, however, it is important to see that he means them in an *e pluribus unum*, individuals-on-the-circumference-gravitating-centerward sense. Freedom and union are not extremes between which a happy medium lies but are rather the happy medium itself. They represent the end result of a process of compromise. They are for all practical purposes equivalent in meaning, a kind of formula for all that Bancroft values in American civilization.

Yet there is no question that, beyond the cheerful sphere of light radiating from America's unique blend of freedom and union, Bancroft is aware of dark and menacing contradictions. The eighth volume contains a key passage, one of the

---

[6] Russell B. Nye, in a recent survey of Bancroft's thought (*George Bancroft*, Great American Thinkers Series, 157–59), identifies freedom and Providence as the *History's* two controlling themes. While granting its great importance in the *History*, I would call Providence more an assumption than a theme. Yet the disagreement may be more semantic than substantive; I agree completely with what Nye has to say, pp. 75–92, concerning Bancroft's belief in compromise, and I also see Providence as central to Bancroft's system, as I explain later.

[7] *History*, I, 3.

[8] *Ibid.*, IX, 5.

most revealing in the *History*, that voices this deeper awareness unequivocally. "Society," says Bancroft,

is many and is one; and the organic unity of the state is to be reconciled with the separate existence of each of its members. Law which restrains all, and freedom which adheres to each individual, and the mediation which adjusts and connects these two conflicting powers, are ever present as constituent ingredients; each of which, in its due proportion is essential to the well being of a state, and is ruinous when it passes its bounds. It has been said that the world is governed too much; no statesman has ever said that there should be no government at all. Anarchy is at one extreme, and the pantheistic despotism, which is the absorption of the people into one man as the sovereign, at the other. All governments contain the two opposite tendencies; and were either attraction or repulsion, central power or individuality, to disappear, civil order would be crushed or dissolved.[9]

Although America may have succeeded in creating one from many, society at large, Bancroft here asserts, "is many and is one"—the many cannot be completely homogenized. Individual freedom does not inevitably lead to cooperation. In the form of anarchy and despotism, freedom and union are appalling dangers between which the ship of state must inch its way. America's political development between the beginning and 1782 is a unique historical case, an extraordinary compromise between mutually repulsive extremes. Speaking of the state of the nation in 1777, Bancroft says the "child that was then born was cradled between opposing powers of evil; if it will live, its infant strength must strangle the twin serpents of separatism and central despotism."[10]

In the one form or the other, either as desirable compromises or as undesirable extremes, freedom and union dominate the *History*. In the first three volumes, which narrate the story of the colonies to 1748, Bancroft isolates the colonial

[9] *Ibid.*, VIII, 118.
[10] *Ibid.*, IX, 451.

charters, the limitless possibilities of free enterprise, and the tradition of English liberties as the major sources of the American tradition of freedom. Then in Volume IV he shows how the war against France in Canada led not only to the unification of the colonies in a common cause but ultimately to the removal of the French threat from the north which had tended to make the colonies dependent on England. Volumes V and VI, recounting the increasing tension between England and America in the decade 1763–1774, are designed to show the colonies gradually uniting against England, first over the Stamp Act controversy of 1766 and then in the series of commercial battles culminating in England's Penal Acts against Massachusetts in 1774. Finally, in the seventh, eighth, ninth, and tenth volumes, open fighting breaks out, independence from England is declared, and the new states begin groping their way, by means of the Articles of Confederation, toward political union. He is at pains, especially in the final four volumes, to show that the process of unification was slow and inductive, growing out of the actual experiences and needs of the colonists and not from abstract theories. It was their deeply ingrained sense of freedom that led them to revolution and their slowly matured sense of community that led them to union.

Bancroft's treatment of the freedom-union theme, despite his somewhat florid and oratorical manner, is on the whole surprisingly sober and intelligent. The colonists revolted from England and set up a representative, federative government, he argues, because they took freedom and independence for granted and found England's rule irksome from the first and finally intolerable. He is keenly aware, for instance, of the importance of economic factors in the history of the colonies, and his treatment of these factors is remarkably astute and free of cant. Two ideas dominate his discussion of economics. One is that the political success of the British colonies was the result in large part of their success in subduing and cultivating the wilderness. The other is that the whole mercantilist system of restrictive trade was so detrimental to the colonies that it forced them to break away from England and establish a policy of free trade. Both ideas, of course, have since become standard interpretations of the period. And both are fundamental to Bancroft's concept of a uniquely American liberty. The wilderness emerges in passage after passage, especially in the earlier volumes, as "useless magnificence" and "fruitless fertility"[11] waiting for the fructifying hand of the colonist. Near the end of Volume III, contrasting French and English efforts along these lines, Bancroft points to the fact that

> still the valley of the Mississippi was nearly a wilderness. All its [French] patrons . . . had not accomplished for it, in half a century, a tithe of the prosperity which, within the same period, sprung naturally from the benevolence of William Penn to the peaceful settlers on the Delaware. The progress of the Anglo-American colonies was advanced, not by anticipating strife with the natives, but by the progress of industry.[12]

According to Bancroft, the key to such progress was always, in town as well as on the frontier, economic *laissez-faire*: "Manhattan began to prosper, when its merchants obtained freedom to follow the impulses of their own enterprise."[13] The New World offered a unique field for free enterprise which the English colonies alone adequately exploited.

These lessons of economic liberty, learned in the American wilderness, doomed the imperial, mercantilistic system of restrictive trade. Bancroft argues not only that "the great topic of variance between England and her continental colonies of America, lay in the mercantile system and its conse-

---

[11] *Ibid.,* II, 266 f.

[12] *Ibid.,* III, 369.

[13] *Ibid.,* II, 294. The virtues of *laissez-faire* capitalism are especially stressed in Volume I. See, for example, pp. 161 and 340 on the economic arrangements in the Virginia and Plymouth colonies.

quences"[14] but further that when the colonies broke away in 1776, "[a]bsolute free trade took the place of hoary restrictions."[15] Benjamin Franklin's "truly American heart" always drove him away from mercantilism toward "the more agreeable system of economy that promised to the world freedom of commerce, a brotherhood of the nations, and mutual benefits from mutual prosperity."[16] Yet for all their brotherliness and egalitarianism Americans never violated each other's property rights: they "were industrious and frugal; accustomed to the cry of liberty and prosperity, they harbored no dream of a community of goods; and their love of equality never degenerated into envy of the rich."[17] Their revolution succeeded in freeing the American capitalist from the shackles of medieval economics.

At the same time, Bancroft has no illusions about entrepreneurial morality. Although all ten volumes support the idea that "legislation, though it can favor industry, cannot create it,"[18] they also insist that the ends of the political state are in some ways profoundly inconsistent with those of the economic corporation. "A corporation," he says,

whether commercial or proprietary, is, perhaps, the worst of sovereigns. Gain is the object, which leads to the formation of those companies, and which constitutes the interest, most likely to be fostered. . . . [C]orporate ambition is deaf to mercy, and insensible to shame.[19]

He denounces the slave trade from beginning to end of the *History* as an unpardonable corruption of economic freedom. His condemnation of the Toryism that came to power in England in the 1760's and 1770's rests on similar grounds. "The tory party took the law as it stood," he argues,

[14] *Ibid.*, III, 390.
[15] *Ibid.*, VIII, 323.
[16] *Ibid.*, IV, 368.
[17] *Ibid.*, IX, 257 f.
[18] *Ibid.*, I, 191.
[19] *Ibid.*, I, 198 f.

19

and set itself against reform. . . . The moneyed interest . . . was to become its ally. . . . Woe hangs over the land where the absolute principles of private law are applied to questions of public law; and the effort is made to bar the progress of the undying race by the despotic rules which ascertain the rights of property of evanescent mortals.[20]

Again, looking beneath the rhetoric to the substance of what Bancroft is saying, we find here solid awareness of the contradictions of human experience. The state is obliged to regulate the private freedom of its members for the public good. Individual liberty and collective constraint often contradict each other.

Bancroft's interpretation of the colonies' political development is in general as sober and realistic as his interpretation of their economic history. His basic argument is that "wise legislation is the enacting of proper laws at proper times; and no criterion is so nearly infallible as the fair representation of the interest to be affected." [21] He blames the failure of legislation like that imposed on the Carolinas by the original proprietors and John Locke on the fact that "the constitution of Carolina was invented in England"[22] and did not, like the political institutions of the other colonies, develop from the needs and experiences of the people living under it. The breaking away from England and the forming of the Republic were essentially the products of circumstance, experience, and expediency. "The republic was to America a godsend," he says:

It came, though unsought, because society contained the elements of no other organization. Here, and in that century, here only, was a people, which, by its education and large and long experience, was prepared to act as the depository and carrier of all political power. America developed her choice from within herself; and therefore it is, that, conscious of following an inner law, she never

20 *Ibid.*, V, 419.
21 *Ibid.*, I, 205.
22 *Ibid.*, II, 128.

made herself a spreader of her system, where the conditions of success were wanting.[23]

America's "inner law" emerges from the *History* as the law of majority rule and the habit of governing and legislating on the basis of compromise among conflicting interest groups. Bancroft traces "the prevailing idea of political life in the United States" to very practical motives: "On the one hand, [the states] continued the institutions received from England with as little immediate change as possible; and on the other, they desired for their constitutions a healthy, continuous growth."[24] Admittedly, his fondness for America's slow political mellowing sometimes spills over into glutinous imagery: at one point he says the colonists' habits of freedom and independence "were not planted or watered by the hand of man; they grew like the lilies, which neither toil nor spin."[25] Although he gives his interpretation large doses of romantic and providential enthusiasm that will be discussed shortly, he manages by and large to convey a cool and persuasive sense of the realities of colonial and revolutionary politics.

One reason for this is that despite his frequent statements of faith in democracy and the common man he also implies that the masses must be trained for self-government. In America, he argues, such training did generally take place, but unevenly and with notable lapses. In seventeenth-century Virginia, for instance, the ruling oligarchy refused to support public education. To this Bancroft snaps: "The instinct of liberty may create popular institutions; they cannot be preserved in their integrity except by the conscious intelligence of the people."[26] After applauding William Penn's constitution for the Quaker colony, he adds the curiously deflating remark that "folly and passion, not less than justice and wis-

23 *Ibid.*, VIII, 474.
24 *Ibid.*, IX, 282.
25 *Ibid.*, III, 396.
26 *Ibid.*, II, 191.

dom, had become enfranchised on the Delaware."[27] Explaining why the colonies, after separating from England, resisted unification, he says the "public mind is of slow growth, and had not yet attained the wisdom necessary for regenerating its government."[28] An undercurrent of distrust of man contradicts the flow of optimistic confidence in human perfectibility which sweeps through the *History*. An outburst like "Who denies that the heart of man is deceitful and desperately wicked?"[29] is atypical, yet it tends to confirm less violent comments, such as "How has history been made the memorial of the passionate misdeeds of men of mediocrity?"[30] or "Greatness in the affairs of man is closely attended by that which is mean and low"[31] or "From the nature of man, imperfection clings to all the works of his hands."[32] Although the undercurrent is not strong enough to more than blunt the optimistic thrust of the *History* as a whole, it justifies the feeling of some of Bancroft's readers that his view of mankind was at core more conservative than the general tone of the *History* suggests.[33]

A passage that epitomizes the realistic, empirical, moderate side of Bancroft's interpretation of early American history occurs in Volume IX, where, in trying to explain the significance of the 1777 Articles of Confederation, he not only criticizes the public attitudes that produced them but clarifies his interpretation of the unique relationship between freedom and union in American political experience:

According to the American theory, the unity of the colonies had, before the declaration of independence, resided in the British king. The congress of the United States was the king's successor, and it

27 *Ibid.*, 402.
28 *Ibid.*, IX, 47.
29 *Ibid.*, III, 35.
30 *Ibid.*, 441.
31 *Ibid.*, IV, 339.
32 *Ibid.*, IX, 283.
33 Nye, *Brahmin Rebel*, 306; Hofstadter, *Progressive Historians*, 18 f.

inherited only such powers as the colonies themselves acknowledged to have belonged to the crown. . . . The confederacy was formed under the influence of political ideas which had been developed by a contest of centuries for individual and local liberties against an irresponsible central authority. Now that power passed to the people, new institutions were required strong enough to protect the state, while they should leave untouched the liberties of the individual. But America, misled by what belonged to the past, took for her organizing principle the principle of resistance to power, which in all the thirteen colonies had been hardened into stubbornness by a succession of common jealousies and struggles.[34]

This is a perceptive statement, marred little by the straining for rhetorical effect or the grandiose philosophizing that often creeps into Bancroft's prose. Most interesting, perhaps, is the resolution it suggests of the idea that in America freedom complemented union with the idea that in general freedom and union are incompatible. Americans had never, Bancroft implies, been free in an anarchic sense at all. Before the Revolution, their tendency to cohere around a central authority had been expressed in their loyalty to the king; after the Revolution, they gave to the confederation roughly that same loyalty. Yet their traditions of English liberty, their peculiar geographical position, their political status as colonies, and their historical experience had produced a political, social, economic, and cultural context different from—and more anarchic than—the Anglo-European pattern of centralization. While the Articles of Confederation embodied the past experience of the colonies almost perfectly, they were inadequate to the present and future demands of American unification. The colonies' tradition of union—of loyalty to a central authority—was as deep and strong as their tradition of independence, and within seven years of the end of the War of Independence the two traditions were to merge in the Constitution.

[34] *History*, IX, 437.

In economic and political terms, then, Bancroft's interpretation of the relationship between diffusion and centralization in early America often seems quite sophisticated and convincing. In religious and philosophical terms, however, it equally often seems simplistic, strident, chauvinistic. From the opening pages of the *History* on, we are never allowed to forget for long that a benevolent, progress-minded deity rules history. The final lines of Volume II pledge that in succeeding volumes "we shall still see that the selfishness of evil defeats itself, and God rules in the affairs of men"[35]—and the pledge is kept. The complexity of Indian language is attributed in Volume III to "a Power higher than that of man."[36] Than in the founding and growth of the American colonies, we are told at the beginning of the fourth volume, "God never showed more visibly his gracious providence and love."[37] Volume VII opens by defining the Revolution as a "change which Divine Wisdom ordained, and which no human policy or force could hold back."[38] Volume VIII recommends "those inspirations of the beautiful and the good, which lift the soul above the interests of the moment, demonstrate our affinity with something higher than ourselves, point the way to principles that are eternal, and constitute the vital element of progress";[39] and Volume X avows that there is "in the world a force tending to improvement, and making itself felt within us and around us, with which we can work, but which exists independently of us, and which it is above our ability to call into being or to destroy."[40]

The central articles of this religious faith are not easy to define. By his own admission, Bancroft was deeply impressed by his reading of Jonathan Edwards while he was a

[35] *Ibid.*, II, 468.
[36] *Ibid.*, III, 265.
[37] *Ibid.*, IV, 15.
[38] *Ibid.*, VII, 21.
[39] *Ibid.*, VIII, 117.
[40] *Ibid.*, X, 366.

student at Harvard. Throughout his life he claimed that "Edwards' was his creed,"[41] and in the *History* he argues that Edwards had taught New England to understand God primarily as Love rather than Wrath and to see Him as the source of "happiness, of human perfectibility, and of human liberty."[42] Moreover, Bancroft seems to find in Edwards' thought justification for his own concept of progress. He ranks Edwards' theory of progress above those of other eighteenth-century progress philosophers:

In America, the first conception of [progress'] office, in the mind of Jonathan Edwards, though still cramped and perverted by theological forms not derived from observation, was nobler than the theory of Vico: more grand and general than the method of Bossuet, it embraced in its outline the whole "work of redemption,"—the history of the influence of all moral truth in the gradual regeneration of humanity.[43]

Several of Bancroft's central ideas—his faith in progress superintended by a benevolent deity, his concept of America as a chosen nation, and his view of history as the gradual unfolding of divine decree—can be traced back to the New England Puritan tradition, for which Edwards is his chief spokesman.

Yet the differences between Bancroft's melioristic, intuitionalistic faith and Edwards' orthodox, rationalistic Calvinism are always sharp, and it is hard to be sure that at all times the theism of the *History* is actually Christian. Bancroft's God, for all His goodwill and providence, is an extremely vague and generalized being. At some points He seems to be little more than simple fate—than the mere consecution, that is, of events in time—as when Bancroft apostrophizes "Happy America! to which Providence gave the tranquillity neces-

[41] Nye, *Brahmin Rebel*, 28. In his later book *George Bancroft*, Nye offers a valuable discussion of Bancroft's religious ideas, pp. 127–35.
[42] *History*, IV, 155.
[43] *Ibid.*, III, 399.

sary for her growth, as well as the trials which were to discipline her for action."[44] Although perhaps Protestant in the sense that He does not seem to require formal, ritualistic worship, Bancroft's God is definitely not Protestant in a theological sense. "Protestantism is not humanity," Bancroft says at one point; "its name implies a party struggling to throw off some burdens of the past, and ceasing to be a renovating principle when its protest shall have succeeded."[45] Despite his disapproval of the feudal trappings of Catholicism, Bancroft sees it as commendable: "The Catholic church asserted the unity, the universality and the unchangeableness of truth; and this principle, however it may have been made subservient to ecclesiastical organization, tyranny, or superstition, rather demanded than opposed universal emancipation and brotherhood."[46] Yet in the *History*, Christianity itself sometimes seems to be merely one manifestation of an instinct in all men toward religious faith. Christianity is a truth, Bancroft suggests, but not the whole truth. "To have asserted clearly the unity of mankind," he says, "was the distinctive glory of the Christian religion,"[47] yet he implies that other religions have already contributed and may in the future contribute as much to mankind. The same tone is audible in the remark that it was "the common people, whose craving for the recognition of the unity of the universe and for a perfect mediator between themselves and the Infinite, bore the Christian religion to its triumph over every worldly influence."[48] Mankind gave the religion its authority, he seems to say, not the other way round.

However he interpreted Christianity, Bancroft nonetheless seems to have had no doubt that absolutely fixed moral laws were everywhere at work in the cosmos. "[T]he laws of the

[44] *Ibid.*, 371 f.
[45] *Ibid.*, IV, 271.
[46] *Ibid.*, VII, 158.
[47] *Ibid.*, IV, 7.
[48] *Ibid.*, VIII, 248.

moral world are unyielding"[49] and "Justice and Truth are the same, everywhere, at all times and for every mind"[50] are the kind of statements that, however startling they may sound to a modern historian, seem bland in comparison with others, such as the following, which Bancroft offers from time to time: "For it always holds true, that Heaven plants division in the councils of the enemies of freedom."[51] It is the argument that moral laws are immutable which Bancroft follows when he defends the concept of natural rights enunciated in the Declaration of Independence. The Revolution, he says, "was destined on every side to lead to the solution of the highest questions of state. Principles of eternal truth, which in their universality are superior to sects and separate creeds, were rapidly effacing the prejudices of the past."[52] Because they were superior to particular religions, Bancroft says, such principles received a sort of absolute expression in the Declaration of Independence:

The bill of rights which [the Declaration] promulgates, is of rights that are older than human institutions, and spring from the eternal justice that is anterior to the state. . . . The heart of Jefferson in writing the declaration, and of congress in adapting it, beat for all humanity; the assertion of right was made for the entire world of mankind and all coming generations, without any exception whatever; for the proposition which admits of exceptions can never be self-evident.[53]

The passage contains much discountable rhetorial flourish, of course, yet the phrase "without any exception whatsoever" is uncompromising. Bancroft really seems to believe that the Declaration reveals truths that are eternally valid.

Accordingly, his notion of progress must be understood as

[49] *Ibid.*, II, 168.
[50] *Ibid.*, X, 65 f.
[51] *Ibid.*, IV, 66.
[52] *Ibid.*, VII, 155 f.
[53] *Ibid.*, VIII, 472.

change moving along tracks of fixed moral law and propelled by an absolute, guiding intelligence. Though not millennialist in a doctrinal Christian sense, it has strong affinites with the American millennialist tradition outlined by Ernest Tuveson in a recent study,[54] and the view of the universe it implies seems to be one of order and stasis rather than expansive, open-ended dynamism. In and of itself, Bancroft's idea of progress reflects the ebullient mood of mid-nineteenth-century America; but in the *History* it is tied to a religious conservatism so peculiar and, in light of the generally liberal tone of the work, so unexpected that it has generally escaped the analysis it invites. Obviously, Bancroft's religious doctrines are not rigorous or dogmatic. His theism, as has already been suggested, may not even be specifically Christian. What *is* dogmatic is his insistence that religious faith itself—faith, that is, in some kind of supernatural, providential being—is absolutely necessary to the well-being of mankind. Infidelity and skepticism are the *bêtes noirs* of the *History*. Almost without exception, Bancroft blames what he seems to see as the curse of modern secularism on the English empirical tradition including, among others, Bacon, Locke, and Hume, and on Frenchmen like Descartes and Voltaire, and he sees the eighteenth century as epitomizing a materialism and sensualism that are the reverse of true religiosity.

As is well known, the key to Bancroft's stand is his sympathy with the transcendental idealism developed in Germany by Kant, Fichte, Hegel, and others in protest against the eighteenth-century tradition of rationalism and empiricism and transported to America through Coleridge and Carlyle by Emerson and others in the New England transcendental movement, though Bancroft himself doubtless cut short the process of cultural transmission to some extent through his study

---

[54] *Redeemer Nation: The Idea of America's Millennial Role.* See especially Chaps. IV and V, pp. 91–186.

in Germany between 1818 and 1822.[55] Central to this movement was the idea that men have an innate, intuitive faculty which enables them to perceive a realm of truth beyond that available to the senses and common understanding. Affirmations that individual men possess such an instinct saturate the *History*. "Man feels that he is a dependent being," we are told. "The reverence for universal laws is implanted in his nature too deeply to be removed."[56] Or: "From the depths of man's consciousness, which envelopes sublimer truths than the firmament over his head can reveal to his senses, rises the idea of right."[57] Part and parcel of this general moral instinct is a special instinct for religion. "Atheism is the folly of the metaphysician, not the folly of human nature. . . . Men revolt against the oppressions of superstition, the exactions of ecclesiastical tyranny, but never against religion itself."[58] One of the things that interested Bancroft most about the Indians was their presumably universal adherence to some sort of religion. "It is natural to the human mind," he says, "to desire immortality; the natives of Carolina believed in continued existence after death and in retributive justice."[59] There were no atheists in a wigwam: "Infidelity never clouded [the Indian's] mind; the shadows of skepticism never darkened his faith."[60]

[55] For a general discussion of the German-American cultural flow during the period, see Henry A. Pochmann, *German Culture in America: Philosophical and Literary Influences 1600–1900*. For discussions of Bancroft's specific debt to German thought, see Nye, *Brahmin Rebel*, 100f., and *George Bancroft*, 110ff. and 125ff.; J. W. Rathbun, "George Bancroft on Man and History," *Transactions of the Wisconsin Academy of Sciences, Arts, and Letters*, Vol. XLIII (1954), 54; and F. L. Burwick, "The Göttingen Influence on George Bancroft's Idea of Humanity," *Jahrbuch für Amerikastudien*, Vol. XI (1966), 194–212. David W. Noble argues in *Historians Against History* that Bancroft's attack on Enlightenment thought stemmed as much from his New England Puritan background as from his contact with German idealism (pp. 18–36).

[56] *History*, III, 73.

[57] *Ibid.*, VIII, 117.

[58] *Ibid.*, I, 484f.

[59] *Ibid.*, 112.

[60] *Ibid.*, III, 288.

Bancroft's most elaborate presentation of the idea occurs in Volume II in his chapter on Quakerism. Treating the Quaker doctrine of the Inner Light as though it were virtually synonymous with his own belief in moral intuition, he concludes that for the Quaker

[e]very moral truth exists in every man's and woman's heart, as an incorruptible seed; the ground may be barren, but the seed is certainly there. . . . The Quaker is no materialist; truth and conscience are not in the laws of countries; they are not one thing at Rome, and another at Athens; they cannot be abrogated by senate or people.[61]

In a revealing passage he contrasts a major spokesman for the Quakers, William Penn, against a major spokesman of British empiricism, John Locke, in a series of point-by-point comparisons:

Locke sought truth through the senses and the outward world; Penn looked inward to the divine revelations in every mind. Locke compared the soul to a sheet of white paper, . . . on which time and chance might scrawl their experience; to Penn, the soul was an organ which of itself instinctively breathes divine harmonies. . . . Locke derives the idea of infinity from the senses, describes it as purely negative, and attributes it to nothing but space, duration, and number; Penn derived the idea from the soul, and ascribed it to truth, and virtue, and God.[62]

Throughout the *History*, Bancroft's hostility to eighteenth-century rationalism and sensationalism is equally plain: at the heart of his notorious patriotism is his belief, apparently sincere, that the American colonists' religious instincts remained unsullied by skepticism during the seventeenth and eighteenth centuries.

It is this insistence that in one form or another causes many of Bancroft's problems as a historian. Vague though his own religion is, he nevertheless seems compelled to justify Amer-

[61] *Ibid.*, II, 352.
[62] *Ibid.*, 379 ff.

ica religiously, with the result that a cloudy idealism becomes his ultimate rationale for a whole series of questionable historical judgments. One of these is the claim that "the colonists . . . were neither skeptics nor sensualists, but Christians. The school that bows to the senses as the sole interpreter of truth, had little share in colonizing our America."[63] As historical interpretation this seems at best doubtful; it acquires meaning in the context of what amounts to a crusade on Bancroft's part against religious slackness. Viewed in that context, it helps explain the many other passages in the *History* which contrast American religiousness with European sensualism. We know, for instance, what Bancroft is really saying when he argues that "in America, free inquiry, which dwelt with the people, far from being of a destructive tendency, was conducting them towards firm institutions, and religious faith was not a historical tradition, encumbered with abuses of centuries, but a living principle,"[64] or that while "English statesmen were . . . inattentive to the character of events which were leading to the renovation of the world," Americans "studied the book of Revelation* to see which seal was next to be broken, which angel was next to sound his trumpet."[65] He is protesting against modern, allegedly European, secularism. Though the entire *History* makes this protest in various ways, nowhere are the lines of connection between Bancroft's belief in Providence, his rejection of rationalism and secularism in favor of religious idealism, his mythicization of America, and his concept of freedom and union more revealingly tied than in a passage from Volume VIII which deserves to be quoted at length:

The eighteenth century refused to look for anything better; the belief in the divine reason was derided like the cowering at spectres and hobgoblins; and the worship of humanity became the prevailing

[63] *Ibid.*, 455.
[64] *Ibid.*, IV, 258.
[65] *Ibid.*, VI, 167 f. The asterisk here and in all succeeding quotations stands for the historians' own footnote numbers.

31

idolatry. Art was commissioned to glorify taste; morality had for its office to increase pleasure; forgetting that the highest liberty consists in being forced by right reason to choose the best, men cherished sensualism as a system, and self-indulgence was the law of courts and aristocracies. A blind, unreasoning, selfish conservatism, assumed that creative power was exhausted . . . ; not knowing that this conception is at war with nature herself and her eternal order, men substituted for true conservatism, which looks always to the action of moral forces, the basest form of atheism and the most hopeless theory of despotic power.

The age had ceased to wrestle with doubt, and accepted it not with anguish as the despair of reason, but with congratulation and pride. . . . The prevailing philosophy . . . scoffed at all knowledge that transcends the senses, limited itself to the inferior lessons of experience, and rejected ideas which are the archetypes of things for ideas which were no more than pictures on the brain; dethroning the beautiful for the agreeable; the right for the useful; the true for the seeming; knowing nothing of a universal moral government, referring everything to the self of the individual. . . . Away, then, with the system of impotent doubt, which teaches that Europe cannot be extricated from the defilements of a selfish aristocracy or despotism, that the British constitution, though it may have a happy death, can have no reform. Let scepticism, the wandering nomad, that intrudes into every field only to desecrate and deny, strike her tents and make way for a people [the Americans] who have power to build up the house of humanity, because they have faith in eternal truth and trust in that higher foresight, which over all brings forth better things out of evil and out of good.[66]

Especially striking is the way Bancroft equates "the highest liberty" with "true conservatism." Real liberty is actually moral self-restraint, and true conservatism is the belief that the principles underlying the moral self-restraint have divine sanction. He reveals that his whole religion and philosophy have a strong conservative bias and that the specter of atheistic, an-

[66] *Ibid.*, VIII, 364 ff.

archistic freedom in America deeply disturbs him.[67] His exhortations at the end of the passage protest too much: they appear to be little more than confessions of worry that in time skepticism might infect America. It has been argued that Bancroft's histories tend to portray America as a new Eden from which the future opens outward in spectacular vistas of hope and progress;[68] yet it is also plain that the promise is tied to the condition that Americans never doubt God's providence or the immutability of moral law. The implication in the passage above, and throughout the *History*, is that if they do, they, like Adam and Eve, will fall. The forbidden fruit in the new Eden is as lethal as it was in the old. It may be, of course, that Bancroft saw eighteenth-century skepticism and infidelity as merely a temporary monstrosity which nineteenth-century transcendental idealism had buried for good. Certainly the tone of the *History* as a whole is buoyant and confident. Yet the frequency with which Bancroft comes back to the problem of faith and doubt and the shrillness with which he tends, as here, to attack skepticism suggest otherwise.

In any event, the religious-philosophical tide of the ten volumes often overwhelms their practical, inductive, reasonable undercurrent. A case in point is Bancroft's claim that history in general and the *History* in particular is scientific.

[67] In his stimulating book *Unquiet Eagle: Memory and Desire in the Idea of American Freedom, 1815–1860*, Fred Somkin argues that the prosperity of those years confronted Americans with the possibility of losing their sense of community to economic greed. He sees the dichotomies of freedom *versus* union, individualism *versus* community, and selfishness *versus* self-sacrifice as the key to the spiritual and social history of America between the War of 1812 and the Civil War. Although I think Somkin tends to overlook the hardheadedness and realism of much of Bancroft's treatment of economics and politics in the *History*, I find his analysis, pp. 196–206, of Bancroft's uneasy defense of Americans against the charge of selfishness generally convincing.

[68] For discussions of Bancroft's view that men would regain a prelapsarian innocence in America, see Richard W. B. Lewis, *The American Adam*, 159–73, and Merrill Lewis, "Organic Metaphor and Edenic Myth in George Bancroft's *History of the United States,*" *Journal of the History of Ideas*, Vol. XXVI (1965), 587–92.

The argument can be summarized from key passages sprinkled throughout the *History*. According to Bancroft, the historian approaches a historical subject the way an astronomer views an unknown constellation or a botanist studies a new species of plant. Like them, he needs first to observe his subject as accurately as he can, using "instruments that may unfold" it "without color and without distortion."[69] His basic instrument is "unwearied"[70] research, based on "the principles of historical scepticism,"[71] which demands exhaustive reading and comparison of all the available documents. After completing this step, he extracts from his study, first, "facts faithfully ascertained," second, "chronological sequence, which can best exhibit the simultaneous action of general causes,"[72] and finally and most important, "the vestiges of moral law [in] the practice of the nations in every age."[73] By following this method, the historian "proves experimentally the reality of justice, and confirms by induction the intuitions of reason."[74] Facts thus verified and set in chronological order will demonstrate, Bancroft asserts again and again, "the superintending providence of God."[75] But the historian must free himself from the "arrogance" that presumes "to know intuitively, without observation, the tendency of the ages."[76]

In all of this Bancroft seems to refer to the historian's general, preliminary study, undertaken well before he begins to consider the problems of actually writing a narrative. The empiricism he recommends is restricted, in other words, to that somewhat narrow range of possibilities lying between his own

[69] *History*, III, 397.
[70] *Ibid.*
[71] *Ibid.*, I, v.
[72] *Ibid.*, VI, x.
[73] *Ibid.*, VIII, 117.
[74] *Ibid.*
[75] *Ibid.*, III, 398.
[76] *Ibid.*, 397.

a priori religious-philosophical interpretation of all history and the body of evidence about a specific period, such as colonial America, which he imagines lying unread and unsifted, as when he first approached it. The yardstick against which he measures these documents is not the one normally used for the purpose of empirical testing, namely the tough reality of human experience itself, but rather the perfect, supernatural moral law or idea that he believes skewers history. For Bancroft, historical statements have validity chiefly as they conform to this divine law; yet at the same time he argues that in order to comprehend the full grandeur of the law the historian must know the whole pattern of historical causes and effects through which it reveals itself. Having grasped the broad threads of historical development suggested by his sources as a whole, he then works them backward into the fabric of supernatural predestination. It is in finding them in his sources that he behaves empirically or inductively, like a scientist observing natural phenomena.

Bancroft seems to be thinking in the terms of this upside-down empiricism whenever he celebrates what he calls the harmony of historical truth. "For the historic inquirer to swerve from exact observation," he says, "would be as absurd as for the astronomer to break his telescopes, and compute the path of a planet by conjecture. Of success, too, there is a sure criterion; for, as every false statement contains a contradiction, truth alone possesses harmony."[77] Since he never fully explains this idea, Bancroft forces us to conclude that his central test of the success or failure of historical writing is whether or not it expresses the moral harmony which radiates from the mind of God through history and which men can best comprehend intuitively. Plainly, there is a kernel of induction and workable common sense in his calling history a science—like his teacher at Göttingen, Heeren, he even recommends a critical approach to the documents—but the idea

[77] *Ibid.*

ultimately vanishes in the mists of his transcendental philosophy.

Yet it seems to me that Bancroft's philosophizing should be seen for what it is—a defense of religious faith and an attack on religious skepticism—and not be allowed to invalidate what is on the whole an intelligent and perceptive reading of early American history. While the philosophy undeniably encouraged many of Bancroft's most glaring weaknesses—excessive patriotism, grandiose generalizing, rhetorical bombast, and black-and-white moral judgments—it did not blind him to historical reality. It may in fact help explain his handling of the basic themes of freedom and union, since it parallels the argument he makes throughout the *History* for a central authority strong enough to be capable of keeping the United States from disintegrating yet not so strong that it threatens economic, political, and religious freedom. Both religiously and politically, he prefers order to anarchy, unity to diffusion, effacement of self to self-glorification. Faith in an omnipotent but benevolent and unjealous deity reinforces loyalty to a strong but democratic nation. His celebration of the American compromise between separatism and centralization foreshadows the argument of Parkman's and Adams' histories, and in this respect he is unquestionably the founder and guiding light of their tradition.

Furthermore, he sets forth in the *History* an interpretation of the individual's role within American democracy to which Parkman and Adams both were obliged to respond. Although Bancroft has his heroes, he argues overall that in colonial America the individual was less important than the community and that leaders tended more to follow than to lead. Volume I repeatedly contrasts the heroism of the industrious, self-effacing founders of the American colonies with traditional military heroism. "In the history of the world," says Bancroft at one point, "many pages are devoted to commemorate the heroes, who have besieged cities, subdued provinces, or overthrown empires. In the eye of reason and of truth, a colony is a better offering than a victory."[78] Succeeding volumes clarify and reinforce the idea. In Connecticut, the "husbandman who held his own plough, and fed his own cattle, was the great man of the age; no one was superior to the matron, who, with her busy daughters, kept the hum of the wheel incessantly alive, spinning and weaving every article of their dress."[79] The masses, thinking and acting in concert, provide democracy's real leadership:

The multitude may always defend itself against the pride of any one, by claiming for itself a collective wisdom superior to that of the wisest individual. The same is true of the moral qualities; there exists in the many a force of will which no violence can break, a firmness of conviction which no bribery can undermine.[80]

Even Washington, the most autogenously heroic figure in the *History*, gave "an impulse to human affairs" only "as far as events can depend on an individual,"[81] the implication being that individuals do not determine history.

The real determinant in history, as many of the passages already quoted suggest, is the divine will expressed through the people at large, who, because of their intuitive religious faith, will instinctively move forward in harmony with God's plan of progress if encouraged to do so. Thus the effective leader keeps in tune with the will of the majority. "The statesman," says Bancroft, "like others, can command nature only by obeying her laws; he can serve man only by respecting the conditions of his being; he can sway a nation only by penetrating what is at work in the mind of its masses, and taking heed of the state of its development."[82] In some cases he is, like William Pitt, a "man of the people," their "noblest

[78] *Ibid.*, I, 349.
[79] *Ibid.*, II, 58.
[80] *Ibid.*, 176.
[81] *Ibid.*, III, 468.
[82] *Ibid.*, VIII, 359.

37

representative and type."[83] But for Bancroft it is generally sufficient if the leader simply conforms his will to theirs by making a conscious effort to understand and to follow them. If anything, Bancroft tends to distrust the charismatic leader, preferring instead the prudent, thoughtful, self-effacing American type best represented by Thomas Jefferson, Benjamin Franklin, and George Washington.

The quality in Jefferson that most impressed Bancroft

was the sympathetic character of his nature, by which he was able with instinctive perception to read the soul of the nation. . . . No man of his century had more trust in the collective reason and conscience of his fellow men, or better knew how to take their counsel; and in return he came to be a ruler over the willing in the world of opinion.[84]

Jefferson took the counsel of the people at large. Only in following public opinion was he able to mold it, and Bancroft's implication is that his genius lay in not aspiring beyond what the masses were willing to allow. Franklin, who in the *History* rivals Washington as Bancroft's favorite leader, is presented as the archetypal American. He "fearlessly defended absolute freedom of thought and speech, and the inalienable power of the people"; his "love of man gained the mastery over personal interest"; his "blandness of temper, his modesty, the benignity of his manners, made him the delight of intelligent society"; and he "separated himself so little from his age, that he has [mistakenly] been called the representative of materialism."[85] More than any other of Bancroft's American heroes, Franklin represents the democratic pragmatist who adjusts himself to the will of the majority and whose fine sense of the limitations of the individual leader in America

---

[83] *Ibid.*, IV, 247. See Levin, *History as Romantic Art*, 49–73, for a general discussion of the representative man in the histories of Bancroft, Parkman, Prescott, and Motley.

[84] *History*, VIII, 462 f.

[85] *Ibid.*, III, 376–80.

gives him most of his effectiveness. Washington, of course, is the *History*'s nonesuch. His character dominates the last four volumes, and the key to his greatness in Bancroft's eyes was his uncanny ability to appreciate and, in terms of military-political strategy, to take advantage of America's sprawling decentralization even as he drove relentlessly toward the goal of effectively centralized nationhood:

Combining the centripetal and the centrifugal forces in their utmost strength and in perfect relations, with creative grandeur of instinct [Washington] held ruin in check, and renewed and perfected the institutions of his country. Finding the colonies disconnected and dependent, he left them such a united and well ordered commonwealth as no visionary had believed to be possible.[86]

Though loved by his soldiers and by the rebels at large, Washington was not, argues Bancroft, a leader in the great-man tradition. His greatness lay in his recognition of the limitations of his power and of the need for continual balancing and harmonization of the "centripetal and the centrifugal forces" in American society. Like Jefferson and Franklin, he was as much a follower as a leader of his countrymen, and therein, according to Bancroft, lay the marvel of his statesmanship.

Of course all three, like virtually all of Bancroft's heroes, are described as intuitive idealists, seeking truth not on earth but in a transcendent realm of Providence and moral law and relying on mankind at large as the reservoir of religious faith. Jefferson was "an idealist in his habits of thought and life, as indeed is every one who has an abiding and thorough confidence in the people."[87] Despite his empiricism and his being "free from mysticism, even to a fault," Franklin "discerned intuitively the identity of the laws of nature with those of which humanity is conscious,"[88] "passed beyond reliance on

[86] *Ibid.*, VII, 400.
[87] *Ibid.*, VIII, 464.
[88] *Ibid.*, III, 378.

sects to faith in God," and "founded the freedom of his country on principles that know no change."[89] Washington's "whole being was one continued act of faith in the eternal, intelligent, moral order of the universe";[90] "the praise which he coveted, was the sympathy of that moral sentiment which exists in every human breast, and goes forth only to the welcome of virtue."[91] Here, again, as is usually the case when Bancroft combats rationalism and skepticism, the *History* has become formulaic. Franklin, Jefferson, and Washington played leading roles in the Revolution: *propter hoc* they reveal all the virtues of transcendental idealists and none of the vices of rationalistic skeptics.

When Bancroft laid down his pen at the end of Volume X in 1874, he had finished a work whose interpretation of America had not only saturated the historical consciousness of his countrymen but had given Parkman and Adams a formidable point of reference for their own great narratives. What he had told them was that the threat of divisiveness and anarchistic individualism in America was slight so long as Americans held to their faith in divine providence and moral law, and in asserting that such faith was instinctive he minimized the threat yet further. Immutable moral law ensured the unity not merely of the American nation but of the race. America was but a preview of the future brotherhood of man. On the other hand, America's tradition of individual freedom—economic, political, philosophical, religious—was a sure bulwark against the tyranny and despotism that had so often in the past been the result of unification and centralization of every kind. In the American system of federative union, with its series of delegations of powers beginning with the individual as the basic source of power and spreading outward from him to community, state, and national levels, Bancroft believed man had

[89] *Ibid.*, 380.
[90] *Ibid.*, VII, 398.
[91] *Ibid.*, 399.

found the solution to the age-old problem of freedom and union. Every human being's religious instinct led him inevitably toward cooperation with his fellow men. In their turn, the leaders of American democracy instinctively sought the collective will of their constituents. The result was the virtual absence of conflict between the many and the one: the many *were* the one, the one *was* the many. The compromise between anarchy and despotism was as perfect as imperfect man could make it. It promised to improve yet further and to spread throughout the earth as God's will prevailed.

Thus astute analysis of American history, unabashed chauvinism, Yankee common sense, and a peculiar type of religious exhortation are the major ingredients in Bancroft's sprawling yet unified, simplistic yet sophisticated, and annoying yet challenging volumes. No less intriguing is the way it was composed. What Bancroft has to say invariably controls how he says it, and comparison of his own text with that of the sources he used reveals a literary method highly consistent with the spirit of the ideas he tries to convey. His pioneer work in method was as important as that in interpretation, providing Parkman and Adams with a stylistic pattern which neither actually adopted or broke away from entirely. The ten volumes cast technical as well as thematic light along the path the two younger historians were later to follow.

★ ★ ★ ★ ★ ★

The Methodological Revolt

WHEN Bancroft's first volume appeared in 1834, it was as though a fresh wind had blown through the stale air of American historiography. Praised immediately, everywhere, as the best history of early exploration and colonization yet written, it must have made Bancroft feel he had finally vindicated himself from the kind of remark Emerson had made in 1823: "[Bancroft] hath sadly disappointed great expectations."[1] For none of his other books was acclaim so quick in coming or so widespread, and in this case the judgment of contemporaries, often a questionable gauge of permanent literary worth, seems accurate. The volume is, in many ways, the best he wrote.[2]

---

[1] Quoted in Nye, *Brahmin Rebel*, 64.

[2] When Bancroft revised the *History*, he did not restudy his sources but instead simply imposed new language on the existing narrative, unconcerned with the impact such revisions might have on the integrity of the evidence he had originally used. Thus his first editions reflect his fullest immersion in the evidence. For an analysis of Bancroft's revisions, see R. J. Oard's Ph.D. dissertation "Bancroft and Hildreth: A Critical Evaluation." Because of the absence of footnotes in Volumes VII and VIII and in Bancroft's two major revisions of the *History* and because of the spottiness of footnoting in Volumes IX and X, I have used the first editions of Volumes I through VI as the basis of this study. I have, of course, relied on Bancroft's footnoting as my basic guide to his use of source material.

The Methodological Revolt

Bancrofts' Initial Step: Volume I

Its tone is more analytical and moderate, less religious and philosophical, than any of the others. Comparison of his sources and his own text shows that he prefers developing the theme of freedom and union to asserting the need for transcendental idealism when he paraphrases. Moreover, the book's subject matter is not as controversial as that of the later volumes. There is relatively little oppression from England to complain about or to use as a foil for American superiority, relatively little evidence of the baleful effects of rationalism and skepticism, and relatively little testimony that has to be discredited. Most of the book consists of straightforward narrative sculpted from coherent, consistent, and substantially agreeing source accounts, and while Bancroft often heightens the narrative for literary or moral effect, he tends on the whole to let good source material speak for itself. In certain sections, such as the passages on the colonial charters or the economic meaning of colonization, his historical insight is often keen. As a fledgling historian, he doubtless felt constrained to check some of the philosophical energy to which, having savored the heady critical applause that greeted his first volume, he later gave freer rein.

Volume I narrates the sixteenth-century English, French, and Spanish voyages of discovery and exploration of North America and the efforts to colonize the eastern seaboard during the sixteenth and seventeenth centuries, ending with the restoration of the Stuart line in England in 1660. In it Bancroft follows published sources exclusively: not one of the documents on which it is based was read by him in manuscript form. Moreover, at many points he prefers eighteenth- and nineteenth-century historians to eyewitness or contemporary accounts, especially when the secondary writer has himself elegantly paraphrased the originals and so provided him with a good narrative model to follow. This fact seems to have been responsible for some of the book's praiseworthiness. Bancroft's reliance on eighteenth-century narrative histories and on several key nineteenth-century scholarly monographs and editions probably encouraged the cautious and critical tone he adopts toward his sources. Eighteenth-century New England historians like Jeremy Belknap, Benjamin Trumbull, and Thomas Hutchinson, all of whom Bancroft used heavily, tended to explore archival and other unpublished material surprisingly thoroughly, to detach themselves from what they wrote, and to footnote well. Other historians, such as George Chalmers, who in 1780 published his superb *Political Annals of the Present Colonies*, were equally good. The scholarliness and neoclassical reasonableness of such sources almost certainly served in Volume I to bridle Bancroft's penchant for grandiose moralizing. Though in succeeding volumes he also follows these sources, he no longer seems to respect them as much.

As in all the volumes of the *History*, the speaker of Volume I stands between the reader and the past, telling him in no uncertain terms what it means, how it should be judged, how much it is worth. Yet such moral certitude, or perhaps arrogance, is in Volume I an indulgence that Bancroft tends to allow himself in intrusions distinct from the narrative—not, as in later volumes, the basic tone that governs much of his editing of his materials. When, for instance, the narrator makes one of his overt and ubiquitous moral judgments—"A government, which could devise the massacre of St. Bartholomew, was neither worthy nor able to lay the foundation of new states"[3] or "It was not the will of God, that the new state should be formed of these materials"[4]—he is merely irritating. His treatment of the documents themselves is generally restrained.

In his preface to the book Bancroft gives a clue to his ap-

[3] *History*, I, 28.
[4] *Ibid.*, 154.

proach to his sources when he says, "I have endeavored to impart originality to my narrative, by deriving it entirely from the writings and sources, which were the contemporaries of the events that are described."[5] Although the book is based as often on secondary as on primary sources, belying Bancroft's claim to having used primaries exclusively, it is nevertheless "original" in its method, as Bancroft claims, in two major ways. In the first place, as Bancroft knew from having read virtually all the secondary works on American colonial history available to him, most of the earlier historians had merely rephrased or copied the best or most recent secondary works at hand, achieving, as a result, little more in much of their prose than crudely spliced editions of large blocks of material copied from prior histories. Some sense of the deadliness of the practice and of Bancroft's effort to avoid it can be gathered from the following example. In preparing his account of a French expedition to Canada in 1604, he was confronted with several versions of the discovery of Port Royal, or Annapolis, in Nova Scotia. The basic eyewitness account, by a man named Lescarbot, was included by Samuel Purchas in his *Purchas His Pilgrimes*, intended as a continuation and amplification of Hakluyt's more famous *Voyages:*

This port is invironed with Mountaines on the North side: Towards the South bee small Hills, which . . . doe poure out a thousand Brookes, which makes that place pleasanter then any other in the World . . . . All this distance is nothing of both sides the River but faire Medowes, which River was named *L'Equille.* Monsieur de Poutrincourt having found this place to bee to his liking demanded it . . . of Monsieur de Monts . . . , intending to retire himselfe thither with his Family . . . .[6]

In 1794, Jeremy Belknap published his *American Biography*, containing a life of Champlain in which the following paraphrase of Lescarbot's account appears:

[5] *Ibid.,* v.
[6] Lescarbot in *Purchas His Pilgrimes,* IV, 1621.

On the eastern side of this bay they discovered a narrow strait, into which they entered, and soon found themselves in a spacious bason, invironed with hills, from which descended streams of fresh water; and between the hills ran a fine navigable river, which they called L'Equille. It was bordered with fertile meadows, and full of delicate fish. Poutrincourt, charmed with the beauty of the place, determined here to take his residence, and having received a grant of it from De Monts, gave it the name of Port Royal.* [Belknap's note: "*Annapolis."][7]

Belknap's account became standard for the chroniclers and annalists who followed him during the next thirty-five years. In 1806, Abiel Holmes, the father of Oliver Wendell, wrote *The Annals of America*, reissuing it in 1829 in revised form. Though he cites twelve sources in a long footnote to his version of the Port Royal discovery, with Lescarbot prominently in first and Belknap inconspicuously in tenth place, Holmes simply copied Belknap for his first sentence without using quotation marks and then followed his phrasing for the rest:

On the eastern side of this bay they discovered a narrow strait, into which they entered, and soon found themselves in a spacious bason, environed with hills, and bordered with fertile meadows. Poutrincourt was so delighted with this place, that he determined to take his residence here; and, having received a grant of it from De Monts, he called it Port Royal.[8]

Thomas C. Haliburton was an even more dutiful copier of Belknap. Except for several substituted words, a reworking here and there of phrases, and the addition of Poutrincourt's delight in the "harbour" and "praries," his version, which first appeared in 1829, is identical to Belknap's; but unlike Holmes, Haliburton makes no footnote acknowledgments whatsoever.

On the Eastern side of the Bay they discovered a narrow Straight,

---

[7] *American Biography*, I, 325.
[8] *The Annals of America*, I, 121.

into which they entered, and soon found themselves in a spacious
Basin, environed with hills, from which descended streams of fresh
water. To one of these, they gave the name Laquille. It was bordered
with beautiful meadows, and filled with delicate fish. Pontrincourt
[*sic*] was so charmed with the beauty and safety of the harbour, the
extent and fertility of the praries, that he chose it for his residence
and having received a grant of it from De Monts, he called it Port
Royal.[9]

In 1832, two years before Bancroft finished the first volume
of the *History*, William D. Williamson published a history
of Maine in which he narrates the episode by using less of
Belknap's actual phrasing than either Holmes or Haliburton
but more of Belknap's than Lescarbot's:

[S]ailing . . . eastwardly along the northern shores of the peninsula,
[they] entered a spacious basin, environed by hills and meadows,
and anchored in a good harbour. Poutrincourt was so charmed
with the beautiful appearance of the place, that he chose it for his
future residence. Obtaining readily a grant of it from de Monts, . . .
he gave it the name of Port Royal.[10]

Complicating our judgment of Williamson's version is the
fact that in his footnote to the passage he identifies Holmes
as his leading source, Lescarbot next. He cites no others. That
he knew Belknap's work is obvious from his heavy citation
of it on nearby pages and throughout the book. In this case
he either failed to see that Holmes had copied Belknap or,
more probably, wanted to create an impression of scholarly
depth by varying his notes.

To a greater or lesser degree, such parroting was typical of
the histories Bancroft read in preparing Volume I. In deliberately setting out to break the dreary habit, he changed the
course of American historiography. No serious historian could

[9] Thomas C. Haliburton, *An Historical and Statistical Account of Nova
Scotia*, I, 15.
[10] William D. Williamson, *The History of the State of Maine*, I, 188 f.

return to such simpleminded editing after Bancroft's repudia-
tion of it in his first book, which was in effect a declaration of
independence from the slavish methods of his predecessors.
His originality in this sense is visible in his own account of the
discovery of Port Royal. Citing Lescarbot first in his footnote
and then, somewhat oddly, Haliburton, he in fact follows no
one source but blends elements from several with much of his
own phrasing:

The harbor, called Annapolis after the conquest of Acadia by
Queen Ann, as excellent harbor, though difficult of access, possessing
a small but navigable river, which abounded in fish and is bordered
by beautiful meadows, so pleased the imagination of Poutrincourt,*
a leader in the enterprize, that he sued for a grant of it from De
Monts, and, naming it Port Royal, determined to reside there with
his family.[11]

Although Bancroft combines the Lescarbot and Belknap
(Haliburton) versions, there is a vigor and forcefulness in his
that results from his compressing the incident into a single
tight sentence whose syntax propels the reader toward the
period. Throughout the *History* a similar determination not
to copy is clear in paraphrase after paraphrase.

This is one of the two major kinds of originality Bancroft
claims for his book. The second is a direct outgrowth of his
conviction that it is always the historian's duty to philosophize
history. To Bancroft, history achieves originality when it
explains, not merely recounts, particulars. The more it is
merely a record or chronicle of an unjudged past, the less its
value. His aim is to raise his narrative to the level of philosophy by finding in it levels of meaning probably unsuspected,
as he himself would grant, by the writers whose records he
follows. Fitting ideas and language from the sources into his
own interpretive context, he uses them for his own ends without much concern for the context in which they originally

[11] *History*, I, 31.

appeared. Having freed himself from the obligation of following the "authorities" page after page, Bancroft can utilize those passages from the sources which offer him the most literary and interpretive help. The flaws in such a method occasionally come home to roost in his later volumes, but in his first he manages to keep it under control and to realize its potential.

So satisfactory a technique was it, in fact, that Bancroft used it much more often than quotation in Volume I. Although he does occasionally set words, sentences, and even paragraphs within quotation marks, he tends to revise the phrasing of quoted material as freely as when he paraphrases. The longest quotation in Volume I ostensibly reproduces part of a letter, sent by the General Court of Massachusetts to the Long Parliament in 1646, protesting efforts by settlers disenchanted with the Bay Colony theocracy to introduce Presbyterianism in New England. Bancroft's view is that these efforts "struck at the very life and foundation of the rising commonwealth" and that had they succeeded "the tenor of American history would have been changed"[12] for the worse. Furthermore, he views the incident as a test of popular liberty. "The harmony of the people," he says, "had been confirmed by the courage of the elders, who gave fervor to the enthusiasm of patriotism."[13] He introduces the letter by praising its "noblest frankness."[14]

Bancroft has rewritten the letter in such a way as to give it a no-nonsense, straight-from-the-shoulder tone missing in the original. He begins his version by stressing the firmness and straightforwardness of the court's protest: " 'An order from England,' they say, 'is prejudicial to our chartered liberties and to our well-being in this remote part of the world.' "[15]

12 *Ibid.*, 476.
13 *Ibid.*, 480.
14 *Ibid.*, 477.
15 *Ibid.*, 478

In contrast, the letter itself oozes with humility and professions of loyalty:

And whereas, by order from your honours, dated May 15, 1646, we find that your honours have still that good opinion of us, as not to credit what hath been informed against us before we be heard, we render humble thanks to your honours for the same; yet forasmuch as our answer to the information of the said Gorton etc. is expected, and something also required of us, which (in all humble submission) we conceive may be prejudicial to the liberties granted us by the said charter and to our well being in this remote part of the world, (under the comfort whereof, through the blessing of the Lord, his majesty's favor, and the special care and bounty of the high court of parliament, we have lived in peace and prosperity these seventeen years,) our humble petition [follows].[16]

By substituting "order" for the roundabout phrasing of the letter, "is prejudicial" for "we conceive may be prejudicial," and, more subtly, "chartered liberties" for "liberties granted us by the said charter," Bancroft emphasizes that the colonists were upset and that relations between mother country and colony were sorely strained in 1646. Equally revealing is his disregard of the conventional submissiveness in the original. Had it actually been left out as it is in Bancroft's version, it would by its absence have signaled extreme defiance, as Bancroft knew. What Bancroft gives us in quotation marks is in effect his estimate of the letter's impact in London.

Almost all of the quotations in Volume I are similarly geared to Bancroft's style, which in turn he has geared to the expectations of his assumed audience. He "modernizes" the documents so that the reader will sense a minimum of discrepancy between the narrator's and the document's tone and diction. Evidence from the *History* as a whole indicates that Bancroft never felt comfortable with quotation as a historiographical tool. It too sharply crossed the grain of his

---

[16] John Winthrop, *The History of New England from 1630 to 1649*, II, 295 f.

wish to translate the past into the terms of his own interpretation. Although he used it increasingly more heavily in his later volumes, he never really mastered it. The fact that he quotes relatively rarely in Volume I, and then always to conform the quotation to his own speaking voice, suggests that he may have quoted not from choice but because he felt it was expected of him as a historian. The drift of his art is away from the past toward the present and the future, and of all the techniques available to him, quotation most opposed that drift.

Paraphrasing was more congenial. As has already been mentioned, the paraphrases in Volume I are of material that is relatively uncontroversial and straightforward, and their tendency is away from religion and philosophy toward economics and politics and toward narratives of action. A frequent technique for Bancroft is to blend a paraphrase of an interpretation set forth in a source into his own interpretation, especially if the source author stresses the economic vigor or love of liberty of the colonists. George Chalmers, who emigrated from England to Maryland but who, as a Loyalist, returned to England in 1775, published in 1780 a history of the American colonies which was the best general work of its kind available to Bancroft. Forceful, cogent, suave, the book argues the illegality of the colonists' rebellion against Great Britain and at the same time the stupidity of England's colonial administration. Although in later volumes Bancroft tries to discredit Chalmers' anti-American argument by means of an *ad hominem* attack on Chalmers himself, an attack similar to the one he mounts against Thomas Hutchinson and his *History of the Colony of Massachusetts Bay*, in Volume I he gives Chalmers all due credit, often closely following his interpretations as well as his narrative. Concerning the founding of Maryland, Chalmers says:

The wisdom and vigour of lord Baltimore successfully performed what the colonial companies had been unable to atchieve. And, at an immense expence, he established a colony; which, after various revolutions, has descended to his posterity, and has added to the importance and power of the English empire.[17]

Bancroft, who sees Baltimore as unusually praiseworthy in that his colony was not only a haven of religious freedom but from the beginning a sound commercial enterprise, shows his approval of Chalmers' judgment by virtually copying it, with two key changes:

[Baltimore] obtained the high distinction of successfully performing, what the colonial companies had hardly been able to achieve. At a vast expense, he planted a colony, which for several generations descended as a patrimony to his heirs.[18]

First Bancroft's changes. Deleting Chalmers' compliment to the empire, he substitutes for it a remark that brings Chalmers, who in 1780 could not know England was to lose Maryland and all the other colonies within three years, up to date, a revision that suggests the concern for accuracy and detail that pervades Volume I. Furthermore, it diverts the flow of Chalmers' statement from praise of British imperialism to praise of American independence. Chalmers' intention is to suggest Baltimore's value to England; even as he echoes Chalmers' language, Bancroft claims Baltimore for America. Less obvious but equally significant is his deletion of Chalmers' "after various revolutions." Throughout Volume I, Bancroft pictures Maryland, along with Connecticut, as a model of orderly growth. Since Chalmers' suggestion that Maryland's colonial history was turbulent does not agree with his own basic viewpoint, he simply leaves it out.

Yet perhaps more remarkable, from the modern point of view, is the similarity between Bancroft's and Chalmers' language. Though unquestionably jarring to the modern ear, it

[17] *Political Annals of the Present United Colonies,* 205 f.
[18] *History,* I, 263.

should be judged in Bancroft's own methodological context. At a time when historians copied each other's work out of a sense of duty and a belief they were performing real historical service, Bancroft expressed his contempt for such orthodoxy by using the language of the sources in his own work strictly on his own terms and to suit himself. In such paraphrases, his first volume demonstrates the extent of his methodological revolt: in repudiating and in effect reversing the purpose of the hard-core plagiarism of his day, they declare his independence of his sources not less forcefully than paraphrases which, like the Port Royal example, deliberately avoid source phrasing. With them he merely capitalizes on fragments that in some way further his own purposes.

The type of paraphrasing most often found in the book, however, is that in which Bancroft follows one or more narratives of action, sometimes for several pages at a time. While it is hard to discriminate between pure narrative and moral judgment in even the most neutral narrative prose, in Bancroft's case such discrimination is impossible. When he narrates an action, he judges it as well, so that the explicit judgments he either borrows from writers like Chalmers or formulates himself permeate the passage. Happily, most of the sources for Volume I narrate events from a point of view compatible in some way with his own, and as a result he is able to concentrate more on improving and clarifying the story they tell than on arguing with them. At many points he manages to produce rousing accounts of what happened by closely paraphrasing good narrative models. One of the most effective passages of this kind occurs during his retelling of the landing at Plymouth in 1620, which he bases on the selections from William Bradford's *Plymouth Plantation* contained in Thomas Prince's *Chronological History of New England*. Like Bradford, Bancroft heightens the importance of the discovery of Plymouth Bay by stressing the hardships the Pilgrims suffered in finding it. Both Bradford and Bancroft describe the afternoon and evening of December 8, 1620, as especially trying:

Source:	*History:*
[They] find no convenient harbor, and hasten on to a port, which Mr. Coppin their pilot assures them is a good one, which he had been in, and they might reach before night. But after some hours sailing it begins to snow and rain; at midafternoon the wind rising, the sea grows very rough, they break their rudder, it is as much as two men can steer her with a couple of oars; and the storm increasing, the night approaching, and bearing what sail they can to get in, they break their mast in three pieces, their sail falls over board into a very grown sea, and they are like to founder suddenly; yet by the mercy of heaven, they recover themselves, and the flood being with them strike into the imagined harbor; but the pilot being deceived cries out, Lord be merciful! my eyes never saw this place before! And he and the mate would have run her ashore in a cove full of breakers before the wind; but a steersman calling to the rowers, 'about with her, or we are cast away,' they get her about immediately, and providence showing a fair sound before them, though it be very dark and rains hard, they get under the lee of a small rise of land; but are divided about going ashore, lest they fall into the midst of savages; some therefore keep the boat, but others being so wet, cold, and feeble, cannot bear it, but venture ashore, and with great difficulty kindle a fire.[19]	But no convenient harbor is discovered. The pilot of the boat, who had been in these regions before, gives assurance of a good one, which might be reached before night; and they follow his guidance. After some hours' sailing, a storm of snow and rain begins; the sea swells; the rudder breaks; the boat must now be steered with oars; the storm increases; night is at hand; to reach the harbor before dark, as much sail as possible is borne; the mast breaks into three pieces; the sail falls overboard; but the tide is favorable. The pilot, in dismay, would have run the boat on shore in a cove full of breakers; 'about with her,' exclaimed a sailor, 'or we are cast away.' They get her about immediately, and passing over the surf, they enter a fair sound; and get under the lee of a small rise of land. It is dark and the rain beats furiously; yet the men are so wet and cold and weak, they slight the danger to be apprehended from the savages, and after great difficulty, kindle a fire on shore.[20]

Though unusually exciting and fast moving, the example fairly represents the kind of straightforward, unpretentious narrative that makes much of Volume I very readable. Bancroft's purpose here is the same as in the Chalmers example: finding Bradford's account well suited to his own, he absorbs it almost verbatim into his book. Bradford does not serve him as an authority in the traditional sense but simply as a useful literary vehicle. Here, though, his aim is not so much to interpret the event as to tell it well, and his editing of Bradford is craftsmanlike. Cutting those portions of the original that slow down the action, he follows Bradford's use of the historical present and strings together brief explosions of movement with semicolons, creating an effect of rapidity, immediacy, and danger, as though every disaster in the sequence were happening at once.

More typical of Bancroft's handling of narrative passages in Volume I is his editing of a section of Benjamin Trumbull's history of Connecticut which tells the story of the hundred settlers who under Thomas Hooker blazed a trail from Massachusetts Bay to Connecticut in 1636. Writes Trumbull:

> About the beginning of June, Mr. Hooker, Mr. Stone, and about a hundred men, women and children, took their departure from Cambridge, and travelled more than a hundred miles, through a hideous and trackless wilderness, to Hartford. They had no guide but their compass; made their way over mountains, through swamps, thickets, and rivers, which were not passable but with great difficulty. They had no cover but the heavens, nor any lodgings but those which simple nature afforded them. They drove with them a hundred and sixty head of cattle, and by the way, subsisted on the milk of their cows. . . .

[19] William Bradford as quoted in Thomas Prince, *A Chronological History of New England*, 166 f. Bradford's work was of course unavailable to Bancroft. Taken to England after Prince had extracted portions of it for his chronicle in 1736, it was not rediscovered until 1856 and was not returned to America until 1897.

[20] *History*, I, 337.

This adventure was the more remarkable, as many of this company were persons of figure, who lived, in England, in honor, affluence and delicacy, and were entire strangers to fatigue and danger.[21]

Rearranging some of Trumbull's phrases and sentences, Bancroft ornaments the passage with semipoetic language designed to prepare us for the two rhetorical questions and the two semi-epic ejaculations with which he concludes:

In June the principal caravan began its march, led by Thomas Hooker, "the light of the Western Churches." There were of the company about one hundred souls; many of them, persons accustomed to affluence and the ease of European life. They drove before them numerous herds of cattle; and thus they traversed on foot the pathless forests of Massachusetts; advancing hardly ten miles a day through the tangled woods, across the swamps and numerous streams, and over the highlands that separated the several intervening vallies; subsisting as they slowly wandered along, on the milk of the kine, which browsed on the fresh leaves and early shoots; having no guide through the nearly untrodden wilderness, but the compass, and no pillow for their nightly rest but heaps of stones. What hardships did they endure in crossing the hills of Worcester county? What dangers in following the windings of the Chickapee, and fording with their cattle its rapid current? How did the hills echo with the unwonted lowing of the herds! How were the forests enlivened by the loud and fervent piety of Hooker! Never again was there such a pilgrimage from the seaside "to the delightful banks" of the Connecticut.[22]

Although Trumbull is his chief model, Bancroft has worked in another source that helps account for the heightened style of his version. Cotton Mather's *"The Light of the Western Churches*: or the Life of Mr. Thomas Hooker" provided him not only with the epithet in his first sentence but with his estimate of the expedition's daily mileage, his stone-pillow

21 *A Complete History of Connecticut*, I, 64 f.
22 *History*, I, 427 f.

figure, and the quoted phrase in his final sentence. Writes Mather:

Accordingly in the month of *June*, 1636, they removed an hundred miles to the westward, with a purpose to settle upon the delightful banks of the *Connecticut River*: and there were about an hundred persons in the first company that made this removal; who not being able to walk about ten miles a day, took up near a fortnight in the journey; having no pillows to take their nightly rest upon, but such as their father *Jacob* found in the way to *Padan-Aram*.[23]

Between them, Mather and Trumbull provide the information and at least a hint of the orotund rhetoric Bancroft uses in his own version. Especially Mather, whose striving for epic effect in the *Magnalia* is well known, seems to have inspired Bancroft's heroic muse, for the *History* elsewhere echoes the *Magnalia* in similar situations. The Hooker passage represents the norm of Bancroft's paraphrasing more closely than the one based on Bradford, reflecting his relatively greater independence of both Trumbull's and Mather's language. As is usually the case, Bancroft is here more interested in interpreting the event than in narrating it. Awe at the difficulties of the march and at the bravery and resourcefulness of the wanderers in meeting them, pleasure at the pastoral simplicity of the whole enterprise and the natural, unsophisticated piety that prompted it, melancholy at the passing of what Bancroft elsewhere calls "the romantic age of American history"[24]—communicating such ideas is Bancroft's main purpose in the passage. Also obvious is his method of viewing an incident from the vantage point of the contemporary reader. His concluding five sentences require us to see the event as extremely remote and hazy, as if it were enveloped in a rich penumbra of legend, in order that it will seem epic, larger than life. Final-

[23] *Magnalia Christi Americana: or, The Ecclesiastical History of New England*, I, 310f.
[24] *History*, I, 150.

ly, Bancroft's religious impulse is at work, and although most readers would probably agree that here it is relatively bland, they would also probably agree that Jacob's stones are uncomfortable in more ways than one.

Taken together, the examples in this brief sampling of the scores to be found in the book suggest Bancroft's brand of what I earlier termed the *e pluribus unum* method of using source material. Availing himself of the scissors-and-paste techniques of the annalist-plagiarist tradition, he isolates useful chunks of prose from his sources and rewrites them to match his own style and argument. Consequently, his narrative is in effect the opposite of what is today called documentary history, despite the fact that he echoes his documents continually and at many points copies them verbatim without quotation marks. He speaks with a gnostic authority and omniscience that has its roots in the philosophy and religion previously discussed. His is as active, aggressive, imaginative a narrating stance as is likely to be found in conventional narrative history. Particular sources become useful to him only insofar as they coincide with the conclusions, historical and metaphysical, he has reached before he sets pen to paper. He sifts his evidence like a prospector who knows what he wants and who expertly secures his findings in his literary gold bag after the dross has been discarded. His sources are absolutely Bancroftized, as it were: trimmed and woven together in an extraordinarily uniform texture. Continually visible just beneath the surface of his own prose, their ideas and phrasing are nonetheless no longer the literary property of the men who originally wrote them but Bancroft's, even in quotations. From his many pieces of prior evidence he creates a wholly original historiographical artifact.

In Volume I the strategy works better, perhaps, than in his other volumes because there his sources are more neutral and his own interpretations more cautiously expressed. Ending at 1660, the book falls short of the era (the Restoration and its rationalistic, skeptical eighteenth-century aftermath) and the events (the deepening and ultimately decisive conflict with England) which fuel his hottest argumentative fires. When he moves beyond 1660 in succeeding volumes, he comes to the core of his interpretation of America, with the result that his deepest convictions are stirred. Also, many of his sources begin to contradict his interpretation, forcing him to a more free-wheeling kind of revision than in Volume I. Whereas in Volume I we find only occasional hints of the basic themes of the *History* in his reworking of source material, in Volumes II–VI he runs the themes through his paraphrases continually. The result is both a loss and a gain. Lost is the relative coolness, realism, and cautiousness of the first volume. Gained is the relative consistency and clarity of philosophical theme and the interpretive force of the next five. Yet the break should not be overemphasized. Bancroft's method remains essentially the same from beginning to end. In the later volumes, the method of the first simply fills out to its true shape.

The Method Extended: Volumes II–VI

Bancroft's second volume, published in 1838, four years after the first, reveals an unmistakable sharpening of argumentative edge. Lacking conclusive evidence, we can only speculate about the reasons for the change, but it seems likely that, along with the suggestions already made, the phenomenal success of Volume I and Bancroft's serious involvement in politics after 1834 were important factors. Reviewing Volume I in the influential *North American Review* (*NAR*), Edward Everett put greatest weight in explaining its success on those qualities that proved in the end to be most characteristic of Bancroft as a historian. "The writer," he insists, "who would produce a classical history, must carry his heart to his task. While learning instructs and judgment guides him, a lofty patriotism must take possession of his soul." This, Everett implies, Bancroft had accomplished, thereby fulfilling Burke's dictum that a historian's " 'passion must instruct his reason.' "[25] Everett rejoices at "the favorable reception which Mr. Bancroft's first volume has met" and concludes that when the whole work is finished, Bancroft will "stand in a position toward the American people, which the most gifted and successful may envy."[26] Although Everett, speaking from conservative Unitarian ground, could not have wished to encourage the transcendentalistic antirationalism that permeates Bancroft's second volume, it seems almost certain that his and praise like it from other quarters had such an effect. After discovering the philosophical line of Bancroft's later volumes, the reviewers for the *NAR*, at the time the organ of the conservative Boston intelligentsia, cooled considerably toward the *History*, leaving the burden of praise to kindred spirits like George Ripley.[27] But in the mid-1830's virtually all American and European critics joined in applauding Bancroft's first book, which within a year had been added to one of every three household libraries in New England alone.[28]

Furthermore, Volume I seems to have interested leading Democratic politicians who saw the value of enlisting the services of a pro-Jacksonian intellectual to oppose the likes of Daniel Webster and Everett in the political arena.[29] The

[25] "Bancroft's History of the United States," *North American Review*, Vol. XL (January–April, 1835), 100.

[26] *Ibid.*, 121 f.

[27] The next review of the *History* to appear in *NAR*, though on the whole still favorable, is more critical than Everett's, concluding with the warning that "no pet theory, nor party predilections, can justify [the historian] in swerving one hair's breadth from truth" (*NAR*, Vol. LII [January–June, 1841], 102). Then, in 1852, *NAR* gave a few curt and hostile pages to Bancroft's fifth volume, finding the book's purpose fuzzy, its points wrong, and its style inflated ("Continuation of Bancroft's History," *NAR*, Vol. LXXIV [1852], 507–15). In contrast, Ripley's review of Volume V in *Putnam's Monthly Magazine*, Vol. I (1853), 300–308, is as enthusiastic as Everett's was eighteen years earlier, concluding that the *History* as a whole "cannot fail to be one of the noblest achievements of American literature" (p. 308).

[28] Nye, *Brahmin Rebel*, 102.

[29] *Ibid.*, 106.

political rise that began for Bancroft in 1835 and culminated in his appointment to high political posts later was hardly slowed by the book, which, together with a radically Jacksonian oration, "The Office of the People in Art, Government, and Religion,"[30] he gave at Williams College in 1835, served to clarify his politics. Nowhere in the body of his writings does he sing the praises of democracy and intuitive morality more loudly than in that address, which can be seen as sharpening the muted political doctrines in Volume I for the benefit of potential political employers. Because the politics of Volume I were so subdued as to seem unexceptionable even to a conservative like Everett, Bancroft may have wanted to make its orientation unequivocally clear in the speech. In any case, such an orientation is unmistakable in Volume II.

Volume II opens with a long chapter whose tone is far more pugnacious than anything in Volume I. The chapter contends that the overthrow of Cromwell and the return of Charles II to the English throne was bad in that Charles represented the triumph of decadent feudalism over the spirit of popular liberty that had emerged during the early years of the Commonwealth. Its tone is one of indignation at the conduct of the English kings who opposed the tide of popular liberty. Charles I, who in 1640 opposed the Puritan revolution, is pictured as a pusillanimous cheat "who had neither firmness to maintain his just authority, nor sincerity to effect a safe reconciliation."[31] His son Charles II is described as fit for the gutter: "It was his misfortune, in very early life, to have become thoroughly debauched in mind and heart; and adversity, usually the rugged nurse of virtue, made the selfish libertine the more reckless in his profligacy. He did not merely indulge his passions; his neck bowed to the yoke of lewdness."[32] James II, who was deposed in 1688, "floated between the sensuality of

---

[30] George Bancroft, *Literary and Historical Miscellanies*, 408–35.
[31] *History*, II, 8.
[32] *Ibid.*, 48

indulgence and the sensuality of superstition, hazarding heaven for an ugly mistress, and, to the great delight of abbots and nuns, winning it back again by pricking his flesh with sharp points of iron, and eating no meat on Saturdays."[33] Complementing this scourge of English monarchy is the systematic attack on Lockeian sensationalism already mentioned, which, Bancroft argues, contributed directly to the licentiousness and materialism of the period and which he equates, as above, with the private debauchery of England's kings.

The change in tone between Volumes I and II reflects the change in method. In Volume II Bancroft no longer keeps his argument more or less separate from his editing of sources but instead lets it govern what he paraphrases and how he paraphrases it. It is interesting, for example, to contrast his treatment of Chalmers' *Political Annals* in the first and second volumes. In Volume I, as we have seen, he follows Chalmers' phrasing closely, merely adjusting it in minor ways to his argument. Volume II reveals a more aggressive approach. When Chalmers fled to England in the 1770's, he undertook to explore the Carolina papers in the Old Paper Office archives, from which he wrote the only account of the founding and development of Carolina between 1670 and 1688 before Bancroft's time based on solid research. Accordingly, all historians before Bancroft relied almost entirely on Chalmers for the history of the Carolinas during these years. The two principal American-written histories used by Bancroft for Volume II, Hugh Williamson's 1812 *History of North Carolina* and François-Xavier Martin's 1829 book of the same title, are little more than slightly altered copies of Chalmers' *Annals* for the period, though neither acknowledges the debt. Chalmers' thesis is that although the proprietary rulers of early Carolina governed their colony with a "mistaken policy" verging on "imbecility"[34]—giving the settlers so much free-

[33] *Ibid.*, 408.
[34] Chalmers, *Political Annals*, 538.

dom that, when an insurrection under John Culpepper did break out in 1678, the proprietaries were unable to put it down —they were nevertheless justified, as the duly constituted authority in the colony, in trying to keep order.

Bancroft, seeing Culpepper's revolt as one of the earliest triumphs of the American concept of freedom, brushes Chalmers' interpretation aside with two footnotes. The first appeals to the reader's patriotism: "Chalmers, with great consistency, condemned Culpepper, just as he condemned Bacon and Jefferson, Hancock and John Adams."[35] The second questions Chalmers' open-mindedness: "His account, in all cases of the kind, must be received with great hesitancy. The coloring is always wrong; the facts usually perverted. He writes like a lawyer and a disappointed politician; not like a calm inquirer."[36] What makes the situation especially intriguing is that Bancroft himself depends on Chalmers' basic narrative and that Williamson, Martin, and other pro-American writers agree with Chalmers, prompting Bancroft to remark somewhat testily in the first footnote, "Williamson has allowed himself to be confused by the judgments of royalists, and vol. i. p. 135, calls the fathers of North Carolina a set of 'rioters and robbers,' " and in the second that Chalmers' "statements are copied by Graham, obscured by Martin, and strange to say, exaggerated by Williamson, i., 138."

Accordingly, whenever Bancroft paraphrases Chalmers, he is forced to reverse Chalmers' argument. As the following example suggests, the editorial fencing that results is often lively. Bancroft's first and third sentences reveal his effort to set the rebels in the best light possible, and his second sentence, containing the nub of his argument, simply denies Chalmers altogether.

Source:	History:
They imprisoned the president, who was the chief object of their	Having deposed and imprisoned the president and the deputies of

[35] *History*, II, 161, n. 2.
[36] *Ibid.*, 162, n. 6.

indignation, and seven proprietary deputies; they seized the royal revenue, amounting to three thousand pounds, which they appropriated for supporting the revolt; they established courts of justice; they appointed officers; they called a parliament: And they, for years, exercised all the authority of an independent state. . . . And thus the people are made the constant bubbles of their own credulity and of others crimes: We may deplore their miseries, though it seems to little purpose to lament, what cannot possibly be in the future prevented!

When Eastchurch at length arrived, to whose commission or conduct there could be no objection, the insurgents derided his authority and denied him obedience.[37]

the propietaries, and set at nought the acts of parliament, the people recovered from anarchy, tranquilly organized a government, and established courts of justice. The insurrection was a deliberate rising of the people against the pretensions of the proprietaries and the laws of navigation; the uneducated population of that day formed conclusions as just as those which a century later pervaded the country. Eastchurch arrived in Virginia; but his commission and authority were derided; and he himself was kept out by force of arms* . . . . [*Bancroft's footnote*:
*Williamson, i. 264.][38]

Bancroft's revision embodies his major themes in the *History*. In the first place, the "people," having achieved political freedom through an act of rebellion, resist the centrifugal drive toward "anarchy" and "tranquilly" draw themselves into political order. Their behavior thus mirrors the fundamental American tendency to centralize politically under the pressure of anarchic circumstances, a tendency best shown in the Revolutionary War and its aftermath of steadily strengthening confederation. Second, they are able to do this because the "population," "uneducated" though it was at the time, was intuitively able to form "conclusions as just as those" which inspired the rebels in the 1770's and which revolted at the economic tyranny of the "laws of navigation." While Chalmers sees what happened as a plunge into anarchy,

[37] Chalmers, *Political Annals*, 535 f.
[38] *History*, II, 159 f.

Bancroft sees it as a heartening example of democratic revolution. Bancroft does not mention the confiscated money, stressing instead how peacefully the revolt was conducted and concluding his first sentence on the note of "justice." His second sentence, challenging Chalmers' "bubbles of credulity" remark, prepares us for the third, which, again reversing Chalmers' tone, applauds the rebels for having "derided" Eastchurch. Bancroft's method, though reflecting the originality of Volume I, goes beyond it by tackling a hostile source. Even while echoing Chalmers' language, he negates his argument.

The example represents the norm of Bancroft's treatment of sources, not only in Volume II but in Volume III, which simply extends the themes and techniques of Volume II into a narrative of the colonies between 1690 and 1748. Between the publication of the third volume in 1840 and Volume IV in 1852, however, Bancroft changed his style of writing history considerably. Although he based his first three books almost completely on published sources and, within that framework, largely on the best secondary histories he had at hand, in Volumes IV, V, and VI, published virtually as a unit between 1852 and 1854 and written with greater consistency of style and method than the first three, he incorporated the fruits of wide research in European and American archives and private manuscript collections. Much of his narrative in these later volumes is based on unpublished primary documents, and, while he by no means stops using secondary sources, roughly speaking he reverses the proportion between secondary and primary material which he has followed before. Furthermore, as a result partly of reduced chronological scope (Volumes I through III cover more than two hundred years, Volumes IV through VI only twenty-six), partly of the increased richness and complexity of his materials, and, partly, perhaps, of the competition posed by Richard Hildreth's doggedly unphilosophical *History of the United States*, issued in

1849,[39] he is generally less emotional, poetic, and didactic than in the earlier volumes.

This is not to say that the oratorical lushness of Volumes II and III comes to an end. Nothing in Bancroft's basic method or philosophy has changed. Yet the passages in which he defends the religion of democracy seem once again, as in Volume I, to be more or less separate from the narrative line. The overall pomposity of his language has been reduced, and we are conscious of breaks in tone between, say, his account of what actually happened in a British cabinet meeting and his judgment of the cabinet's moral behavior. One reason for this seems to have been the technical problem of welding together diffuse primary documents, a problem aggravated by the fact that in these later volumes, especially the fifth, which covers only three years, he was forced to go into single events in greater detail than before, thus encountering more of those stubborn and not easily generalized minutiae of historical fact that tend to resist his kind of God-in-history interpretation.

In the preface to Volume VI he discusses his new style briefly. After describing his research in the archives and manuscript collections, he concludes with this statement: "The abundance of my collections has enabled me, in some measure, to reproduce the very language of every one of the principal actors in the scenes which I describe, and to represent their conduct from their own point of view."[40] The first part of the remark, concerning his use of the actors' language, alludes to a noticeable increase in the number and length of quotations he includes in all the volumes after the third. More startling is his claim to have represented the actors' conduct "from their own point of view." If this were really the case, it would represent a radical break from his earlier *e pluribus unum* practice of ruthlessly homogenizing all source material

[39] Nye, *Brahmin Rebel*, 186.
[40] *History*, VI, x.

with his own style and argument. It is not the case; his method in this respect has not changed. What he seems to be referring to is the curious device of using quotations from eighteenth-century pro-American writers to support his own nineteenth-century transcendental interpretation of history.

An example of the device occurs in Volume VI in a chapter titled "An American Empire is in the Divine Decrees." There Bancroft sympathetically quotes a host of American preachers and pamphleteers of the 1760's who argue that God has predestined American independence and nationhood. The words of John Dickinson, author of the Farmer's Letters, form part of Bancroft's argument: " 'Almighty God himself,' wrote Dickinson, 'Will look down upon your righteous contest with approbation. . . . [elisions mine] You are assigned by Divine Providence, in the appointed order of things, the protector of unborn ages, whose fate depends upon your virtue.' "[41] No less persuasive in Bancroft's eyes is the comment of an unknown pamphleteer: " 'The land we possess is the gift of Heaven to our Fathers, and Divine Providence seems to have decreed it to our latest posterity.' "[42] Four pages later Bancroft quotes an anonymous column in the *Boston Gazette* as though it carried the same kind of weight: " 'The grand design of God in the settlement of New England' began to be more clearly discerned." Here Bancroft has concluded with words of his own that in effect increase the authoritativeness of the source over those he merely quotes. The device simply extends Bancroft's basic strategy in paraphrasing to quotation. It shows not how concerned he had become with his sources' points of view but instead how indifferent he was to them. It also suggests his unsureness over quotation as a historiographical technique.

So much for the new style in terms of quotation. In terms of paraphrasing, it resembles what we have already seen, but

[41] *Ibid.*, 139.
[42] *Ibid.*, 141.

in many cases the masses of primary documents Bancroft used demanded even more editorial *sang-froid*. A representative example is his narrative of a struggle for power between William Pitt and George Grenville in the eighth chapter of Volume V. The Pitt-Grenville episode is composed largely of snippets taken from primary evidence and edited to form a running narrative. Unlike Bancroft's first three volumes, in which he often follows a single source for some time, Volumes IV–VI, particularly Volume V, usually shift quickly from source to source, echoing within single sentences the phrasing of as many as three or four different models. Though less congenial to Bancroft than the one-to-one technique of the earlier volumes, the new method nevertheless seems to have muted the open warfare with the sources found in the account of the Carolina revolt and throughout Volumes II and III. What Bancroft does now is to run his style and argument through the sources more subtly, by means of systematic, piece-by-piece selection among and rewriting of the evidence. We have the sense of being plunged into the middle of the documents and of being only gently guided by Bancroft through the maze, yet in many cases we are actually thundering toward Bancroft's own conclusions on a locomotive of source material aimed in the opposite direction. The Pitt-Grenville chapter, as saturated with sources as any in the *History*, is in fact as contemptuous of the orthodoxies of the scissors-and-paste tradition as the most devout disciple of Collingwood could wish.

The historical background of the episode is as follows. In October, 1761, William Pitt, appointed prime minister of England in 1757 and largely responsible for England's victories over France between 1757 and 1760, was forced out of office by George III and a peace faction in Parliament. By 1763, after several political realignments, power had passed to a so-called triumvirate consisting of George Grenville, the Earl of Egremont, and the Earl of Halifax; in August and September of that year the war party under Pitt challenged the triumvirate and partly succeeded in reestablishing itself in power. In the course of the struggle, however, the king rejected Pitt's bid to supplant Grenville as prime minister.

The key to Bancroft's presentation of this tortuous affair lies in his opinion of its chief antagonists. On the one hand, Pitt emerges from the *History* as its greatest non-American hero, rivaling Washington himself. "[C]alled to the ministry neither by the king, nor by the parliament of the aristocracy . . . , but 'by the voice of the people,' " says Bancroft, Pitt "bent all factions to his authoritative will, and made 'a venal age unanimous.' . . . His presence was inspiration; he himself was greater than his speeches. Others have uttered thoughts of beauty and passion, of patriotism and courage; none by words accomplished deeds like him."[43] Pitt was, Bancroft concludes, "the greatest minister of his century, one of the few very great men of his age."[44] On the other hand, George Grenville is portrayed as a sodden and avaricious bureaucrat who showed his true colors by nourishing "a rankling grudge against Pitt" and who, "austere and rigidly inflexible," was simply a "dull, plodding pedant in politics." In an extravagant simile Bancroft describes him when he came to power in 1761 as being "at that period of life when the gentler passions are quiet, and ambition rules without restraint, . . . like the bird that croaks whilst enjoying the fullest meal."[45] Pitt draws his strength from the common will of his countrymen; Grenville draws his from an autocratic, self-willed king.

So repugnant to Bancroft were Grenville and the other members of the triumvirate that in his account of their contest with Pitt in 1763 he praises even George III, who emerges from the *History* as a whole as its worst tyrant, for encouraging Pitt. Yet it is clear from the sources Bancroft followed that the king was duplicitous throughout, simultaneously

43 *Ibid.*, IV, 275f.
44 *Ibid.*, 409.
45 *Ibid.*, V, 98–101.

promising Grenville full support and bargaining secretly with Pitt over Grenville's ouster. It is also clear that Pitt's demands were so outrageous that the king finally had no choice but to confirm Grenville in power. Grenville himself seems to have stayed remarkably calm, allowing himself a few bitter comments only when he discovered at the end of August that the king, after openly committing himself to Grenville, was still carrying on with Pitt. In order to keep his favorable image of Pitt intact, Bancroft not only makes the king's relations with Pitt seem noble and upright but pictures Grenville as the guilty party gnawing his lip with jealousy and rage.

The task of sustaining this image was complicated by the fact that Bancroft's best sources were written by members of Grenville's camp, and as a result he repeatedly turns them around to fit his interpretation. He begins his account by applauding Lord Hardwicke's advice to the king to replace the triumvirate with a new cabinet: "The wise answer of the illustrious jurist was reported to the king, who, disregarding the most earnest dissuasions of Grenville, desired ten days for reflection, on which Grenville went into the country to await the decision."[46] The bias against Grenville is clear. The king wants to "reflect" on the "wise answer" of an "illustrious jurist" while Grenville clamors in protest. Yet there is no evidence in the sources Bancroft used that Grenville acted with the tactlessness connoted in Bancroft's "most earnest dissuasions." On the contrary, the sources suggest that he worked hard to make the other members of the cabinet behave themselves during the ten-day grace period. On August 4, for example, he wrote Egremont in a note Bancroft never mentions that "to wait ten days or a fortnight, if it is wished, for the decision of an alternative which has been so temperately and so firmly stated, is certainly more decent than to insist upon the conclusion of it in eight-and-forty hours."[47]

[46] *Ibid.*, 139 f.

[47] Grenville to Egremont, 4 August 1763, *The Grenville Papers* (ed. by William J. Smith), II, 85.

Next Bancroft turns to Egremont. After derogating his behavior with such words as "harangue," "extorting," "insulting," "uncivil," and "impertinent," Bancroft goes on to paraphrase Egremont's August 6 reply to Grenville. In this letter Egremont complains about the hidden influence of the king's favorite, Lord Bute, who, Egremont suspects, may have inspired the attack on Grenville's ministry but who may be losing control of the situation he created. Egremont speaks of "absolute necessity and fear" being felt by Bute, which it is clear from the context he means may result from pressure brought against Bute by persons or circumstances beyond the control of the triumvirate. Says Egremont:

[W]hether any proposal may not have been already, or intended to be extended by other hands, I cannot tell; should rather fancy it is so intended to be, for I think nothing will make the fluctuating mind of the chief spring [Bute] of all this confusion resolve to do fairly by us, but absolute necessity and fear; most probably when it will be too late.[48]

Egremont's "other hands" seems to refer to politicians, other than those allied either with Grenville or Pitt, who were also jockeying for position and who might have been so dangerous to Bute as to make it an "absolute necessity" for him to support the triumvirate for "fear" of losing his own favor with the king if these "other hands" came to power. Though complicated and suggestive, Egremont's comment seems to have no sinister intent. Bancroft gives it a marvelously dark reading:

Instead of hastily resigning, Egremont was ready to concert with Grenville how to maintain themselves in office in spite of the king's wishes, by employing "absolute necessity and fear."[49]

This is a prime example of the way Bancroft points the lan-

---

[48] Egremont to Grenville, 6 August 1763, *ibid.*, 89.
[49] *History*, V, 140.

guage of sources that contradict him toward his own ends in the volumes published after 1850. Here, as elsewhere, the technique is quick, subtle, and devastating: it demonstrates how, despite his apparent detachment in these volumes, Bancroft uses snippets from his sources to bolster his interpretations at any cost.

The interpretation in this case is plain throughout the episode. Unknown to Grenville until August 26, the king entered into negotiations with Pitt on August 10, and these continued into September. In his diary for August 20 and 21, Grenville, referring to himself in the third person, recorded the following conversation with the king:

Saturday, 20th.—The King . . . spoke . . . with great praise of Mr. Grenville, and said he could never have anybody at the head of his Treasury who would fill that Office so much to his satisfaction as he did.

Sunday, 21st.—The King sent to Mr. Grenville at nine o'clock, to order him to come to him immediately; he went directly, and the King told him that he had fully considered upon the long discourse Mr. Grenville had held to him on the Friday . . . [and] that by his advice he meant to conduct himself.[50]

Unwilling to allow Grenville the credit he claims for himself here, Bancroft reworks the passage into an attack on Grenville's abilities as a speaker:

For a day or two the king hesitated, and had to endure the very long and tedious speeches of Grenville on the inconveniences of sacrificing his ministry.* 'I have fully considered your long discourse on the Friday,' said he to his minister on Sunday the twenty-first; 'by your advice I mean to conduct myself.'[51]

Far from boring the king, Grenville's speech apparently convinced him to break off with Pitt, though the break was not

---

[50] "Mr. Grenville's Diary," *Grenville Papers*, II, 192 f.
[51] *History*, V, 141 f.

actually made until early in September. Bancroft's "inconvenience of sacrificing his ministry" is a sarcastic phrase he has worked together from two sentences in Grenville's diary entry for Friday, August 19. It especially shades the meaning of the second, in which Grenville, protesting the king's "sacrificing his servants in Mr. Wilkes's affair,"[52] refers to an event totally unconnected with the current struggle.

Partly because Pitt left few records of the negotiation and partly because all the sources agree that his behavior throughout was arrogant and unreasonable, Bancroft keeps the spotlight trained on Grenville's alleged defects rather than on Pitt's virtues. The result, as the examples suggest, is a sort of running assassination of Grenville's character. As in Volumes II and III, Bancroft conforms the particulars of his evidence and his narrative to an interpretation diametrically opposed to that of the sources themselves. Yet here he buries the judgment beneath an avalanche of footnotes and documents, thus making it seem that his own bias is weaker than in the earlier volumes. In such passages he reaches the logical end of his rebellion against the tradition he inherited. No source, no matter how primary, is sacred; all individual documents are merely grist for the interpretive mill, to be manipulated as Bancroft sees fit.

Neither Volume VII of the *History*, published in 1858, nor Volume VIII, published two years later, contains a single footnote, and the omission of footnotes from the two books, of course, puts them beyond the reach of the kind of analysis that has here been applied to the first six. Volumes IX and X, written in Bancroft's old age, contain a smattering of notes that are insufficient for close study, and revisions of the entire *History*, done in 1876 and 1882, offer none whatsoever. There may be significance in his almost total omission of notes from the *History* after the publication of Volume VI. At last he seems to have taken the step which freed him completely

[52] "Diary," *Grenville Papers*, II, 192.

from the scissors-and-paste methodology against which he revolted in his first volume twenty-five years earlier and which he resisted even more vigorously in his next five. With his powerful urge to write not merely original but transcendental history, he never could be content with the slavish adherence to particular documents which characterized the tradition he inherited. Footnoting may have been identified in his mind with that tradition. If so, the abandonment of notes in his late volumes may simply have been his refusal to give individual sources an important role in his narrative.

However we judge the propriety of Bancroft's methods, we will perhaps at the least grant that they were well adapted to his themes. The thesis that the God who rules history is knowable through the intuition of the common man, is sure to defeat the rationalist and the skeptic, and is bent on uniting all mankind in democratic brotherhood could never in any case be proved by historical induction. In effect, Bancroft admitted as much from the beginning in the way he used sources, though Volume I was less revealing in this respect than later volumes. On the basis of his religious assumptions he was able to set early American history at the center of the cosmic drama and to give what he saw as the triumph of that history—the achievement, through experience, of a perfect compromise between the anarchic and despotic impulses in man by means of the American method of confederation—divine sanction. Perhaps unwittingly, he paralleled his argument that Americans gravitated, because of instinctive faith in divine providence and fixed moral law, away from the outer darkness of despotism and anarchy toward the light of unified freedom with a method in which he himself imposed verbal and intellectual unity on the jumble of his historical sources. As God drew Americans inexorably to union, Bancroft drew the documents inexorably to unity. Bancroft may never have admitted, even to himself, that there was a similarity between God's method as ruler of the universe and his own method as a historian, of course. Yet the contemporary American writers who most fully shared Bancroft's transcendental conception of the universe—Emerson, Thoreau, and Whitman—all maintained that the creativity of the artist is godlike. Whether or not Bancroft consciously acknowledged such a parallel, his method reflects and realizes many of the implications of his argument in the *History*.

That this interlocking of theme and method resulted in weaknesses as well as strengths in the *History* cannot be denied. The manipulations of documentary evidence in the Pitt-Grenville episode, for example, come close to breaking the rules of the game, and similarly dubious practices occur often in the volumes that followed the first. The two types of originality—verbal and interpretive—that Bancroft introduces and keeps under relatively tight rein in Volume I come into conflict with his sources thereafter, with the result that the delicate editorial balance between fidelity to the evidence and fidelity to his own argument which he strikes in Volume I seems often on the verge of collapse. He works his generalizations directly into his rewriting of particular documents in the later books, and despite the muting of his earlier oratorial style in Volumes IV, V, and VI, he disregards the original context of borrowed language there more than in Volume I.

Yet on the whole, making the necessary allowances for his defense of transcendental theism, his attack on eighteenth-century sensationalism and rationalism, his overbearing patriotism, and his questionable editorial techniques, it is arguable that Bancroft's interpretation of the contradictory traditions of individual freedom and collective restraint in America, his shrewd and realistic reading of particular men and events in the past, and his revolutionary method of incorporating evidence into his narrative constitute an impressive literary achievement. More to the point, he established thematic and methodological norms from which Parkman and Adams often departed but were never able completely to ignore. Bancroft stands, pioneer like, at the beginning not only of the tradition the three men form but of U.S. historiography itself. In 1865, the year before Bancroft issued his ninth volume, a thin, compulsive Bostonian published the first of another monumental series of books on the colonial history of North America. Francis Parkman had set his *France and England in North America* on its journey into the wilderness.

★ ★ ★ ★ ★ ★

The Wilderness,
New France,
and English Liberty

IF BANCROFT's *History* floats on the optimistic, egalitarian
flood tide of nineteenth-century American thought, Parkman's nine-volume *France and England* rides its agnostic,
pessimistic, aristocratic undercurrents. Where Bancroft sees
a benevolent God ruling history, Parkman sees the amoral
and indifferent forces of physical nature; where Bancroft sees
endless panoramas of material progress, Parkman sees the
possibilities of greed and corruption; where Bancroft sees
democracy blossoming into a brotherhood of man, Parkman
sees the danger of the rise of demagogues and the extinction
of individual self-control and heroism. While Bancroft embraced the optimistic side of Edwards' Calvinism, which he
then developed into a benevolent and democratic transcen-
dentalism of his own, Parkman professed an agnosticism
that, rejecting the formal doctrines of pre- and post-Edward-
sean Calvinism, nevertheless retained most of its pessimism
about life, its distrust of mankind in the mass, and its allegori-
zation of existence into an exhausting but supremely dramatic
struggle between the forces of good and evil.

Part of the explanation for these contrasts lies in the difference between the lives the two men led. Born twenty-three
years after Bancroft in 1823 to a wealthy Boston family with

impeccable social credentials, Parkman never had to worry about making his way in the world. Although critical of some aspects of the tightly knit New England society in which he grew up, he was comfortable enough within it never to break away, as Bancroft did, and settle elsewhere. Moreover, at the age of fifteen, he says, he got involved in a love affair that changed the course of his life:

I became enamoured of the backwoods. This new passion—which proved permanent— . . . soon got full possession of me, and mixed itself with all my literary aspirations. . . . It was not till some years later that I enlarged the plan to include the whole course of the American conflict between France and England; or, in other words, the history of the American forest; for this was the light in which I regarded it. My theme fascinated me, and I was haunted with wilderness images day and night.[1]

At an age when Bancroft was reading Jonathan Edwards cover to cover and preparing himself for a four-year grind in German universities, Parkman was out tramping the Middlesex Fells and taking rugged hikes through the wilderness of northern New England and New York. And when in the fall of 1843 he had his first bout with what he called "the Enemy"—the mysterious and doubtless psychosomatic complex of illnesses that plagued him all his life—he simply left Harvard and took a year-long recuperative tour through Europe at his family's expense. Moreover, as his statement shows, he discovered his ruling passion for the American wilderness and its history before he graduated from college, and although he began studying law after his return from Europe in 1844 and a year and a half later earned a law degree, he spent most of his time during these years exploring historical sites and writing stories of wilderness adventure. While Bancroft did not settle on writing history till he was

[1] Francis Parkman to Martin Brimmer, in Henry D. Sedgwick, *Francis Parkman*, 329 f.

in his thirties, Parkman seems to have known from adolescence where his life's work lay.

Yet the path between ambition and final achievement was a bitterly hard one for Parkman. Though by 1852 he had been able to publish *The Oregon Trail*, his account of a camping expedition to the far west in 1846, and *The Conspiracy of Pontiac*, his apprentice work in history for the later *France and England,* he had already begun experiencing serious attacks from the Enemy that laid him low for long periods of time. Insomnia, indigestion, partial blindness, numbness in the hands and feet, and vertigo gripped him and left him unfit for work. Yet it seemed that in 1852, having inherited his father's wealth, married, and brought his illness more or less under control, he was ready to push his historical work forward rapidly. Then the Enemy struck with a force that kept him *hors de combat* for thirteen years and for the rest of his life reduced his literary productivity to a fraction of what it might have been. For days on end he had to lie in a darkened room without moving, since the slightest stimulation would set his brain whirling. In addition, arthritis partly crippled his legs, a particularly frustrating debility for someone who so loved the outdoors. To crown his suffering, his four-year-old son died in 1857 and his wife a year later. Prostrated, he dragged himself to various sanitariums to try to regain his health, traveling as far as Paris in 1858–59 to be treated by a brain specialist, but recovery was slow. Tormented by relapses, he nevertheless managed to work out a system of study in which he would first listen to people read from sources and then dictate his own narrative. He also devised a writing grid with wires a half-inch apart to guide his pencil. Through the Civil War years he somehow learned to live with his handicaps, and by 1865, thirteen years after he had begun, he was able to bring out the first volume of *France and England*, entitled *Pioneers of France in the New World.*

Was Parkman helped through these trials by some form of

deep religious faith like Bancroft's? Though there is some evidence that Parkman was attracted to religion at several points in his life,[2] his histories are unmistakably agnostic in tone. The word "Providence" occurs in them hardly more than a dozen times, and in all but two or three cases it is attributed to a point of view distinct from Parkman's own. At the two or three points where Parkman does use the term in a personal sense, he seems merely to be dabbling in the kind of providential rhetoric that saturates Bancroft's work. "Supernaturalism," as he calls it,[3] is for him almost always a term of disparagement, and he criticizes even his most sympathetic Catholic heroes, such as Samuel de Champlain,[4] for indulging in it. On this score, Protestants fare no better than Catholics. Parkman never tires of mocking the "redhot Calvinism" which led New Englanders to teach "their duty to other people, whether by pen, voice, or bombshells."[5] The men he admires most are those like La Salle, who, seeing the comet of 1680, "coolly noted down the phenomenon, not as a portentous messenger of war and woe, but rather as an object of scientific curiosity."[6]

For religion, Parkman seems in *France and England* to substitute a partly naturalistic, partly sociological environmentalism. The ultimate reality in Parkman's *Weltanschauung* is physical nature, as Howard Doughty has pointed out,[7] and within that ultimate reality a second "nature" consisting of human civilization. The larger context of physical nature that emerges from *France and England* is basically static or, like the seasons, at best cyclical and thus incompati-

[2] Howard Doughty, *Francis Parkman*, 393 f.

[3] *The Old Regime in Canada*, 8. All subsequent references to the text of *France and England in North America* will be to the nine-volume set edited by Allen Nevins, of which *The Old Regime* is Volume IV.

[4] *Pioneers of France in the New World*, 217.

[5] *A Half-Century of Conflict*, II, 131.

[6] *La Salle and the Discovery of the Great West*, 198 f.

[7] *Francis Parkman*, 190–97.

ble with a dynamic, meliorative interpretation of history like Bancroft's. To Parkman the laws of nature are fixed, yet they offer little sign of the moral order that Bancroft assumes controls all history. On the contrary, Parkman repeatedly describes natural law in tooth-and-claw terms, as when he remarks that the primeval Maine forest "survives, in some part, to this day, with the same prodigality of vital force, the same struggle for existence and mutual havoc that mark all organized beings, from men to mushrooms."[8]

Yet human civilization has to some extent modified this struggle for existence, and it is within the context of this second, sociological environment that Parkman establishes the criteria for most of his ethical judgments. For example, he is more apt to explain human behavior in terms of race or national character than Bancroft. While Bancroft analyzes Indian life in his third volume chiefly to show the unity of mankind, Parkman sets out in *The Jesuits in North America in the Seventeenth Century* to prove that red men are racially inferior to whites. "If the higher traits popularly ascribed to the race are not to be found [in the Huron-Iroquois tribes]," he begins, "they are to be found nowhere,"[9] and he concludes that despite their superiority to other Indians, "there is no indication whatsoever [in the Iroquois] of a tendency to overpass the confines of a wild-hunter and warrior life. They were inveterately attached to it, impracticable conservatists of barbarism, and in ferocity and cruelty they matched the worst of their race."[10] On the other hand, he views the Anglo-Saxon as superior to other Caucasians. England, "vitalized by a stable and regulated liberty, has peopled a continent and spread colonies over all the earth, gaining constantly new vigor with the matchless growth of its offspring."[11] He explains these racial-national differences in

8 *A Half-Century of Conflict*, I, 32.
9 P. xliii.
10 *Ibid.*, lxvf.
11 *Pioneers*, 413

terms of the centuries-long development that has produced them. "Not institutions alone," he says, "but geographical position, climate, and many other conditions unite to form the educational influences that, acting through successive generations, shape the character of nations and communities."[12] Physical and social environment determines racial and national character, which in its turn determines civilization. Providence, if it exists, is too remote to matter.

In addition to these general philosophical differences between Parkman and Bancroft, there are a host of specific differences in the argument, style, tone, and subject matter of their works. To be sure, in his introduction to *Pioneers*, Parkman, discussing the scope and subject of the series of books he plans to write, pays an unmistakable tribute to Bancroft's *History*. Saying that although he, Parkman, will be describing the "springs of American civilization," he will not "enter upon subjects which have already been thoroughly investigated and developed" but instead "restrict himself to those where new facts may be exhibited, or facts already known may be placed in a more clear and just light."[13] Though historians other than Bancroft, most notably Hildreth, had written on early American history, it is Bancroft to whom Parkman here chiefly refers. And though from the first Parkman had been attracted more to the history of the wilderness, the Indians, and French exploration of the interior continent than to the English colonies, part of his reason for focusing on Canadian history in *France and England* was undoubtedly the fact that in his opinion Bancroft had not only "done" English America but done it well.

Yet at the same time he implies that he disagrees with Bancroft's *History* in many ways. He wants to set "facts already known . . . in a more clear and just light." As often as not he seems in *France and England* to carry on a running debate

12 *The Old Regime*, 394.
13 *Pioneers*, xxxi.

with Bancroft, not merely at the points where they discuss the same subjects but throughout, in their fundamental attitudes toward human experience. Bancroft sees the Quaker sect as triumphantly democratic and, in its doctrine of the Inner Light, as embodying the best in religious intuitionalism; Parkman sees the Quakers as a faction not only "capable of extreme bitterness towards opponents" and "jealous for the ascendancy of their sect" but especially imbecile in arguing that it is a "sin to fight, and above all to fight against Indians."[14] In contrast to Bancroft's picture of the Indian as an instinctively religious and thus worthy member of the human family, Parkman draws a portrait in acid, concluding that the "primitive Indian, yielding his untutored homage to One All-pervading and Omnipotent Spirit, is a dream of poets, rhetoricians, and sentimentalists."[15] It seems likely that Parkman is here consciously pointing to Bancroft as one of the dreamers, but the identification is even more certain when he describes those who deplore the Acadian deportation in 1755 as infected with "New England humanitarianism, melting into sentimentality at a tale of woe."[16] Though Longfellow's *Evangeline*, published in 1847, undoubtedly set the tone Parkman ridicules, it was not until Bancroft's fourth volume in 1852 that Longfellow's pro-French, anti-British bias found its way into the mainstream of American historical writing, and Parkman's treatment of the Acadian question is almost a point-by-point rebuttal of Bancroft's.

The contrast between the two men is perhaps clearest in the style and tone of their works. Parkman's style, though by no means plain in a twentieth-century, Hemingwayesque sense or always cliché free, as David Levin has pointed out,[17] is nevertheless much simpler, more straightforward, less orator-

14 *Montcalm and Wolfe*, I, 336 f.
15 *Jesuits*, lxxxix.
16 *Montcalm and Wolfe*, I, 284.
17 Levin, *History as Romantic Art*, 221–23.

ical than Bancroft's. Whereas Bancroft often seems to use the heaviest words he can find, Parkman generally avoids self-consciously elegant or epic diction. The flow of his sentences is smoother than Bancroft's. Fewer sentences roll majestically toward their periods, fewer clauses are set in heavy antithesis or parallelism, fewer verbs thunder in the subjunctive mood. With this simplifying of style there is a corresponding lightening of tone, best seen, perhaps, in the humor which is almost completely missing from Bancroft's pages but which fills Parkman's. One of Henry IV's mistresses is described as "the crafty and capricious siren who had awakened . . . conjugal tempests" between the king and queen.[18] Very unlike her is the Canadian heiress Jeanne Le Ber, who shut herself up in a cell behind the altar of a Montreal church for twenty years. Says Parkman:

> Though she rarely permitted herself to speak, yet some oracular utterance of the sainted recluse would now and then escape to the outer world. One of these was to the effect that teaching poor girls to read, unless they wanted to be nuns, was robbing them of their time. Nor was she far wrong, for in Canada there was very little to read except formulas of devotion and lives of saints.[19]

The legends and superstitions of Catholicism regularly provoke caustic comments like that concerning "the Holy House of Loretto,—which, as all the world knows, is the house wherein Saint Joseph dwelt with his virgin spouse, and which angels bore through the air from the Holy Land to Italy, where it remains an object of pilgrimage to this day."[20] Louis XIV's efforts to populate Canada resulted in a matrimonial clearance sale in which "Hymen, if not Cupid, was whipped into a frenzy of activity."[21] A French officer, routed from his post during a

[18] *Pioneers*, 262.
[19] *The Old Regime*, 359.
[20] *Jesuits*, 432.
[21] *The Old Regime*, 226f.

battle near Quebec in 1760, leaves behind "his watch, hat and feather, wine, liquor-case, and mistress."[22]

Parkman is no less amused by Anglo-Americans, especially New Englanders, though because of the weighting of *France and England* toward Canadian history he has fewer chances to chide them. Typical of the tone he often uses on them is his remark at the beginning of his narrative of the New England expedition against Quebec in 1696:

Humility was not among the New England virtues, and it was thought a sin to doubt that God would give his chosen people the victory over papists and idolaters; yet no pains were spared to ensure the divine favor. A proclamation was issued, calling the people to repentance; a day of fasting was ordained; and, as Mather expresses it, "the wheel of prayer was kept in continual motion."[23]

Of course the New Englanders are humiliated in the campaign, with the result, says Parkman dryly, that the "Puritan bowed before 'this awful frown of God,' and searched his conscience for the sin that had brought upon him so stern a chastisement."[24] The habitual tendency of New Englanders toward what he sees as an excess of zeal prompts Parkman to take potshots at his own contemporaries, as when he likens the impractical settlement of Roberval along the St. Lawrence in 1542, with its communal style, to "one of the experimental communities of recent days"[25]—a barb probably aimed in part at Brook Farm. At another point he compares the New Englander of his own day and of the eighteenth century and wryly concludes that the "mixture, which is now too common, of cool emotions with excitable brains, was then rarely seen."[26]

Then, too, the subject matter of Parkman's books is different from Bancroft's. Material to which Bancroft gives at most

[22] *Montcalm and Wolfe*, II, 336.
[23] *Count Frontenac and New France under Louis XIV*, 245.
[24] *Ibid.*, 284.
[25] *Pioneers*, 205.
[26] *Montcalm and Wolfe*, I, 27.

two or three chapters in his first three volumes or does not discuss at all is the meat of Parkman's first five books. The first, *Pioneers*, narrates the ill-fated French Huguenot colony in Florida in the sixteenth century and then shifts halfway through to an account of French exploration of the St. Lawrence Basin and of Acadia in the sixteenth century and the settlement of Quebec and the exploration of the northern Lakes under Champlain in the seventeenth. The second volume, *Jesuits*, published in 1867, begins with a seventy-page description of Indian culture and goes on to narrate the three-pronged story of Jesuit missionary work among the Hurons between 1633 and 1652; the wars between the Hurons and the Iroquois and the subsequent collapse and martyrdom of the Jesuit missions, 1641–52; and the founding of Montreal in 1642 and its first decade of growth. With *The Discovery of the Great West*, first published in 1869 but revised and retitled *La Salle and the Discovery of the Great West* in 1879, Parkman moves away from the Saint Lawrence–Great Lakes region to an account of French penetration of the Mississippi Valley between 1672 and 1689, culminating in La Salle's descent of the Mississippi and his disastrous attempt to found a colony at its mouth in the 1680's.

In *The Old Regime*, published in 1874, Parkman returns for the first third of the book to an account of Quebec and Montreal, carrying the story there forward from roughly the time of the collapse of the Huron missions in the early 1650's to the arrival of Frontenac in 1672. Then, in Part II of the book, he sets forth a description and analysis of the effects of French colonial policy in Canada, abandoning almost entirely the narrative style of the rest of *France and England* and concentrating chapter by chapter on different aspects of Canadian life. *Count Frontenac* (1877) returns to the narrative, quasi-biographical style of *Pioneers*, *Jesuits*, and *La Salle*. Here Parkman goes back over roughly the same time span he covered in *La Salle*, concentrating now, however, on

Canada's central administration and on the beginnings of conflict between New France and the English colonies to the south. Frontenac's stormy career, beginning with his appointment as governor by Louis XIV in 1672 and his recall in 1682, continuing with his reappointment in 1689, and ending with his death in 1698 after his defeat of both the English and the Iroquois, serves as the narrative framework of the book.

These first five volumes of *France and England* seldom overlap Bancroft's *History* in subject matter. With *Montcalm and Wolfe*, however, published in 1884, Parkman retold a part of the story Bancroft had already covered in detail. *Montcalm and Wolfe*, focused on the fighting between France and England during the French and Indian War, coincides almost exactly with the time span and the events covered in Bancroft's fourth volume. Yet even here the contrast between the two historians' aims and approaches is plain. Whereas Bancroft treats the war as a preliminary to the more important conflict between America and England in the 1760's and 1770's, Parkman treats it as the climax of his entire work. Bancroft's prime interest is in the effect of the war on America's relationship with England, Parkman's in its effect on England's struggle with France. Moreover, Bancroft writes more as a political and diplomatic historian, Parkman more as a military historian, and there is a heavier stress on the drama, heroism, and excitement of the fighting itself in *Montcalm and Wolfe* than in Bancroft's book. *Montcalm and Wolfe*, more than twice as long as Volume IV, offers a correspondingly greater wealth of narrative detail, and at many points— the Acadian deportation is an example—Parkman's interpretations completely oppose Bancroft's. The final volume of *France and England*, appearing in 1892 a year before his death, completes Parkman's narrative by returning to Frontenac's death in 1698 and bringing the story up to the beginning of *Montcalm and Wolfe*. Entitled *A Half-Century of Conflict*, the book bears about the same relationship to Bancroft's *History* as the first five volumes of *France and England*.

Thus far the differences between the two historians' works have been underscored. There are many similarities as well, in interpretation, theme, and literary technique.[27] Yet what seems to me to be the most important link between them has never been traced. This is, of course, the conflict between freedom and constraint or union, which is, I believe, woven into the fabric of *France and England* no less pervasively than in Bancroft's *History* and which embodies virtually the same impulse toward compromise, toward finding a workable middle ground between extremes, that is found in the earlier historian's work.

Doughty has shown that the contrast between nature and civilization which permeates all of Parkman's historical writing does not reflect the conventional romantic dichotomy between nature as Rousseauvian innocence and civilization as corrupter of that innocence but instead a complex and even tragic sense of symbiotic relation between the two.[28] In Parkman's nature, argues Doughty, we see the same struggle between creativity and destructiveness, beauty and ugliness, delight and horror, that characterizes human civilization. Constituting merely a part of nature, man reflects all its ambiguities and contradictions, and the penetration of European civilization into the American wilderness results in neither a solution to nor a corruption of nature but instead a continuation, in different form, of nature's basic conflicts and imbalances. On these grounds Doughty agrees with Otis Pease that Parkman does not, despite his biographical approach and his celebration of personal heroism, advocate a "great man" theory of history.[29] Parkman's heroes do not control

[27] The best, indeed only, study of the common literary and thematic ground shared by Bancroft and Parkman, along with Prescott and Motley, is Levin's *History as Romantic Art*.

[28] *Francis Parkman*, 190–96.

[29] *Ibid.*, 229–31; Otis Pease, *Parkman's History: The Historian as Literary Artist*, 31–43.

history; they either resist it, like La Salle or Montcalm, at great personal cost or follow its necessities, often at equally great cost.

Yet what has not been pointed out is that despite the complexity of Parkman's interpretation of them, nature and civilization do nevertheless each have a primary connotation in *France and England* that establishes them as poles between which the whole work develops. The basic connotation of nature, or the American wilderness, is personal freedom, or license; the basic connotation of civilization, or the French and the English colonies, is union, self-sacrifice to the group, centralization. Yet Parkman distinguishes between the civilization of the French and the English colonies. New France emerges as the polar extreme of centralization, opposite the polar extreme of anarchic freedom connoted by the wilderness, while the English colonies with their tradition of "ordered liberty" represent a tough and, in Parkman's eyes, desirable compromise between the two. As Doughty shows, however, neither nature nor civilization is to Parkman altogether good or altogether bad. Correspondingly, the freedom of the wilderness emerges from *France and England* as both desirable and undesirable, similarly ambiguous in this respect to its opposite number, the absolutism of New France. Even the compromise system lying symbolically between them, that of the seaboard British colonies, reveals weaknesses as well as strengths. It is in the self-control, self-discipline, and moral strength of individual men and women that Parkman finds a denominator not only common to the wilderness, the English colonies, and New France but sufficiently stable and universal to serve as a moral criterion valid for the whole range of human experience they embrace.

An analysis first of Parkman's image of the wilderness. In the introduction to *Pioneers* he defines the human meaning of the vast world of sky, sun, storm, water, and thick foliage that greeted the white man in North America. It was a world "of the wildest freedom," and for the French trapper and *coureur de bois* it taught "a lesson of lawless independence."[30] The Frenchmen who tried to found a colony in Florida in 1562, "surrounded by that influence of the wilderness which wakens the dormant savage in the breasts of men, soon fell into quarrels."[31] This corrosive, barbarizing effect of wild country, though a constant threat to every white man, actually occurs in *France and England* in general only among French Canadians of the lower classes. When for example La Salle makes his voyages of discovery into the midcontinent, he keeps losing the rank and file of his expeditions through desertions, which Parkman attributes to "a spirit of lawlessness" that broke out among the men "with a violence proportioned to the pressure which had hitherto controlled it. Discipline had no resources and no guarantee; while those outlaws of the forest, the *coureurs de bois*, were always before their eyes, a standing example of unbridled license."[32] Often these deserters, much to Parkman's disgust, gave up civilization altogether and joined Indian tribes.

The *coureurs de bois*, however, usually did not go this far. Literally "forest runners," they held to a trapping and trading way of life outside both the white man's and the red man's civilizations, escaping "from the control of intendants, councils, and priests, to the savage freedom of the wilderness."[33] Yet "a year or two of bush-ranging spoiled them for civilization,"[34] and although Parkman suggests their life-style was romantic and full of wilderness adventure, he makes it clear that they themselves were anything but poetic: "It would be false coloring to paint the half-savage *coureur de bois* as a romantic lover of nature. He liked the woods because they

---

[30] *Pioneers*, xxxiii.
[31] *Ibid.*, 38.
[32] *La Salle*, 165 f.
[33] *The Old Regime*, 309 f.
[34] *Ibid.*, 313.

emancipated him from restraint."[35] The repressiveness of Canadian society was to blame, argues Parkman, for their defection to the anarchy of the woods, a defection that for Parkman symbolizes the chief weakness of French colonization in North America. Unlike the English, the French tried to exploit the wilderness without taming it, with the result that many of Canada's potentially most useful citizens, such as the *coureurs de bois*, were irrestibly drawn to the license of the forest. Though Canadians "showed an aptitude for mechanical trades, they preferred above all things the savage liberty of the backwoods."[36]

Thus the negative side of the freedom that the wilderness always connotes to Parkman is its anarchy. The woods are often pictured in terms of jungle war, with the fittest alone surviving and they themselves succumbing at last to the inexorable cycle of birth, growth, death, and decay. At one point in *A Half-Century of Conflict* the forest is described as full of "[y]oung seedlings . . . , [which are] rich with the decay of those that had preceded them, crowding, choking and killing each other" and which "survive by blighting those about them. They in turn, as they grow, interlock their boughs, and repeat in a season or two the same process of mutual suffocation." Immediately afterward, Parkman half-playfully connects this carnage with democracy: "Not one infant tree in a thousand lives to maturity; yet these survivors form an innumerable host, pressed together in struggling confusion, squeezed out of symmetry and robbed of normal development, as men are said to be in the level sameness of democratic society."[37] Although his needling of extreme egalitarians here is tongue in cheek, his linking of democracy with the chaos of raw nature reflects one of the basic ideas of *France and England*. The wilderness functions throughout as a metaphor for

[35] *Ibid.*, 315.
[36] *Ibid.*, 364 f.
[37] *A Half-Century of Conflict*, I, 32 f.

complete social diffusion and individualism—that is, for extreme democracy. Correspondingly, it is enervating and meaningless. When the first explorers reach the site of Quebec, they are surrounded by "nameless barbarism"; [38] repeatedly Parkman describes the entire continent as wrapped in "savage slumber"; [39] when La Salle penetrates the Mississippi Valley, he finds a "dark domain of solitude and horror"[40] and, at the mouth of the Mississippi, the "limitless, voiceless" Gulf of Mexico, "lonely as when born of chaos, without a sail, without a sign of life."[41] The history of the continent before the arrival of European civilization is described as "gloomy and meaningless"[42] and Parkman is more than content that in face of the French and English the "long and gloomy reign of barbarism was drawing near its close."[43] Insofar as the wilderness remains without order or discipline of any kind it is a perfect image, in Parkman's eyes, of the lethargy, brutishness, and irrationality of man in the state of nature.

Yet men did live in this wilderness before the white man came and Parkman's portrayal of the Indian lies at the heart of the negative side of his view of forest freedom. Throughout *France and England* he associates the savagery of the Indians with the savagery of physical nature. They are a "fickle and bloodthirsty race"[44] that is "no less fierce, and far more dangerous"[45] than the wolves, bears, and wildcats that prowl the forest with them. As France's allies, they are "like a vast menagerie of wild animals"[46] roaming thousands of miles of wilderness, and Parkman's sympathy with the view of the British colonists that they were more like "vicious and dan-

[38] *Pioneers*, 185.
[39] *Ibid.*, 268; *Jesuits*, 55.
[40] *La Salle*, 194.
[41] *Ibid.*, 285.
[42] *Jesuits*, 246.
[43] *Ibid.*, 336.
[44] *Pioneers*, 250.
[45] *A Half-Century of Conflict*, I, 34.
[46] *Count Frontenac*, 403.

gerous wild animals" than men is obvious in his remark that "the benevolent and philanthropic view of the American savage is for those who are beyond his reach."[47] They are often associated with destructive and ungovernable processes, as when the Iroquois are pictured as seething around the Jesuit missionaries like "the lava-crust that palpitates with the throes of the coming eruption, while the molten death beneath . . . glares white-hot through a thousand crevices."[48] Their pitiless ferocity, which makes the wilderness "dark and bloodstained,"[49] goes hand in hand with an inability to reason inductively. Concerning tales of the Indian's knowledge of natural medicines, Parkman says that here, "as elsewhere, his knowledge is in fact scanty. He rarely reasons from cause to effect, or from effect to cause."[50] In fact, says Parkman, "[i]t is obvious that the Indian mind has never seriously occupied itself with any of the higher themes of thought. . . . His perpetual reference of [natural] phenomena to occult agencies forestalled inquiry and precluded inductive reasoning."[51] The result is that, "like all savages," the Indians are as "unstable as children."[52]

Their instability has a definite political significance for Parkman. Like the wilderness, they represent a sort of democratic chaos. Focusing on the Iroquois as the Indian *par excellence*, Parkman concludes that the political structure of the Iroquois nation was remarkable for "the incongruity of its spirit and its form. A body of hereditary oligarchs was the head of the nation, yet the nation was essentially democratic."[53] Despite the superior position of the chief and the absence of a leveling impulse in Indian society, "each man,

---

[47] *A Half-Century of Conflict*, I, 215.
[48] *The Old Regime*, 31.
[49] *Jesuits*, 295.
[50] *Ibid.*, xl.
[51] *Ibid.*, lxxxviii.
[52] *A Half-Century of Conflict*, II, 221.
[53] *Jesuits*, lxiv.

whether of high or low degree, had a voice in the conduct of affairs, and was never for a moment divorced from his wild spirit of independence. Where there was no property worthy the name, authority had no fulcrum and no hold."[54] All Indian tribes were "wild democracies" in which "a respect for native superiority, and a willingness to yield to it, were always conspicuous."[55] Although Parkman seems to see this deference to natural superiors as good, he makes it clear that the extreme individualism of Indian culture and the corresponding inability of the Indians to organize in really effective political combinations sealed their doom.[56] They could not unify themselves for effective warfare: "They waged war on a plan altogether democratic,—that is, each man fought or not, as he saw fit."[57] Equally disastrous, they were always at the mercy of hotheads and demagogues: "Among savages, with no government except the intermittent one of councils, the party of action and violence must always prevail."[58] Most debilitating of all, the Indian held to his barbarism and the entire tangle of irrational rites, customs, and superstitions which made up his culture with a bulldog tenacity that ruined any chance he might have had to organize against and defeat the white man. He was not only extremely independent and anarchistic but inflexibly set in his ways. Repeating the idea that the Indians "joined the extreme of wildness with the extreme of conservatism"[59] several times in *France and England*, Parkman links them again and again with the irrational, somehow helpless automatism of physical nature. The freedom of

[54] *Ibid.*, lxixf.
[55] *Ibid.*, xlix.
[56] Russell B. Nye, in "Parkman, Red Fate, and White Civilization," *Essays on American Literature in Honor of Jay B. Hubbell* (ed. by Clarence Gohdes), argues convincingly that Parkman viewed the Indians untamable savagery as one of the chief reasons for Anglo-American success in North America (pp. 152–63).
[57] *Jesuits*, 436.
[58] *Ibid.*, 302.
[59] *Count Frontenac*, 94.

the Indian and the wilderness, he argues, is the freedom of chaos and oblivion.

Yet while the wilderness always connotes a fundamentally dangerous freedom in *France and England*, it also connotes refreshment and invigoration. If one opens *France and England* and reads a few pages, he is likely to find evidence of the fascination with woodsmanship and wilderness scenery that distinguishes it from the work of every other nineteenth-century American historian except Theodore Roosevelt, who of course drew much of his inspiration for his *Winning of the West* (1889–96) from *France and England* and dedicated the work to Parkman. Parkman's narrative is regularly punctuated with lush descriptions of natural setting drawn from his own observations. His books shimmer with forest sunrises and sunsets, panoramas of coastlines, mountains, and prairies, and light sparkling from countless rivers and lakes. Storms of rain, snow, and wind whip through his pages with almost visceral force. We smell the frozen air of winter and the hot perfumes of summer. Repeatedly, he suggests that leaving civilization and immersing one's self in nature for a while is excellent spiritual and physical tonic. For example, after describing a part of the Canadian coastline that greeted a group of French colonists in 1612, he says: "Such is the scene that in this our day greets the wandering artist, the roving collegian bivouacked on the shore, or the pilgrim from stifled cities renewing his jaded strength in the mighty life of Nature."[60] Repeatedly, he celebrates the "savage charm" unspoiled by "the handiwork of man"[61] of wilderness scenes like the one revealed to Champlain when he first explored Lake Huron in 1615.[62]

[60] *Pioneers*, 275 f.
[61] *Ibid.*, 366.
[62] In an interesting study, *Wilderness and the American Mind*, Roderick Nash has pointed out (pp. 98 ff.) that Parkman's positive attitudes toward the wilderness reflected the nineteenth-century shift away from the earlier idea of

He lets his unhappiness over the destruction of the wilderness be known in a number of ways. One is to picture the first steps of the forest-clearing process as ugly and scarring. When the French begin a fort at Oswego on Lake Ontario in 1659, he says "a ghastly wound soon gaped in the green bosom of the woodland," filled with the "stumps and prostrate trees of the unsightly clearing."[63] Similarly, the pioneer work of the English settler on the frontier is described as "the repulsive transition from savagery to civilization, from the forest to the farm. The victims of his axe lay strewn about the dismal 'clearing' in a chaos of prostrate trunks, tangled boughs, and withered leaves, waiting for the fire that was to be the next agent in the process of improvement."[64] Parkman's sarcastic "improvement" echoes an undertone in *France and England* of hostility to industrialization and commercialism that we shall look at more closely later, and it is interesting to note that the chaos of the pioneer's clearing is similar to the chaos caused by the struggle for existence in the primeval forest. Man shares the destructive potential of nature. Parkman's doubts about the value of industrialization and the cutting down of the wilderness are suggested in the contrast he makes between the site of Pittsburgh in 1755 and the modern city, "with its swarming population, its restless industries, the clang of the forges, and its chimneys vomiting foul smoke into the face of heaven."[65] He seems to have seen the freedom of the wilderness as a welcome antidote to the restrictions, conformities, and vulgarities of modern civilization. While condemning its anarchy, he was powerfully drawn to its freshness, vitality, challenge.

---

the wilderness in Western civilization as something fearful and hostile to something valuable and beautiful enough to be preserved in national parks. *France and England* supports Nash's interpretation up to a point, yet it is important to remember that basically Parkman saw the wilderness as anarchy.

[63] *The Old Regime*, 29.
[64] *Montcalm and Wolfe*, I, 334.
[65] *Ibid.*, 207.

It was as a challenge to the moral strength and technical skill of the civilized man that Parkman seems to have valued the wilderness most highly. The wilderness tends to bring out the best in his strong-willed, masculine heroes and at least certain good qualities in those who, like the *coureurs de bois*, live a more or less savage life. The *coureurs de bois* are "white Indians, without discipline, and scarcely capable of it, but brave and accustomed to the woods."[66] As "excellent woodsmen, skillful hunters, and perhaps the best bushfighters in all Canada,"[67] they exhibit, like one of their most well-known members, Du Lhut, "a persistent hardihood" born of lives spent "exploring, trading, fighting."[68] The wilderness teaches them and the nobler representatives of civilization who enter it lessons of courage, self-discipline, and resourcefulness unavailable in civilized life yet as useful there, Parkman hints, as in the woods. The process of mastering the wilderness usually implies for Parkman a process of self-toughening and self-improvement, so that the value of contact with it is not only to clear one's brain of the cobwebs of civilization but to strengthen one's moral fiber.

At the opposite extreme from the anarchy of wild nature in *France and England* stands the paternalism and despotism of New France. Although Parkman's repeated contrast of what he calls the absolutism of the French colony with the liberty of the English colonies[69] is a central organizing principle of the nine volumes, it reflects an opposition that on the English side lies inside his more comprehensive contrast between New France and the wilderness. The liberty of the English colonies is of the regulated or ordered variety, as has already been mentioned and will be further analyzed, which represents a compromise between the true political poles of

66 *Count Frontenac*, 150.
67 *Montcalm and Wolfe*, II, 246.
68 *La Salle*, 255.
69 See, for example, *Pioneers*, xxxii f. and 396f., *Jesuits*, 448, and *Montcalm and Wolfe*, I, 35.

wilderness freedom and absolutist centralization in Parkman's work as a whole. These true poles are outlined at the beginning of the fifteenth chapter of *A Half-Century of Conflict*:

> Canada was divided between two opposing influences. On the one side were the monarchy and the hierarchy, with their principles of order, subordination, and obedience. . . . On the other side was the spirit of liberty, or license, which was in the very air of this wilderness continent, reinforced in the chiefs of the colony by a spirit of adventure inherited from the Middle Ages, and by a spirit of trade born of present opportunities. . . . Kindred impulses, in ruder forms, possessed the humbler colonists, drove them into the forest, and made them hardy woodsmen and skillful bush-fighters though turbulent and lawless members of civilized society.[70]

Especially revealing here is Parkman's equation of liberty and license. This is not the liberty represented by the English colonies in the absolutism-liberty dichotomy that Parkman mentions from time to time in *France and England* but rather the more basic—and dangerous—anarchy of the wilderness.

Opposite this liberty as well as English liberty stands New France. On balance, as with wilderness freedom, Parkman sees French-Canadian centralization as representing an undesirable extreme. Its worst flaw, the one Parkman sees as the key to the ultimate collapse of the colony, was its repression of individual initiative and, correspondingly, of self-reliance and self-discipline. Yet while Parkman sees the repressiveness of French absolutism as chiefly to blame for Canada's woes, he also suggests there was a ludicrous, quixotic quality about the whole Canadian venture that should limit the seriousness with which we take the repressiveness. It is in the areas of religion and politics that he takes the despotism of New France most to task.

Like Bancroft, though not so strongly, he argues that the religious despotism of New France contrasted with the reli-

[70] *A Half-Century of Conflict*, II, 2.

gious freedom of the English colonies. "To plant religious freedom on this Western soil," he says, "was not the mission of France. It was for her to rear in Northern forests the banner of Absolutism and of Rome; while, among the rocks of Massachusetts, England and Calvin fronted her in dogged opposition."[71] The main force behind this papist thrust, of course, was Jesuitism, which Parkman interprets as the incarnation of a totally hierarchical and authoritarian view of the universe. The Jesuits "would act or wait, dare, suffer, or die, yet all in unquestioning subjection to the authority of the Superiors, in whom they recognized the agents of Divine authority itself."[72] As the Iroquois was Indian *par excellence*, the Jesuit was priest *par excellence*, "rank," says Parkman, with the "instinct of domination" which, unchecked, "has always been the most mischievous of tyrannies."[73] Yet Parkman argues that the Jesuit was not so much ambitious for himself as "for the great corporate power in which he had merged his own personality."[74] He uses this argument to explain, for example, why the Jesuits encouraged only nuns to support the Canadian mission: "We hear of no zeal for the mission among religious communities of men. The Jesuits regarded the field as their own, and desired no rivals. . . . It was to the combustible hearts of female recluses that the torch was most busily applied."[75] Self-abasement to jealous, despotic power is what Parkman finds most deplorable in the Jesuit system.

It is with dry satisfaction that he reports the failure of this machinelike system to convert the North American Indians to Roman Catholicism. "They would have tamed the wild man of the woods," he says, "to a condition of obedience, un-

---

[71] *Pioneers*, 161 f.
[72] *Jesuits*, 7.
[73] *Ibid.*, 160.
[74] *La Salle*, 30.
[75] *Jesuits*, 153.

questioning, passive and absolute,—repugnant to manhood, and adverse to the invigorating and expansive spirit of modern civilization."[76] The effort was doomed from the start, not because the Indians had caught the modern spirit "but because their own ferocity and intractable indolence made it impossible that they should exist in its presence."[77] The result of all the Jesuits' missionary work was a handful of what Parkman calls tamed savages.[78] More sapping to the energies of New France, however, was the change from the "Canadian Jesuit of the first half of the seventeenth century," who "was before all things an apostle," to "his successor of a century later," who "was before all things a political agent."[79] Although suggestive of the flaws in their world view, the Jesuits' failure to convert the Indians was in many ways a noble failure. But the willingness of all the Catholic priests in Canada after Louis XIV's accession to do political work in return for a Catholic monopoly of the colony's religious life was a different matter. "We have said before," Parkman reminds us at the beginning of *Montcalm and Wolfe*, "and it cannot be said too often, that in making Canada a citadel of the State religion,—a holy of holies of exclusive Roman Catholic orthodoxy,—the clerical monitors of the Crown robbed their country of a trans-Atlantic empire. New France could not grow with a priest on guard at the gate to let in none but such as pleased him."[80]

Parkman finds Canada's religious despotism inseparable from its political. The one fueled the other. Behind them both stood French monarchism, epitomized for Parkman by Louis XIV: "He was a devout observer of the forms of religion. . . . Above all rulers of modern times, he was the embodi-

---

[76] *Ibid.*, 44 f.
[77] *Ibid.*, 320.
[78] *Ibid.*
[79] *A Half-Century of Conflict*, I, 134.
[80] *Montcalm and Wolfe*, I, 21.

ment of the monarchical idea."[81] Summing up the meaning of
Louis' career, Parkman emphasizes its repressiveness:
"Crushing taxation, misery, and ruin followed, till France
burst out at last in a frenzy, drunk with the wild dreams of
Rousseau. Then came the Terror and the Napoleonic wars,
and reaction on reaction, revolution on revolution, down to
our own day."[82] Here Parkman extends the repression-binge
syndrome of French Canada to the entire history of modern
France, warning that excessive political constraint always
engenders its opposite number. Virtually all of *The Old Regime*
is devoted to describing the particulars of Louis' paternalism in New France, which is said to have bound the government of the colony "from head to foot":[83] "Seignior, *censit-
aire*, and citizen were prostrate alike in flat subjection to the
royal will."[84]

The result, as Parkman points out again and again, was a
"spiritual and temporal vassalage from which the only escape
was to the savagery of the wilderness."[85] But what were the
effects on those who remained within the system? Parkman
defines at least three, all baneful. For the common citizen,
the chief effect was an enervation of mind and spirit that
reduced him to almost helpless dependence on higher authority. "The unchecked control of a hierarchy," says Parkman,
"robbed him of the independence of intellect and character,
without which, under the conditions of modern life, a people
must resign itself to a position of inferiority."[86] For those of
the ruling class who remained faithful to the king and their
duty, the effect was endless squabbling among themselves and
tattling to daddy. Parkman portrays this phenomenon very
convincingly by narrating several series of almost incredibly

81 *The Old Regime*, 171 f.
82 *A Half-Century of Conflict*, I, 2.
83 *The Old Regime*, 271.
84 *Ibid.*, 281.
85 *Montcalm and Wolfe*, II, 412.
86 *Ibid.*, I, 23.

childish quarrels among high colony officials, concluding one such series with the comment that "rivalry and jealousy rankled among the French officials, who continually maligned each other in tell-tale letters to the court"[87] and another by justifying "matters worthy of a knot of old gossips babbling around a tea-table" on the grounds that in them we can see "the workings of an unmitigated paternalism acting from across the Atlantic."[88] Parkman finds the deterioration of morale in such a system both sad and funny.

But the third major effect of Louis' paternalism in Canada —its encouragement of corruption in the public service—does not amuse him at all. From the time Canada became a royal colony, Parkman argues, France's mercantilist system of economic restriction, while similar to England's, was much more centralized, so that "the habit [Canadians] contracted, and were encouraged to contract, of depending on the direct aid of government" became fixed. "Not a new enterprise was set on foot without a petition to the king to lend a helping hand."[89] Thus "perverted and enfeebled,"[90] Canada's economy not only never became self-sufficient but tended more and more to become the "prey of official jackals. . . . Honesty could not be expected from a body of men clothed with arbitrary and ill-defined powers, ruling with absolute sway an unfortunate people who had no voice in their own destinies, and answerable only to an apathetic master three thousand miles away."[91] The "apathetic master" Parkman refers to here is Louis XV, but the same problem existed in Louis XIV's reign as well: "Nothing is more noticeable in the whole history of Canada," Parkman says, "after it came under the direct control of the Crown, than the helpless manner in which this

[87] *Count Frontenac*, 385.
[88] *A Half-Century of Conflict*, I, 114f.
[89] *The Old Regime*, 292.
[90] *Ibid.*, 289.
[91] *Montcalm and Wolfe*, II, 30.

absolute government was forced to overlook and ignore the disobedience and rascality of its functionaries in this distant transatlantic dependency."[92] Canadian paternalism not only drove its victims into the wilderness and emasculated those who remained within its grasp but was in its turn victimized by its own parasites.

And yet, like the wilderness, New France also symbolizes certain values that Parkman admires. Though basically undesirable, its drive toward religious, political, military, and social centralization is in Parkman's eyes not simply an unavoidable ingredient in human nature but in some ways a commendable one. In the first place, he sees it as tending to inspire loyalty to great central ideas or organizational systems. For example, despite its "horrible violence to the noblest qualities of manhood," the Jesuit order "has numbered among its members men whose fervent and exalted natures have been intensified, without being abased, by the pressure to which they have been subjected"[93] during their indoctrination. It produced in Canada that "marvellous *espirit de corps*, that extinction of self, and absorption of the individual in the Order, which has marked the Jesuits from their first existence as a body," a faithfulness and selflessness "no less strong than the self-devoted patriotism of Sparta or the early Roman Republic."[94] The loyalty, the sense of duty, the willingness to sacrifice oneself for a higher cause, which Parkman believes characterized the feudal ideal from which modern Catholicism and monarchy developed, attract him powerfully, and throughout *France and England* he pays a real if qualified tribute to these virtues.

In addition, he praises the military efficiency that centralization gave Canada. He finds the whole military atmosphere of Canada bracing. When he says in the introduction to

92 *The Old Regime*, 143.
93 *Jesuits*, 11 f.
94 *La Salle*, 93.

103

Pioneers that the "story of New France is, from the first, a story of war,"[95] he invites us to share his own fascination with it. In his sympathetic portrayal of the Canadians as a military people, he balances their willingness and ability to fight against the torpor other forms of paternalistic centralization produced. "From the moment when the Canadians found a chief whom they could trust," he says, "and the firm old hand of Frontenac grasped the reins of their destiny, a spirit of hardihood and energy grew up in all this rugged population; and they faced their stern fortunes with a stubborn daring and endurance that merit respect and admiration."[96] In other words, the reliance on authority and a chain of command that debilitated them in most areas of their lives equipped them well for military affairs. In the climactic struggle of the 1750's between France and England for control of the continent, says Parkman, the "rulers of Canada knew the vast numerical preponderance of their rivals; but with their centralized organization they felt themselves more than a match for any one English colony alone."[97] Unfortunately for Canada, the English colonies not only pulled themselves together during the war but were joined by thousands of veteran troops from England; yet Parkman concludes that "in this the most picturesque and dramatic of American wars, there is nothing more noteworthy than the skill with which the French and Canadian leaders used their advantages" and "the courage with which they were seconded by regulars and militia alike."[98]

Finally and perhaps most important, absolutist habits of thought produced in the leaders and explorers of New France a largeness and boldness of imagination missing in the English colonies. Although ultimately vain, the growth of New

[95] *Pioneers*, xxxiv.
[96] *Count Frontenac*, 309.
[97] *Montcalm and Wolfe*, I, 62.
[98] *Ibid.*, II, 381f.

France "was the achievement of a gigantic ambition striving to grasp a continent."[99] Parkman is usually critical, as here, of the quixotism of French schemes, yet he admires their breadth and associates them in a sympathetic way with the aristocratic, absolutist temper of French-Canadian culture. "In the French colonies," he says, "the representatives of the Crown were men bred in an atmosphere of broad ambition and masterful and far-reaching enterprise. Achievement was demanded of them."[100] The most striking embodiment of this spirit was La Salle, in whose exploits Parkman sees "a grand type of incarnate energy and will."[101] While the English colonists "plodded at their workshops, their farms, or their fisheries," New France strove behind the "patient gallantry of her explorers, the zeal of her missionaries, the adventurous hardihood of her bushrangers"[102] to realize mighty dreams. Her willingness to gamble for high stakes impresses Parkman as one of the great contributions of her system to American civilization.

At heart, however, Parkman, like Bancroft, is a believer in compromise. Though the extremes of wilderness freedom and Canadian unity attract him in several ways, he never seriously questions that the Anglo-American tradition of "regulated freedom,"[103] despite its imperfections, is the best solution available to mankind of the existential contradictions symbolized in New France and the wilderness. The imperfections in the English colonies, interestingly enough, are not only similar to those which Bancroft argues became evident during the revolutionary era but are, like Bancroft's, the result of too great a tendency to freedom. The three Parkman stresses are economic greed, military inefficiency, and political disunity.

99 *Pioneers*, xxxiv.
100 *A Half-Century of Conflict*, II, 65.
101 *La Salle*, 446.
102 *Montcalm and Wolfe*, I, 124f.
103 *Pioneers*, xxxii.

He implies that greed for wealth will always be a danger in an industrial democracy like America's. In his famous charge to America at the end of *Montcalm and Wolfe*, he asserts that the country must "rally her powers from the race for gold and the delirium of prosperity to make firm the foundations on which that prosperity rests."[104] At the beginning of the same book he condemns the Puritans for their "excess in the pursuit of gain,"[105] and in *Count Frontenac* he equates the materialism of democracy with military weakness: "The conditions of [Massachusetts'] material prosperity were adverse to efficiency in war. A trading republic, without trained officers, may win victories; but it wins them either by accident or by an extravagant outlay in money and life."[106] Hints of Parkman's distaste for the scramble for money which he feels threatens American democracy can be heard throughout *France and England*, and the hints are all connected with his belief that economic selfishness, like other kinds, smacks of the tooth-and-claw savagery of the primeval forest. The man struggling blindly for fortune is like the tree, the animal, or the Indian struggling blindly for existence. Parkman deplores the hucksterism, especially in America, of what he elsewhere favorably calls "the self-relying energies of modern practical enterprise."[107]

The military inefficiency of the British colonies is presented in *France and England* as one of their chief problems from the beginning of hostilities with New France in the 1680's to Pitt's rise to power in 1757. Parkman introduces the seventy-year struggle between the colonies by excoriating "the bungling inefficiency which marked the military management of the New England governments from the close of Philip's war to the peace of Utrecht."[108] At Fort Pemaquid in 1696 the Mass-

104 *Montcalm and Wolfe*, II, 413 f.
105 *Ibid.*, I, 26.
106 *Count Frontenac*, 285.
107 *La Salle*, 73.
108 *Count Frontenac*, 224.

achusetts government acts "with its usual military fatuity."[109] Summarizing the military differences between New France and the English colonies, he says the conflict consisted of "a compact military absolutism confronting a heterogeneous group of industrial democracies, where the force of numbers was neutralized by diffusion and incoherence."[110]

The military shortcomings of the English colonies were only a symptom of what Parkman sees as a deeper political malaise: the political disorder and disunity both within the individual colonies and among them as a whole. Although he sees the New England colonies as relatively stable, the others, especially New York, are pictured as little patchwork kingdoms not far from anarchy. In 1700, he says, "New York was a mixture of races and religions not yet fused into a harmonious body politic, divided in interests and torn with intestine disputes."[111] In the 1750's, Pennsylvania's population, like New York's, was "heterogeneous."[112] Yet the disunity within individual colonies was insignificant compared to their lack of mutual cooperation:

No conscious community of aims and interests held them together, nor was there any authority capable of uniting their forces and turning them to a common object. . . . Each province remained in jealous isolation, busied with its own work, growing in strength, in the capacity of self-rule and the spirit of independence, and stubbornly resisting all exercise of authority from without.[113]

As might be expected, Parkman's view of their situation on the eve of the French and Indian War is a good deal bleaker than Bancroft's. While Bancroft sees them as consciously— and successfully—striving for unity, Parkman argues that results along this line

[109] *Ibid.*, 380.
[110] *Montcalm and Wolfe*, I, 419.
[111] *A Half-Century of Conflict*, I, 7.
[112] *Montcalm and Wolfe*, I, 31.
[113] *A Half-Century of Conflict*, II, 64.

had been most discouraging. . . . They were all subject to popular legislatures, through whom alone money and men could be raised; and these elective bodies were sometimes factious and selfish, and not always either far-sighted or reasonable. Moreover, they were in a state of ceaseless friction with their governors, who represented the king, or, what was worse, the feudal proprietary.[114]

In terms of his major freedom-order symbols, Parkman argues that the English colonies had to move closer to New France, farther from the wilderness, to become politically sound.

Yet there is never any more question in Parkman's mind than in Bancroft's that despite their economic, military, or political flaws the English colonies, with their tradition of "ordered freedom"[115] midway between the extremes of repression and license, were more than equal to the task. They eventually coalesced into the United States, the "eldest and greatest"[116] of Britain's offspring, thereby justifying their wilderness vigor—their "liberty, crude, incoherent, and chaotic, yet full of prolific vitality."[117] Their drive toward order, Parkman implies, diverted their drive toward freedom into productive channels, while the freedom kept the order from becoming "barren and absolutist." Yet unlike Bancroft, Parkman sees nothing predestined or inevitable about the spread of democracy throughout the earth. "The air of liberty," he says, "is malaria to those who have not learned to breathe it. The English colonists throve in it because they and their forefathers had been trained in a school of self-control and self-dependence; and what would have been intoxication for others, was vital force to them."[118] Here as elsewhere he stresses the centuries of growth and experience that produced

114 *Montcalm and Wolfe*, I, 34.
115 *Ibid.*, II, 411.
116 *Ibid.*
117 *Ibid.*, I, 35.
118 *A Half-Century of Conflict*, I, 311 f.

the English concept of freedom and successfully transplanted it to America. Whereas the French-American, suddenly exposed in the New World to a wilderness freedom his background had not prepared him for, either went native or remained the passive tool of monarchy and Catholicism, the Anglo-American, inured to the temptations of freedom through long experience with it, calmly confronted and mastered the wilderness.

Parkman offers another, related, explanation for the success of the British colonies. English colonization was open and voluntary, while French colonization was state controlled. "British America," he says,

> was an asylum for the oppressed and the suffering of all creeds and nations, and population poured into her by the force of a natural tendency. France, like England, might have been great in two hemispheres, if she had placed herself in accord with this tendency, instead of opposing it; but despotism was consistent with itself, and a mighty opportunity was for ever lost.[119]

In other words, the success of the English colonies was due no more to a political tradition innate in their settlers than to a single enormous mistake in French policy which followed naturally from France's absolutism. France's failure was inevitable only in the sense that she held doggedly to her error. Providence played little part in the affair.

Yet the result, according to Parkman, was to introduce into English America a population hardened by the fires of persecution and extremely jealous of its rights and freedoms. Whatever the English colonists achieved was the result of their own choice and their own personal sacrifice. They were not coddled, argues Parkman, by a paternalistic government, nor did they come to North America to renounce the world. The Puritans, for example, "thought that a reward on earth as well as in heaven awaited those who were faithful to the law," and

---

[119] *Count Frontenac*, 396. See also *Montcalm and Wolfe*, I, 24.

although this hardheaded practicality encouraged selfishness it was "manly, healthful, and invigorating" in a way that the religious asceticism of New France, with its constant harping on "the nothingness and the vanity of life,"[120] was not. The motivation for the Puritan exodus came from within: "In their own hearts, not in the promptings of a great leader or the patronage of an equivocal government, their enterprise found its birth and its achievement."[121] In episode after episode Parkman repeats this idea, as when he says of Massachusetts' sacrifices for the war in 1758 that her "contributions of money and men were not ordained by an absolute king, but made by the voluntary act of a free people."[122] He sees a spirit of self-reliance and self-motivation pervading not only New England but all the English colonies, and it is this spirit which for him lies at the heart of the Anglo-American compromise between freedom and order. Discipline and control of one's self is the key to the highest civilization. Each man must master his own appetites for license and for tyranny—for the wilderness and for New France—before he can be said to be truly civilized. Freedom and restraint are ultimately internal contradictions to be fought out on the battlefield of each man's soul.

Consequently, the portrayal of heroic character emerges as one of the most important purposes of *France and England*. That heroism would be a key to all the volumes was made clear in the introduction to the first, *Pioneers*, where Parkman says that in the early history of North America "men, lost elsewhere in the crowd, stand forth as agents of Destiny."[123] His point is not that individuals control history but that much of the meaning of his own historical narratives lies in the examples of heroic character they depict. He clinches the point in

---

[120] *Jesuits*, 329.
[121] *Pioneers*, 30.
[122] *Montcalm and Wolfe*, II, 85.
[123] *Pioneers*, xxxi.

the last sentence of the book when, having just concluded the account of his first major hero, Champlain, he comments that "[h]eroes of another stamp succeed; and it remains to tell hereafter the story of their devoted lives, their faults, their follies, and their virtues."[124] In *France and England* as a whole Parkman attributes heroism to what at one point he calls "that height and force of individual development which is the brain and heart of civilization"[125]—that is, to the self-discipline and self-motivation of each and every man. All his heroes reveal some combination of these essential virtues. The capacity to generate and sustain not merely the drive but also the self-regulation necessary to achieve heroic ends is in Parkman's eyes the monopoly neither of England nor of France. If anything, France produced more individual heroism in North America than did England. The aristocratic, semi-feudal society of France and New France encouraged the "highest growth of the individual"[126] more than the English colonies, at least among its upper classes. On the other hand, individual freedom and initiative were much more widely diffused in England's society. Her colonies took root and flourished because of "the historical training of her people in habits of reflection, forecast, industry, and self-reliance,—a training which enabled them to adopt and maintain an invigorating system of self-rule, totally inapplicable to their rivals."[127]

Plainly, Parkman's concept of character and heroism differs widely from Bancroft's. Bancroft argues that the ideal leader follows or embodies the will of the masses, which is by definition, because it rests on their intuitive perception of divine truth, infallible. Parkman argues that the masses are no better than the self-discipline each one of them has in-

---

[124] *Ibid.*, 420.
[125] *The Old Regime*, 401.
[126] *Montcalm and Wolfe*, II, 414.
[127] *The Old Regime*, 396.

dividually achieved. Leaders are ultimately interesting to him not as individuals to venerate but as examples of a self-mastery all men must strive to win. Bancroft's whole system rests on the idea that to follow the common will is to realize the will of God; Parkman's rests on the idea that there is no improvement beyond self-improvement. "There are no political panaceas," he asserts, "except in the imagination of political quacks. . . . Freedom is for those who are fit for it. The rest will lose it, or turn it to corruption." The rulers of New France erred, he goes on, not in exercising authority but in exercising "too much of it, and, instead of weaning the child to go alone, [keeping] him in perpetual leading-strings, making him, if possible, more and more dependent, and less and less fit for freedom."[128] Parkman's social views are aristocratic only in the sense that he denies Bancroft's faith in the innate goodness of man. He everywhere implies it is the duty of each man, no matter what his station in life, to civilize his own internal wilderness.

Yet this process of self-cultivation implies the whole task of compromise that is suggested in his narrative of the taming of the historical North America. The individual must be subordinate enough to organized society and the restrictions it imposes on him for the commonweal to honor "the true foundations of a stable freedom,—conscience, reflection, faith, patience, and public spirit."[129] Yet at the same time he must be independent enough—imbued enough with the lawless spirit of the wilderness—not to have, as was the case in Canada, his "volition enfeebled" or his "self-reliance paralyzed." "A man, to be a man," says Parkman, "must feel that he holds his fate, in some good measure, in his own hands."[130] In some good measure. Not entirely, but in some good measure. Parkman never tries to define the formula precisely but instead drama-

128 *Ibid.*
129 *Ibid.*, 397.
130 *Ibid.*, 395.

tizes it in dozens of case histories of heroism and in his symbolization of the extremes of the wilderness and New France, with the English colonies lying roughly midway between. Another important and related set of poles is "the modern world of practical study and practical action"[131] which La Salle embodied and the medieval world of knighthood, chivalry, and religious faith which produced its own peculiar strengths and weaknesses. Among all these coordinates Parkman would have us chart the true path of individual character. The liberty of primeval nature and the restraint of New France, and the English compromise between them, are only the most important.

Despite the differences between Parkman and Bancroft as far as philosophy of history, style, interpretation of particular events, and subject matter are concerned, the similarity of their basic themes is remarkable. Both see anarchy and tyranny as extremes between which a middle way to political and social stability should be followed. Each is an advocate, in his own way, of compromise. No less remarkable is the similarity in their handling of source material. Like Bancroft, Parkman uses the scissors-and-paste method of composition to create a narrative style appropriate to his subject, theme, and argument. He, too, achieves a high degree of originality by weaving the language of the sources into his own prose, and although his method is different from Bancroft's in many ways, it is unmistakably Bancroftian in its broad contours. Since the method of *France and England* remains basically the same throughout the nine volumes, we can get a fair sense of its range by looking closely at what have been generally recognized as Parkman's two greatest works. We are, of course, about to enter the rugged, dramatic *La Salle* and the equally rugged and dramatic *Montcalm and Wolfe*.

[131] *La Salle*, 406.

CHAPTER FIVE

★ ★ ★ ★ ★ ★

La Salle and
Montcalm and Wolfe

I F BANCROFT freed American historians from the tyrannies of the scissors-and-paste method, Parkman showed them how to exploit the method for maximum artistic effect. By paraphrasing his sources closely, Parkman gives almost visceral force to the action of *France and England*. As Doughty and Pease have shown,[1] he tries above all to bring the past to life. He spells out his strategy, which remains constant throughout the nine volumes, in the introduction to *Pioneers*:

Faithfulness to the truth of history involves far more than a research, however patient and scrupulous, into special facts. Such facts may be detailed with the most minute exactness, and yet the narrative, taken as a whole, may be unmeaning or untrue. The narrator must seek to imbue himself with the life and spirit of the time. He must study events in their bearings near and remote; in the character, habits, and manners of those who took part in them. He must himself be, as it were, a sharer or spectator of the action he describes.[2]

The narrator must participate in past events—a simple-sounding idea, yet one that sets Parkman's historiography

[1] Doughty, *Francis Parkman*, 163–68, and Pease, *Parkman's History*, 53–67.
[2] *Pioneers*, xxxvif.

114

far apart from Bancroft's. Bancroft normally shapes the past to fit his audience's present expectations; Parkman at his best re-creates the past so vividly that the reader is drawn into it even against his will. Moreover, what Parkman adds to his histories is not so much philosophical argument as personal knowledge of historical sites and lifelong experience with the wilderness. The freedom-order theme outlined in the last chapter is largely implicit in his books. He does not, like Bancroft, tend to state it in elaborate asides. Lush—to some readers overlush[3]—descriptions of nature that are usually based on his own observations rather than on his sources fill *France and England*. Their effect is to draw us backward in time from the civilized, technological present to an earthy, wild, forest-smothered past.

Between them, *La Salle* and *Montcalm and Wolfe* reveal substantially the full range of Parkman's source techniques. *La Salle* portrays a flawed French hero ultimately overcome by the anarchic forces of nature, while *Montcalm and Wolfe* portrays two equally worthy champions, one French and one English, whose careers in North America dramatize the English colonies' superiority to New France. Each book is, in its own way, a masterpiece of historical prose, and each reveals unique aspects of Parkman's compromise between adherence to and independence of source material.

La Salle and the Discovery of the Great West

Almost every line of *La Salle* contributes in some way to the contest between the French explorers of the Mississippi Valley and the midcontinent wilderness. The inhuman energy of nature saturates the book. When early in the narrative Marquette and Joliet, on their way down the Mississippi, pass the

---

[3] For example, Yvor Winters witheringly diagnoses Parkman's set pieces on nature as "a cold delirium of academic pseudo-poeticism." *In Defense of Reason*, 422.

mouth of the Missouri, Parkman describes it as "that savage river, descending from its mad career through a vast unknown of barbarism,"[4] equating its violence with the undisciplined natural world through which it flows. Repeatedly, he contrasts the flicker of order and reason cast by his explorers with the desolation that surrounds them, as when the dying Marquette is carried past a "lonely and savage shore"[5] or La Salle trudges back to Canada "through those vast and gloomy wilds,—those realms of famine, treachery, and death."[6] He has Tonty as well as La Salle find the mouth of the Mississippi "a voiceless desolation of river, marsh, and sea."[7] And as Doughty shows,[8] dominating the book is the "dark and inexorable river" itself, "rolling, like a destiny through its realms of solitude and shade"[9]—a destiny at best indifferent to man.

According to Parkman, the effect of this savage force on the Europeans exposed to it is that of a moral winnow. At the end of one of the most gripping narrative sequences in the book, in which he discovers that an Illinois village has been sacked in his absence, La Salle finds a plank on which a French deserter has scrawled the words *"Nous sommes tous sauvages."*[10] The strange message, appearing literally in the middle of nowhere, represents everything Parkman detests about natural license. Condemning it as "the work, no doubt, of the knaves who had pillaged and destroyed the fort,"[11] he implies that to yield to nature in this way is unforgivably weak and immoral and that no strong man would ever do so. La Salle himself emerges from the book as the toughest and most iron-

[4] *La Salle*, 60.
[5] *Ibid.*, 70.
[6] *Ibid.*, 173.
[7] *Ibid.*, 429.
[8] *Francis Parkman*, 268–83.
[9] *La Salle*, 431.
[10] *Ibid.*, 196.
[11] *Ibid.*, 197.

willed hero of the *France and England* series. Parkman measures his heroism against the sheer bulk of raw nature he challenged:

> To estimate aright the marvels of his patient fortitude, one must follow on his track through the vast scene of his interminable journeyings, those thousands of weary miles of forest, marsh, and river, where, again and again, in the bitterness of baffled striving, the untiring pilgrim pushed onward towards the goal which he was never to attain.[12]

Yet Parkman also argues that La Salle "contained in his own complex and painful nature the chief springs of his triumphs, his failures, and his death."[13] His "vast and comprehensive"[14] ambition, productive as it was in some ways, nonetheless reflected the basic weakness in French colonial policy that Parkman defines in *Count Frontenac*: while the English colony "increased by slow extension, rooting firmly as it spread," New France "shot offshoots, with few or no roots, far out into the wilderness."[15] Perhaps more than any other character in *France and England*, La Salle typifies this weakness. In the face of bitter opposition from the Jesuits and with undependable men to help him, he first tries to establish a personal empire reaching from the St. Lawrence to the Mississippi, then proposes to invade Mexico with an army of fifteen thousand Indians, and finally, without knowing where the mouth of the Mississippi is, tries to establish a major colony there. That Parkman sympathizes with him in many ways is clear, yet he also sees him as a symbol for the disregard of common sense that doomed French Canada. La Salle tries to master the external world of nature without having fully mastered himself.

---

12 *Ibid.*, 407 f.
13 *Ibid.*, 407.
14 *Ibid.*, 406.
15 *Count Frontenac*, 395.

In general, though, Parkman does identify with the point of view of the strong man of civilization, such as La Salle, who strives to master physical nature, and in *La Salle* he tries to re-create the wilderness experiences of La Salle, Tonty, Joutel, and the other civilized men in the book and to draw the reader into these experiences by persuading him that the narrator of *La Salle* was an eyewitness to what he describes. Accordingly, the narrating stance he adopts is not the conventional one of omniscience. Instead, it asks the reader to accept the fiction that the narrator's perception is bound by the chronological unfolding of events or, in other words, that the narrator is merely experiencing and reporting events as they happen. One might distinguish Parkman's technique from Bancroft's by likening Parkman to an on-the-spot radio or television announcer and Bancroft to an editorializer speaking after the fact. Unlike Bancroft, Parkman tries in imagination to participate directly in the experience of his characters.

At his best he succeeds brilliantly, and he is often at his best in *La Salle*. Part of the reason is that in writing *La Salle* he found his sources allowed him to use a method well suited to the book's theme: the word-by-word, paragraph-by-paragraph, page-by-page reconstruction of eyewitness accounts. There is virtually no sign of paraphrasing of secondary writers in the book. Moreover, there is little evidence, except at two points, of synthesis of conflicting evidence and practically none of fusion of diffuse material, such as letters or official documents, into a running narrative. Nearly all of the book rests on a dozen or so records that Parkman tends to follow exclusively in the sections of the narrative they underpin.[16]

[16] There is an interesting body of criticism concerning Parkman's use of the La Salle material controlled by Pierre Margry in Paris and published, at Parkman's urging, by the U.S. government during the 1870's. It begins with John G. Shea's attack on Margry's reliability as an editor in an 1879 pamphlet entitled *The Bursting of Pierre Margry's La Salle Bubble*, continues with Jean Delanglez' *Some La Salle Journeys*, in which Delanglez shows that Margry

La Salle and *Montcalm and Wolfe*

Although it ostensibly narrates the twenty years from La Salle's arrival in New France in 1666, at the age of twenty-three, to his murder in Texas in 1687, *La Salle* actually focuses on half a dozen expeditions—launched usually, but not in every case, by La Salle—into the American midcontinent during those years and lasting from a month or two to several years. Before 1678, when La Salle begins a major effort to secure the Mississippi Valley for France, the only extended expedition Parkman narrates is Marquette's and Joliet's down the Mississippi to Arkansas in 1673, which he bases solely on the journal written by Marquette. For the middle half of the book, which chronicles La Salle's treks back and forth between Canada and the Mississippi Valley between 1678 and 1682, ending with his navigation of the Mississippi to its mouth, Parkman follows only five basic documents. Of these, two—Hennepin's *Description de la Louisiane* and the anonymous *Relation des Déscouvertes et des Voyages du Sieur de la Salle 1679-1681*—dominate more than a hundred of *La Salle's* pages. The final quarter of the book, a narrative of La Salle's attempt to establish a military outpost at the mouth of the Mississippi from 1684 until his assassination in 1687, is drawn almost entirely from

bowdlerized the documents, and concludes with two articles that appeared in the early 1960's in the *William and Mary Quarterly (WMQ)*. In the first of these, "The History of New France According to Francis Parkman," *WMQ*, Vol. XVIII (1961), 163–75, W. J. Eccles uses the Delanglez book as part of his ammunition for a general attack on Parkman's arguments and methods in *France and England* as a whole. In the second, "A Journey into the Human Mind: Motivation in Francis Parkman's *La Salle*," *WMQ*, Vol. XIX (1962), 220–37, William R. Taylor accepts Eccles' strictures on *La Salle* but in part excuses Parkman on artistic grounds. Francis P. Jennings, "A Vanishing Indian: Parkman Versus His Sources," *Pennsylvania Magazine of History and Biography*, Vol. LXXXVII (1963), 306–23, questions Parkman's handling of some source material in *Montcalm and Wolfe* in much the same way Eccles questions *La Salle*. For a defense of Parkman against so-called revisionists like Eccles and Jennings, see David E. Griffin, " 'The Man for the Hour': A Defense of Francis Parkman's *Frontenac*," *New England Quarterly*, Vol. XLIII (1970), 605–20.

the journal of Henri Joutel, La Salle's second-in-command during the expedition.

The key to Parkman's method in *La Salle* is his strategy of ordering the factual content of his source material around the emotional or psychological mood he feels it justifies. To express what it was probably like to paddle with Marquette down the Mississippi or to hike with La Salle across the prairie, he defines the mood of the particular experience and then saturates his narrative with it. Whenever one of his sources offers evidence for such a mood, he milks it dry. As we have seen, Bancroft culls his material for language that will support his generalizations and interpretations. In contrast, Parkman culls his for the direct psychological experience of his characters. To create and sustain his moods, Parkman employs two basic techniques. On the one hand he adds to his narrative details that the sources themselves do not specifically mention but that are, to borrow Pease's phrase, universally "valid in experience,"[17] thus enriching his story not only with the details themselves but with the feeling such details can be made to convey. On the other hand, he revises, reorders, and selects details from the documents to best literary advantage.

The first, more inventive, technique takes a number of forms. Occasionally Parkman moves inside the consciousness of one of his heroes and tries to imagine his thoughts and feelings at a particular moment. Thus at the end of Chapter XII, in which he recounts La Salle's first major voyage through the Great Lakes, he sums up the chapter's psychological meaning by picturing La Salle on the shore, isolated, disappointed, and worried: "He scanned the dreary horizon with an anxious eye. No returning sail gladdened the watery solitude, and a dark foreboding gathered on his heart."[18] Though no source says so, it is reasonable to assume that La

[17] *Parkman's History*, 62.
[18] *La Salle*, 150.

Salle felt something of the sort. The lines invite us to sympathize with La Salle's mood of increasing anxiety in the chapter as a whole. Similarly, Parkman at one point attributes to Marquette an itch to explore that is nowhere directly stated in the sources: "He heard marvels of [the Mississippi] also from the Sioux, who lived on its banks; and a strong desire possessed him, to explore the mystery of its course. A sudden calamity dashed his hopes."[19] Having ascribed both the longing and the dashed hopes to Marquette, Parkman is able to use them to poise the reader, as well as Marquette, emotionally at the starting point of Marquette's voyage.

Equally effective is the psychological fictionalizing in Parkman's version of the following source account of Frontenac's arrival at Montreal in 1673:

[He] arrived June 15 at five in the evening at Montreal, where he was received by M. Perrot, Governor, to the noise of all the cannons and musketry of the inhabitants of the island, who were under arms, and was addressed on the beach by the officers of justice and syndic of the inhabitants, and afterwards by the clergyman at the door of the church, where the *Te Deum* was chanted.[20]

Parkman pokes fun at this Gallic pomp and circumstance by making Frontenac himself seem to suffer through it:

Perrot, the local governor, was on the shore with his soldiers and the inhabitants, drawn up under arms, and firing a salute, to welcome the representative of the king. Frontenac was compelled to listen to a long harangue from the judge of the place, followed by another from the syndic. Then there was a solemn procession to the church, where he was forced to undergo a third effort of oratory from one of the priests. *Te Deum* followed in thanks for his arrival, and then he took refuge in the fort.[21]

19 *Ibid.*, 33.
20 "Voyage du Comte de Fontenac au Lac Ontario, en 1673," in Pierre Margry (ed.), *Découvertes et Établissements des Français dans l'Ouest et dans le Sud de l'Amérique Septentrionale (1614–1754)*, I, 199. The translation is mine.
21 *La Salle*, 77 f.

The revision suggests that Frontenac's boredom at vapid oratory is just one more sign of the good sense with which Parkman credits him throughout. At the same time, its humor is aimed at Frontenac for listening as well as at the speakers for talking.

Far different in mood is Parkman's fictionalization of Tonty's state of mind when he is allowed by the Iroquois to return to the Illinois warriors during a battle between the two nations in the fall of 1680. In the source, Tonty, having explained how he tricked the Iroquois by exaggerating the number of Frenchmen in the Illinois camp, goes on to describe his release:

> That disturbed them and they threw me a necklace so that I might tell the Illinois to retire to their village; that they were hungry and that they were to carry grain to them. Never have I felt such great joy, and having made the two armies retire, I carried the necklace to the Illinois, who drew back to their village and me with them.[22]

In his version, Parkman expands Tonty's joy into this striking passage:

> They sent Tonty back with a belt of peace: he held it aloft in sight of the Illinois; chiefs and old warriors ran to stop the fight; the yells and the firing ceased; and Tonty, like one waked from a hideous nightmare, dizzy, almost fainting with loss of blood, staggered across the intervening prairie, to rejoin his friends.[23]

From the fact that Tonty was earlier wounded by the Iroquois and did lose a good deal of blood Parkman infers his dizziness and staggering. None of the action or emotion he supplies is forced or implausible, and in his likening of Tonty's joy to waking from a nightmare he shows unusual alertness to the psychological possibilities of the experience.

[22] "Relation de Henri de Tonty," *Découvertes et Établissements*, I, 587. The translation is mine.
[23] *La Salle*, 213 f.

The type of invention found most often in *La Salle* and throughout *France and England* and most often discussed by Parkman's critics is his creation of natural setting. In situation after situation, using sometimes his own visits to the actual locations, sometimes his familiarity with the flora and fauna of North America, and sometimes his imagination as guides, he gives to the setting of *La Salle* a tangibleness and sensuousness completely missing from his sources. As is true of the others, this sort of fictionalization serves the dual function of certifying Parkman's narrator as a witness to the action and of helping define the mood of the narrative at any given point. For instance, Parkman's account of Frontenac's embassy to the Iroquois in 1673, which Parkman terms a "complete success" and treats favorably from beginning to end, at one point pictures the scene that supposedly greeted Frontenac as he emerged from the dangerous St. Lawrence and began the sail across Lake Ontario toward Iroquois territory:

[At] length the last rapid was passed, and smooth water awaited them to their journey's end. Soon they reached the Thousand Islands, and their light flotilla glided in long file among those watery labyrinths, by rocky islets, where some lonely pine towered like a mast against the sky; by sun-scorched crags, where the brown lichens crisped in the parching glare; by deep dells, shady and cool, rich in rank ferns, and spongy, dark green mosses; by still coves, where the water-lilies lay like snow-flakes on their broad, flat leaves; till at length they neared their goal, and the glistening bosom of Lake Ontario opened on their sight.[24]

Entirely Parkman's own, the passage vibrates with the mood of hopefulness and success that pervades the episode. The pine tree connoting the companionship of ships meeting at sea; the lichens not shriveled or otherwise brutally tortured but "crisped" by the sun; the dells soft with ferns and moss

[24] *Ibid.*, 79.

and free of the snakelike, grotesque roots or rotting and suffocating vegetation that Parkman elsewhere invokes in similar topographical but different emotional regions; the water lilies likened to snowflakes and hence removed from the steaming violence of organic process altogether; and finally the lake "glistening" with promise—all these cast a subtle vote for Frontenac's undertaking.

Contrast this with the similarly source-free description of the Mississippi as it appears to Joutel and his companions on their return to Illinois in 1687. La Salle has been shot; the murderers have murdered each other; the Texas colony lies in ruins.

With these [Indian guides], the travellers resumed their journey in a wooden canoe, about the first of August,* descended the Arkansas, and soon reached the dark and inexorable river, so long the object of their search, rolling like a destiny through its realms of solitude and shade. They launched forth on its turbid bosom, plied their oars against the current, and slowly won their way upward, following the writhings of this watery monster through canebrake, swamp, and fen.[25]

The connotations of treachery, exhaustion, and inhuman power in the passage are clear, and they all intensify the mood of defeat and bewilderment that fills the chapter in which the passage appears.

More impressive, perhaps, than his technique of adding details he has himself imagined is Parkman's selection and organization of the details he finds in his sources for greatest psychological effect. Several critics have praised Parkman's skill at organizing complex narrative sequences to heighten suspense and tension[26]—for example, his switching back and forth between approaching armies or his building of a narra-

25 *Ibid.*, 430 f.
26 See Levin, *History as Romantic Art*, 210–28, and Wilbur R. Jacobs, "Some of Parkman's Literary Devices," *New England Quarterly*, Vol. XXXI (1958), 244–52.

tive line on an ascending or descending curve of success. While such switching and building is more frequent in *Montcalm and Wolfe*, with its many complicated and simultaneous actions, than in *La Salle*, one section of *La Salle* reveals it well. This is Parkman's account of the events of 1680–81, comprising La Salle's journey to and from Canada in search of men and supplies, Tonty's involvement in the Iroquois-Illinois war, and Hennepin's exploration of the Upper Mississippi, all of which happen at roughly the same time. After opening the sequence of six chapters in which he narrates these events with a scene on the Illinois River showing the setting out of La Salle, Tonty, and Hennepin on their separate paths, Parkman first follows La Salle through terrible hardships to and from Fort Frontenac, concluding this part of the drama with La Salle's horrified discovery that the Indian village where he left Tonty the year before has been devastated. Before allowing either La Salle or the reader to find out what happened, Parkman then goes back to recount Tonty's adventures from the beginning, utilizing our anxiety over Tonty's fate to help motivate the sequence. Finally, having assured us of Tonty's safety, he devotes three chapters to comic relief from the grim excitement of the story just told. These set forth a half-comic account of Hennepin's wanderings and their successful conclusion with Hennepin's return to Green Bay. They also provide contrast to the tension of La Salle's quest for the Mississippi, placed as they are immediately before La Salle makes his successful voyage down the mysterious river.

What has not been appreciated is the extent to which this concern for psychologically effective arrangement of material controlled Parkman's line-by-line construction of his histories. At his best, Parkman made every paragraph so tight and emotionally coherent that the task of following the narrative is effortless. The artistic challenge he faced was this: On the one hand were his sources, usually rambling, colorless, monotonous affairs. On the other was his determination to give his story the intensity of felt life. The easier way for him to bridge the gap was to imagine details not in conflict with or, better, details implied by the sources, add them, and so flesh out the sources with products of his own imagination. This is the technique we have already seen. More challenging is the method he used most of the time—that of analyzing the sources, isolating from them details that suggest a mood or tone, then recombining these details in paragraphs organized to expose the mood or tone most effectively.

A paragraph of high wilderness adventure from *La Salle* can serve as a representative example of this kind of revision. The paragraph occurs after La Salle completes the first voyage on his ship, the *Griffin*, across Lakes Erie, Huron, and Michigan to Green Bay. Having sent the ship back to Niagara with a load of furs, La Salle decides to explore Lake Michigan to the south by canoe. The episode opens as he and his men embark.

<table>
<tr><td>

Source:

We set out the next day, September 19th, with fourteen persons in four canoes, I directing the smallest, loaded with five hundred pounds, with a carpenter just arrived from France, who did not know how to avoid the waves, during rough weather, I had every difficulty to manage this little craft. These four bark canoes were loaded with a forge and all its appurtenances, carpenter's, joiner's and pit sawyer's tools, arms and merchandise.

We took our course southerly towards the mainland four good leagues distant from the island of the Poutouatamis. In the middle of the traverse and amid the most beautiful calm in the world, a

</td><td>

La Salle:

The parting was not auspicious. The lake, glassy and calm in the afternoon, was convulsed at night with a sudden storm, when the canoes were midway between the island and the main shore. It was with much difficulty that they could keep together, the men shouting to each other through the darkness. Hennepin, who was in the smallest canoe, with a heavy load, and a carpenter for a companion, who was awkward at the paddle, found himself in jeopardy which demanded all his nerve. The voyagers thought themselves happy when they gained at last the shelter of a little sandy cove, where they dragged up their canoes, and made their cheerless bivouac in the

</td></tr>
</table>

storm arose which endangered our lives, and which made us fear for the bark, and more for ourselves. We completed this great passage amid the darkness of night, calling to one another so as not to part company. The water often entered our canoes, and the impetuous wind lasted four days with a fury like the greatest tempests of ocean. We nevertheless reached the shore in a little sandy bay, and stayed five days, waiting for the lake to grow calm. During this stay, the Indian hunter who accompanied us, killed while hunting only a single porcupine which served to season our squashes and the Indian corn that we had.

On the 25th we continued our route all day, and part of the night favored by the moon, along the western shore of Lake Dauphin, but the wind coming up a little too strong, we were forced to land on a bare rock, on which we endured the rain and snow for two days, sheltered by our blankets, and near a little fire which we fed with wood that waves drove ashore.[27]

drenched and dripping forest. Here they spent five days, living on pumpkins and Indian corn, the gift of their Pottawattamie friends, and on a Canada porcupine, brought in by La Salle's Mohegan hunter. The gale raged meanwhile with a relentless fury. They trembled when they thought of the "Griffin." When at length the tempest lulled, they re-embarked, and steered southward, along the shore of Wisconsin; but again the storm fell upon them, and drove them, for safety, to a bare, rocky islet. Here they made a fire of driftwood, crouched around it, drew their blankets over their heads, and in this miserable plight, pelted with sleet and rain, remained for two days.[28]

Parkman's paragraph appears in the chapter that concludes with the picture, cited earlier, of La Salle scanning the horizon for the *Griffin*, which did in fact go down during the storm. Parkman organized the paragraph as a microcosm of the chapter as a whole: it moves on a line of descending success, beginning with the image of the lake as "glassy and calm" and concluding with the image of the party reduced to extremes, hunched under their soaked blankets. His topic sentence,

[27] Louis Hennepin, *A Description of Louisiana*, 108 f.
[28] *La Salle*, 143 f.

"The parting was not auspicious," prepares us for the worsening chain of events in the paragraph itself and foreshadows further trials later in the chapter. His final sentence, consisting merely of a picture of the bedraggled group around the fire, expresses the paragraph's whole meaning. We feel the explorers' pain and frustration as they crouch under their blankets, pelted with rain and sleet for two solid days. Without explicit comment, Parkman has captured their feelings superbly.

His success is due to his having rearranged the order of some parts of Hennepin's account and to his having increased or reduced the emotional intensity of others. By making Hennepin's comments on his fellow rower's clumsiness part of the action itself, he brings them to life. And in having them follow at once the powerful scene of the men shouting to each other through the night, he transfers the confusion and fright of the boat-to-boat shouting to the situation in Hennepin's own canoe. We can almost see Hennepin yelling orders and encouragement to his fumbling companion. Next Parkman heightens the contrast between the grimness of this struggle to keep from drowning and the relief of reaching shore by intensifying Hennepin's "we nevertheless reached the shore" into his own "The voyagers thought themselves happy when they gained at last the shelter," a device that also reinforces the illusion the narrator is himself taking part in the action. He at once qualifies this mood, however, by inventing a setting on the island that undercuts their and our sense of relief: "the drenched and dripping forest." He lets their provisions during the five-day wait speak for themselves, skillfully understating their suffering by omitting Hennepin's "only a single" in connection with the porcupine.

In the two sentences that follow these remarks on the provisions, he draws together widely separated elements from Hennepin's account for maximum psychological effect. Both isolate in a single sentence, for example, information that

Hennepin has blended into larger sentences and has separated with intervening material. The first, describing the "relentless fury" of the storm, is based on a remark Hennepin makes before he comments on the provisions; and the second, concerning their fear for the *Griffin*, is based on something he says before that. One effect of Parkman's reversal of Hennepin's order, of course, is to focus attention on the *Griffin* by generalizing the explorers' concern for it over the course of the whole gale. More important, it relates their present suffering to the more expensive and far-reaching loss of the supplies on board the ship, deepening the seriousness of the loss. Finally, the "relentless fury" of the storm, which causes them to "tremble," is placed in such a way as to reinforce Parkman's consistent personification of the storm as a malignant and vicious enemy, an image introduced with the word "convulsed" to describe the storm's effect on the lake, as though the lake itself were an organism and the storm its sentient torturer; amplified with "relentless fury"; and concluded with the phrase "again the storm fell upon them," which suggests some great, stalking animal. The storm represents nature at its wildest.

In sum, Parkman has reorganized Hennepin's account in the chronological sequence in which the action happened and, furthermore, isolated from it for special emphasis, by means of short sentences and heightened language, those elements that contribute most to its mood of increasing misery and decreasingly effective action. We ourselves seem to have gone through an experience that ends by placing us in that mute and static circle of sufferers around the fire, balked from further movement by the elemental ferocity of nature. Gradually the action loses its momentum, bogs down, and grinds to a halt. In its artistry the paragraph resembles many others that also narrate the kind of forest experience that seems to have stirred Parkman most deeply, though of course it only dramatizes one of the moods and utilizes a few of the techniques he developed to help him recreate the life buried in his sources.

Its theme is consistent with the theme of *La Salle* as a whole. Just as the paragraph dramatizes the conflict between civilization and nature and hints at the defeat of the former by the latter, so the book narrates the gradual defeat of La Salle's ambition to tame the Mississippi Valley in the face of the barbarism both within his followers and outside them in physical nature. Passage after passage of closely revised source material in *La Salle* tells the same story: civilization temporarily baffled by barbarism. The implication throughout is that La Salle's own character and the civilization he represented were inadequate to the task he undertook. His scheme, though bold, was, like the paternalistic civilization that created him, unrealistic, overcentralized, too much the product of a single mind and will. The English, with their plodding yet self-disciplined and balanced democracy, were better equipped to conquer the West after they had conquered New France.

The crucial difference between Bancroft's method and Parkman's in *La Salle* lies in Parkman's relatively greater interest in the inner, psychological experience of the men who wrote his primary sources. Virtually all of his fictionalized passages, in which he adds details of feeling or setting not specifically sanctioned by the sources, seem to be designed to make that inner, psychological experience as vivid and life-like as possible. They reinforce the historical action that he assembles from the sources themselves in episodes like the Lake Michigan storm with fitting imagery and mood. Bancroft's rebellion against the annalist-plagiarist approach to history is so total and his own goal of writing philosophically and artistically original history so strong as to reduce his interest in the personal experience even of authors of primary sources to a minimum. Parkman's aim is precisely to revivify such experience—to make his narrator seem to be taking part in the events he describes. Although he tries in *Montcalm and*

Wolfe to achieve the same end, there, as we will now see, his subject and his sources lead him back to a more Bancroftian method.

Montcalm and Wolfe

Parkman's opinion that *Montcalm and Wolfe* was his masterpiece[29] is probably right. In terms of range and quantity of source material used, complexity of narrative line, and sheer length it is unquestionably his big book. Its subject, the fourteen years of war between France and England, ending with France's expulsion from North America in 1763, was, as he remarked to Henry James, "an old hobby" of his [30]—he had spent forty years collecting materials and planning before he saw it into print in 1884. Whereas *La Salle* deals with the relatively simple struggle of a handful of men against the wilderness, *Montcalm and Wolfe* narrates a complex war between France and England for control of a continent and a population of hundreds of thousands. *La Salle* is his consummate statement of his wilderness theme; *Montcalm and Wolfe* is his consummate tribute to Anglo-American civilization. Though each book has its peculiar strengths and expresses a major aspect of Parkman's world view, *Montcalm and Wolfe* is focused more on his central thesis in *France and England*: the superiority of a tradition of ordered freedom to the extremes of anarchy and despotism.

Montcalm and Wolfe differs from *La Salle* in that the wilderness stands more at its periphery. The sort of struggle that La Salle waged against nature is incidental to its main action, which consists almost entirely of battles fought by the book between already civilized powers, its occasional incidents of forest barbarism notwithstanding. The book concentrates on the contest between Montcalm and Wolfe, two

[29] Charles H. Farnham, *A Life of Francis Parkman*, 204.
[30] Francis Parkman to Henry James, 15 September 1885, in *Letters of Francis Parkman* (ed. by Wilbur R. Jacobs), II, 178.

eminently civilized heroes, instead of on a struggle between a hero and physical nature: the French and Indian War was historically an altogether different affair from the exploration of the Mississippi, and in this sense Parkman had no choice but to tell it as he did. Yet to say that nature stands at the edges of *Montcalm and Wolfe* is not to say that it lacks meaning. Again and again Parkman reminds us of its chaos. The "skeletons" of dead trees clog the "sullen water" of a stream as "a bristling barricade";[31] the forests of western Pennsylvania are "a leafy maze, a mystery of shade, a universal hiding-place, where murder might lurk unseen at its victim's side";[32] Cape Split is "some misshapen monster of primeval chaos."[33] On the other hand, its invigorating, refreshing purity stands as a rebuke to the clutter and selfishness of modern industrial civilization: "The most beautiful lake in America lay before them; then more beautiful than now, in the wild charm of untrodden mountains and virgin forests."[34] The wilderness encapsulates the action of *Montcalm and Wolfe*, framing without dominating it.

The action itself consists of the climactic struggle between English liberty and French absolutism. Carried on by thousands of men in dozens of separate events spread over a continent, it made it impossible for Parkman to achieve the immediacy and unity of psychological effect which characterizes *La Salle*. The emotion generated in the reader by *Montcalm and Wolfe* is strong, but it consists of the reader's wanting the English colonies as a whole to beat New France as a whole. Only in isolated and momentary ways can Parkman re-create the psychological experience of his characters. There were simply too many of them. The result is a return to the Bancroftian method of fitting together bits and pieces of source

31 *Montcalm and Wolfe*, I, 322.
32 *Ibid.*, 335.
33 *Ibid.*, 268.
34 *Ibid.*, 295.

material without much concern for the point of view or tone of the source author. Like Bancroft, Parkman deliberately overpowers his sources with his own narrating voice, borrowing their language when it suits his purposes.

The Bancroftian flavor of his approach is plain in his use of secondary sources. In *La Salle* he blends the language of virtually no secondary writer into his own prose, in part because virtually no secondary works on the subject existed when he wrote the book. *Montcalm and Wolfe*, however, recounting historical events that had been written about by many historians before Parkman, lets him take advantage of useful snippets from earlier histories. For instance, he occasionally uses Smollett's *History of England* in Chapters XXV and XXVII. At one point Smollett says: "The disaster at the falls of Montmorenci made a deep impression on the mind of General Wolfe."[35] Parkman places the line, in slightly altered form, directly at the beginning of the climactic chapter, "The Heights of Abraham": "Wolfe was deeply moved by the disaster at the heights of Montmorenci."[36] Later in the chapter, at the critical moment when Wolfe and his men are drifting silently toward their landing place beneath the cliffs of Quebec, Smollett appears again. Parkman bases a long paragraph listing the difficulties of the attack on the first part of a long footnote in Smollett's work; and on the following page he paraphrases a wonderfully dramatic exchange between a French sentry and the English landing barges directly from the second part of Smollett's note, filling it out with details from Robert Wright's *Life of Wolfe*.[37]

Wright's work, published in 1864, is Parkman's source for all his information on Wolfe's early life, much of his account of Wolfe's expeditions against Louisbourg and Quebec, and

[35] Tobias Smollett, *The History of England*, IV, 227.
[36] *Montcalm and Wolfe*, II, 259.
[37] Compare *Montcalm and Wolfe*, II, 286, with Smollett, *History*, IV, 230f. (note), and Wright, *The Life of Major-General James Wolfe*, 576.

several of his tributes to the heroism of Wolfe's character. Echoes of Wright's language can be heard at many points in *Montcalm and Wolfe*, as in the following description of England's response to the news of Wolfe's victory and death:

Source:	*Montcalm and Wolfe*:
Great Britain blazed with bonfires. . . .One spot alone—Blackheath—was dark, for there the mourning mother wept for the loss of the best of sons; and her neighbors, in sympathy with her sorrow, refrained from the display of their participation in the national joy.[38]	England blazed with bonfires. In one spot alone all was dark and silent; for here a widowed mother mourned for a loving and devoted son, and the people forebore to profane her grief with the clamor of their rejoicings.[39]

As the passage shows, Parkman strives as conscientiously as Bancroft for verbal originality, even when he follows a secondary source closely. At one or two points he paraphrases Bancroft himself. To describe the effects of a skirmish between a squad of colonials under Washington and a French scouting party in 1754, Bancroft uses a bold metaphor: " 'Fire!' said Washington, and, with his own musket, gave the example. That word of command kindled the world into a flame."[40] Parkman uses it too. "Judge it as we may," he says, "this obscure skirmish began the war that set the world on fire."[41] His final sentence in the same chapter, comparable to the opening line he borrowed for Chapter XXVII from Smollet, also incorporates one of Bancroft's figures:

Source:	*Montcalm and Wolfe*:
In the whole valley of the Mississippi, to its headsprings in the Alleghanies, no standard floated but that of France.[42]	Not an English flag now waved beyond the Alleghanies.[43]

[38] Wright, *Wolfe*, 593.
[39] *Montcalm and Wolfe*, II, 324.
[40] Bancroft, *History*, IV, 118.
[41] *Montcalm and Wolfe*, I, 150.
[42] Bancroft, *History*, IV, 121.
[43] *Montcalm and Wolfe*, I, 161.

Similar borrowings from secondary writers can be found in Chapter V, "Washington." There Parkman paraphrases Jared Sparks's *Life of George Washington* and Winthrop Sargent's *History of an Expedition Against Fort Duquesne in 1755* at considerable length.[44]

The sheer number and diversity of the materials Parkman gathered for *Montcalm and Wolfe* seems to have led him to use even his primary sources differently than he did in *La Salle*, more as Bancroft had in the *History*. In the first place, he often had to condense them sharply. While it is clear from the few examples presented that in *La Salle* Parkman trimmed or at least carefully selected from his materials, it is also clear that not only the subject but the scope of his narrative there conformed closely to the subject and scope of a handful of sources, so that the evidence he used and the narrative he wrote were often in a one-to-one quantitative proportion or at least very near it. Often, in fact, he used significantly more words than his sources. In contrast, *Montcalm and Wolfe* forced him continually to cut.

In a way this technique, probably the one used most often in *Montcalm and Wolfe*, is also the most revealing in terms of theme, since it involved not simply deleting unwanted words but, more important, running the basic ideas of the book through the material that was kept. Parkman's handling of the opening section of a journal written by Washington after his expedition to the Allegheny River in 1753 is a case in point. His portrayal of Washington in the chapter containing the episode sums up his whole heroic ideal. Washington emerges as a man who, like all of Parkman's heroes, confronts and, through self-discipline and practical reason, overcomes immense obstacles.

Washington begins his journal as follows:

[44] Compare, for example, Sparks's *Washington*, 52 ff., with *Montcalm and Wolfe*, I, 156–59, and Sargent's *Expedition*, 53f., with *Montcalm and Wolfe*, I, 161.

I . . . set out on the intended Journey the same Day: The next, I arrived at *Fredericksburg,* and engaged Mr. *Jacob Vanbraam,* to be my *French* Interpreter; and proceeded with him to *Alexandria,* where we provided Necessaries. From thence we went to *Winchester,* and got Baggage, Horses, etc. and from thence we pursued the new Road to *Wills-Creek,* where we arrived the 14th of *November.*

Here I engaged Mr. *Gist* to pilot us out, and also hired four others as Servitors, *Barnaby Currin, John Mac-Quire,* Indian Traders, *Henry Steward,* and *William Jenkins;* and in Company with those Persons, left the Inhabitants the Day following.[45]

Cutting the number of words Washington uses by half, Parkman sets the whole in a single sentence that subtly distinguishes between civilization—the journey to Will's Creek, with its connotations of ease and safety—and the "wilderness" into whose perils Washington unhestitatingly "struck";

Washington set out for the trading station of the Ohio Company on Will's Creek; and thence, at the middle of November, struck into the wilderness with Christopher Gist as a guide, Vanbraam, a Dutchman, as French interpreter, Davison, a trader, as Indian interpreter, and four woodsmen as servants.[46]

Not only does Washington determinedly strike into the wilderness, but he does so "at the middle of November," a poor time of the year to have to begin, with only a handful of men to accompany him.

Parkman's next few lines—"They went to the forks of the Ohio, and then down the river to Logstown, the Chiningúe of Céloron de Bienville. There Washington had various parleys with the Indians; and thence, after vexatious delays, he continued his journey towards Fort Le Boeuf"—are a condensation of ten pages of Washington's journal. Most important to Parkman's theme are the "vexatious delays" that threaten to keep Washington from fulfilling his mission. But, continues

[45] George Washington, *The Journal of Major George Washington,* 5f.
[46] *Montcalm and Wolfe,* I, 132f.

Parkman, Washington pushed on "towards Fort Le Boeuf, accompanied by the friendly chief called the Half-King and by three of his tribesmen. For several days they followed the traders' path, pelted with unceasing rain and snow, and came at last to the old Indian town of Venango, where French Creek enters the Alleghany." It is clear that Parkman wants to stress the hardships of traveling over a "path" through "unceasing rain and snow": the adverbial phrase "at last" suggests relief at having made it through. The passage Parkman based these lines on is remarkable for its lack of a sense of heroism. Says Washington calmly: "We set out about 9 o'Clock with the Half-king, *Jeskakake, White Thunder,* and the Hunter; and travelled on the Road to *Venango,* where we arrived the 4th of *December,* without any Thing remarkable happening but a continued Series of bad Weather. This is an old *Indian* Town, situated at the Mouth of *French* Creek on *Ohio.*"[47] In Parkman's view, Washington's "Road" and "without any Thing remarkable happening" are insufficiently challenging, and he recasts them as we have seen. His only real economy appears in his passing over the Indians with a brief mention.

He concludes his paraphrase by confronting Washington with an unexpected disappointment, the seizure by the French of an English trading post, and at the end he quotes Washington's description of a dinner during which the Frenchmen get drunk and reveal their designs on the Ohio Valley:

Source:	*Montcalm and Wolfe:*
We found the *French* Colours hoisted at a House from which they had driven Mr. *John Frazier,* an *English* Subject. I immediately repaired to it, to know where the Commander resided. There were three Officers, one of whom, Capt. *Joncaire,* informed me, that he had the Command of the *Ohio:* But	Here there was an English trading-house; but the French had seized it, raised their flag over it, and turned it into a military outpost. Joncaire was in command, with two subalterns; and nothing could exceed their civility. They invited the strangers to supper; and, says Washington, ... [There fol-

47 Washington, *Journal,* 16 f.

there was a General Officer at the near Fort, where he advised me to apply for an Answer. He invited us to sup with them; and treated us with the greatest Complaisance. [The passage that Parkman has quoted follows.][48]

lows an eleven-line quotation describing the dinner and the French threats.][49]

With "but" in the second clause Parkman sharpens our sense of Washington's disappointment, and his trimming of the information about Joncaire, along with his deletion of Washington's comments about the general officer, brings us quickly to the long quotation in which yet another obstacle, the hypocrisy of Joncaire's "civility," is made clear. As Parkman uses it, the quotation about the dinner hints at one more of Washington's virtues: his ability to sound out weaker men by staying sober during a drinking bout. Not only was Washington tough and steadfast, suggests Parkman, he was shrewd.

Wishing, then, to demonstrate Washington's heroism, Parkman cuts from his account all unnecessary information, trims that of secondary interest to its sparest form, and concentrates on that which will expose the heroism most efficiently. He lacks the space to immerse us in Washington's psychological experience. We see Washington from the outside, the way we see most of Bancroft's heroes, including Washington himself in the *History*. It is Washington's conflict with the French rather than the wilderness that Parkman stresses, with all the political, social, and military complications it implies.

Parkman's method in *Montcalm and Wolfe* is also more Bancroftian than in *La Salle* in that in *Montcalm and Wolfe* he tends to impose his own narrating point of view on his primary sources more aggressively. In paraphrasing these sources he tends, like Bancroft, to erase their point of view and incorporate merely their information or language. In the

---

[48] Washington, *Journal*, 17.
[49] *Montcalm and Wolfe*, I, 133 f.

example that follows he practically turns the source inside out. Pierre Roubaud, a Jesuit missionary who accompanied Montcalm's expedition against Fort William Henry, wrote this account of some British scouts who approached the French camp:

About eleven o'clock, two boats that had left the fort appeared on the lake. . . . One fairly large flatboat held all us missionaries. A tent had been set up there to give us protection from the open air, during the nights that were quite cold in this climate; this awning, thus arranged, created a kind of shadow in the air that could be easily discovered by the light of the stars. Curious to identify it, it was directly towards us that the Englishmen moved. . . . Few, in short, would have escaped, if luckily for them a trifle had not betrayed us a few moments too soon. One of our army's sheep began to bleat; at this cry, which uncovered the ambush, the enemies spun around and made for the opposite shore, rowing furiously to save themselves under cover of the shadows and the woods.[50]

Parkman takes every detail from Roubaud, including the information about the lake's geography and the location of the sheep, which come from earlier passages in Roubaud's letter. Yet by narrating the action as though it had been seen by the Englishmen in their boats, he succeeds in elbowing Roubaud completely off the stage:

About ten o'clock at night two boats set out from the fort to reconnoitre. They were passing a point of land on their left, two miles or more down the lake, when the men on board descried through the gloom a strange object against the bank; and they rowed towards it to learn what it might be. It was an awning over the bateaux that carried Roubaud and his brother missionaries. As the rash oarsmen drew near, the bleating of a sheep in one of the French provision-boats warned them of danger; and turning they pulled for their lives towards the eastern shore.[51]

[50] Pierre Roubaud, "Lettre," in *Lettres Édifiantes et Curieuses,* VI, 277 f. The translation is mine.

[51] *Montcalm and Wolfe,* I, 492 f.

Parkman's shift in point of view is so severe that it requires him to make an interesting extrapolation from the information Roubaud gives. Since no English account of the incident was available to him, he was forced to guess what time the scouts left Fort William Henry. Roubaud says merely that they approached "about eleven o'clock." Parkman, assuming that a boat on patrol would move slowly, sets the time of their departure at "about ten o'clock." Without seeing Roubaud's letter, no reader could know that a French source was Parkman's model.

Finally, a technique of great service to Parkman in *Montcalm and Wolfe*, though rarely used in *La Salle*, was one Bancroft adopted in his fourth, fifth, and sixth volumes: blending snippets from a number of primary sources into a single, unified account. Generally speaking, the action of *Montcalm and Wolfe*, far more complicated and incorporating many more sources than the action of *La Salle*, required a more synthetic approach. To meet this challenge, Parkman often had to shift rapidly among bits and pieces of evidence, his skill at which is impressive. At his best, he comes close to achieving the psychological immersion of *La Salle*: actions that are so unified in terms of mood and feeling as to seem to have been reported by a single intelligence are in fact stitched together from sources with sometimes radically different points of view. For instance, his account of the British army's camp on Sunday, September 7, 1755, the day before the Battle of Lake George, is based on the testimony of two eyewitnesses, Seth Pomeroy, captain of a Massachusetts regiment, and William Johnson, commanding general of the army. Pomeroy made this entry in his journal for September 7: "Sabath Day 7th a fair Day but Some Small Showers about 200 wagons Came this Day Load Chiefly with battoes I attened public worship this Day news at night of larg body men Traviling South up or near yᵉ wood Creek."[52] Parkman follows Pomeroy closely,

[52] *The Journals and Papers of Seth Pomeroy* (ed. by Louis E. DeForest),

but, by cleaning up his grammar and by adding, among other phrases, the sly "not wholly a day of rest," he succeeds in taking Pomeroy's place as the viewer watching the day's events: "It was a peaceful day, fair and warm, with a few light showers; yet not wholly a day of rest, for two hundred wagons came up from Fort Lyman, loaded with bateaux. After the sermon there was an alarm."[53] Pomeroy has disappeared. What remains is a narrator who by placing himself in Pomeroy's mind manages to persuade us that he saw those events.

Immediately, without warning, Parkman begins to paraphrase an altogether different kind of document—Johnson's official report of the battle:

Source:	*Montcalm and Wolfe*:
Gentlemen,	An Indian scout came in about
Sunday evening the 7th. instant	sunset, and reported that he had
I received intelligence from some	found the trail of a body of men
Indian scouts I had sent out, that	moving from South Bay towards
they had discovered three large	Fort Lyman. Johnson called for a
roads about the South Bay, and	volunteer to carry a letter of
were confident a very considerable	warning to Colonel Blanchard, the
number of the enemy were	commander. A wagoner named
marched, or on their march to-	Adams offered himself for the
wards our encampment at the	perilous service, mounted, and
Carrying-place. . . . I got one	galloped along the road with the
Adams, a waggoner, who volun-	letter.[55]
tarily and bravely consented to	
ride express with my orders to	
colonel Blanchard of the New	
Hampshire regiment, commanding	
officer there. I acquainted him	
with my intelligence, and directed	
him to withdraw all the troops	
there within the works thrown	
up.[54]	

113. The manuscript of DeForest's edition was used by Parkman for *Montcalm and Wolfe.*

53 *Montcalm and Wolfe*, I, 296.

54 William Johnson to the Governors of the Several Colonies, September 9, 1755, in *The Documentary History of the State of New York* (ed. by E. B. O'Callaghan), II, 691.

55 *Montcalm and Wolfe*, I, 296.

While Parkman's motive in reducing Johnson's "scouts" to a "scout" is not entirely clear, it may be akin to the one that prompts him to have Johnson call for a volunteer and to have Adams step forward, vault into the saddle, and gallop off. All these changes seem to be the result of his wish to dramatize the passage with invented details of action. Equally important are the devices by which he brings the narrator close to the action. The narrator seems to have seen the scout (or scouts) come into camp, Johnson emerge from his tent, explain the mission, and call for a volunteer. Then Adams speaks up and rides away. The events are described as they might have been seen by an onlooker, not as they are reported by Johnson, whose role, which Johnson himself sees as the lead, Parkman reduces to a minimum. Thus the passage contributes to the impression developed in the chapter as a whole that Johnson is not a true hero but a hollow, self-aggrandizing man, a tone that provides the passage with its emotional unity. According to Parkman, the scout did not necessarily report to Johnson; he merely reported, perhaps to everyone else in the army first. And Parkman ignores Johnson's remarks about the letter to Blanchard, choosing instead to invent Adams' probable movements. Finally, Parkman may have felt that a single scout running in with the news would strike the reader as more dramatic than Johnson's vague "some scouts"; it is clear in any case that his "sunset" is more vivid than Johnson's "evening."

Yet for all its polish, the method is essentially the same as Bancroft's. It, too, lies somewhere between verbatim copying and total abandonment of the language of the sources at a point of compromise artistically comfortable to the historian. Parkman was no more interested than Bancroft in paraphrasing his sources to meet scissors-and-paste obligations. Like Bancroft, he used the sources for his own ends and to suit himself. Where he seems to have moved beyond Bancroft, methodologically speaking, and indeed beyond most other narrative historians of his era, was in his use of the accounts of eyewitnesses as a means of reliving the past. More in *La Salle* and the volumes of *France and England* like it than in *Montcalm and Wolfe*, he was able to re-create the psychological experience of civilized men performing heroic feats in the wilderness by adding his own experience to theirs and by revising their narratives for greatest emotional impact. The method was consistent with his basic theme that between the anarchy of the wilderness and the despotism of the absolutist state there lay an area of self-regulated freedom best represented by the Anglo-American political tradition. By telling histories from within the point of view of the heroes who embodied the self-sacrificing self-reliance he felt was crucial to a sane and balanced civilization, he was able not only to bring the past to life but to express his own ideals.

Montcalm and Wolfe is at bottom like *La Salle* and the rest of Parkman's books in asserting a pessimistic, nonmeliorative philosophy of life. When in the final lines of the book Parkman challenges democracy to "give the world a civilization as mature and pregnant, ideas as energetic and vitalizing, and types of manhood as lofty and strong, as any of the systems which it boasts to supplant,"[56] he denies that the world improves. Much of his force as a historian stemmed from this belief in the essential uniformity of nature and human experience, for in it he felt sure that his readers in the present could relive the experience of the past with him. Unlike Bancroft, who held that the best lay in the future, Parkman felt that all the heroism of human civilization, past, present, and future, was implicit in the taming of the North American continent. *Montcalm and Wolfe* appeared in 1884. Five years later Henry Adams began publishing his nine-volume history of the Jefferson-Madison era. With this work, the tradition came to its fitting conclusion.

---

[56] *Montcalm and Wolfe*, II, 414.

★ ★ ★ ★ ★ ★

Character and Compromise in Adams' *History*

ADAMS' *History of the United States During the Adminis-trations of Jefferson and Madison,* published between 1889 and 1891, has received more attention in recent decades than Bancroft's *History* or Parkman's *France and England.* This is partly because Adams' other writings—most notably *The Education of Henry Adams*—are of major literary im-portance; partly because, as the great-grandson and grandson of U.S. presidents and as a central figure in American cultural history of the late nineteenth and early twentieth centuries, Adams is a compelling biographical subject; and partly be-cause the *History* itself is seen by working historians, as Mer-rill D. Peterson puts it, as ranking "with the magnificent achievements of American historiography, if indeed it does not outrank all others."[1] While only one book-length study of Bancroft and two of Parkman have been published since World War II, more than a dozen books on Adams have come out. Although most of these devote only a chapter or two to the *History,* they have sifted it with a thoroughness necessari-ly missing from the critical canon on Bancroft and Parkman. This is not to say that Nye's studies of Bancroft, Pease's and

[1] "Henry Adams on Jefferson the President," *Virginia Quarterly Review,* Vol. XXXIX (1963), 187.

Doughty's analyses of *France and England,* or Levin's book on both writers are not as valuable as any of the books on Adams. They are. Yet they stand in isolation. They have not been probed and tested the way the studies of Adams' *History* have been. This probing and testing has progressively clarified the *History*'s meaning: no clearer proof of the value of repeated critical examination of a work of history could be found.

That said, the inevitable qualification clamors to be heard. Impressive though the criticism of the *History* is, it tends to explain the work chiefly as a stepping-stone to Adams' later work and to measure it against ideas he developed late in life. The effect has been to split the *History* off from the tradition of Bancroft's *History* and Parkman's *France and England.* Adams' biography, around which most of the criticism is organized, encourages such a splitting off. Up to the age of fifty, when he finished the *History,* Adams spent most of his adult life producing conventional history at Harvard and then as intellectual-in-residence and social lion in Washington. His *Essays in Anglo-Saxon Law* (1876), written by his students at Harvard, his *Documents Relating to New England Federalism* (1877), *The Writings of Albert Gallatin* (1879), *The Life of Albert Gallatin* (1880), *John Randolph* (1882), and of course the *History* were all produced during a twenty-year immersion in historical study. Then, perhaps partly as the result of his wife's suicide in 1885, he abruptly changed course. He gave up conventional history, dabbled in radical historical speculation, and produced the celebrated *Mont-Saint-Michel and Chartres* and *The Education of Henry Adams* before his death in 1918. Making sense of his entire literary career has been a more engrossing problem to modern scholars than linking any part of it to writers like Bancroft and Parkman. There has in fact been a tendency to deny his debt to the earlier historians.[2]

[2] A recent example of this tendency can be found in J. C. Levenson's "Henry

Yet despite its heavily biographical, somewhat insular tone, explication of the *History* has worked progressively closer to the heart of the onion, and what seem to me to be the two most convincing general interpretations are among those most recently to appear. In the first, published in 1962, George Hochfield rejects the consensus, reached during the 1950's, that the *History* embodies a scientism drawn chiefly from the mechanistic determinism of Herbert Spencer and the positivism of Auguste Comte.[3] Hochfield argues that Adams' final chapter, in which he calls for a science of history and from which the scientistically oriented critics have drawn their most convincing evidence, is merely "casual" in its scientism and that, in terms of the definitions of science Adams himself offers in the chapter, "the *History* is not scientific."[4] While conceding that the *History* is permeated with "the idea of necessary movement in history"[5] and that "Adams tends to think of events as forced, as issuing out of their precedent circumstances, more or less beyond the control of individual wills,"[6] Hochfield denies that it expresses a mechanistic philosophy. Adams "is still," he says, "too much the moralist for that."[7] Like Yvor

---

Adams," *Pastmasters*, 43–46. At one point (p. 45) Levenson remarks that "Parkman's most characteristic accomplishments in defining his subject differ so much from Adams' at so many points that the older historian seems to have been an ironic model for the younger."

[3] For interpretations stressing the *History*'s debt to Comte and positivism, see Max I. Baym, *The French Education of Henry Adams*, 96, and, more importantly, William H. Jordy, *Henry Adams: Scientific Historian*, 73–120 and especially 116–17; for those stressing its debt to Spencerian determinism, see Henry Wasser, *The Scientific Thought of Henry Adams*, 54–60, and Ernest Samuels, *Henry Adams: The Middle Years*, 349–86. Timothy P. Donovan, *Henry Adams and Brooks Adams*, 35–46, generally follows the scientistic thesis and in particular Samuels' argument that the scientism of the *History* conflicts with its literary or moral thrust in such a way as to mar it as a work of art.

[4] George Hochfield, *Henry Adams: An Introduction and Interpretation*, 70.

[5] *Ibid.*

[6] *Ibid.*, 68.

[7] *Ibid.*

Winters and to a lesser degree William H. Jordy and J. C. Levenson,[8] Hochfield contends that Adams' major concern is the moral behavior of his characters in general and the defeat of Jefferson's idealism in particular. "The true center of the *History*, after all," he says, "is not a concern with the laws of mechanical development but with the idealism of democracy."[9] In Hochfield's view this concern resulted for Adams in an almost tragic awareness of the gap between Jefferson's ideals and the hard reality of the human condition, and, further, in his rejection of the democratic ideal as a "harmful, or at best enfeebling, illusion."[10] Yet far from resulting in the bitter pessimism of the later works, continues Hochfield, this realization freed Adams in the *History* from the tyrannical idealism of his heritage and allowed him for the first time in his life to accept, calmly, not only the frustrations of his own and other men's experience but also the "knowledge of the hardness and solidity of life."[11]

Especially helpful is Hochfield's suggestion that in the *History* Adams judges all act and motive strictly within the context of what is historically possible. The *History* is not concerned with whatever natural—or supernatural—forces have caused the world to be. It is trained instead, argues Hochfield, on what men have done and what they can reasonably be expected to do within the context of the world as it exists. The interest it occasionally seems to evince in the mysterious givens that enclose human experience is irrelevant to its main concerns. Man in relation to political society is Adams' mat-

---

[8] Winters, *In Defense of Reason,* 416–17 and 422–29, applauds the *History*'s precise moral intelligence; Jordy calls the work "the greatest moral history ever produced in America," *Scientific Historian,* 67; and J. C. Levenson, *The Mind and Art of Henry Adams,* 126 f., argues that in the *History* Adams did not completely break away from the tradition of moral history he had inherited from earlier American historians.

[9] *Introduction and Interpretation,* 71.
[10] *Ibid.,* 83.
[11] *Ibid.,* 84.

ter, and throughout the *History* he assumes that men and nations are sufficiently interesting in and of themselves to justify the closest study and that moral judgments which issue from such study are limited in their finality to purely pragmatic, empirical standards.[12] The *History* assumes nothing about the nature of the forces surrounding man except that to ignore the limitations they impose is to court, as Hochfield says, "inevitable disaster."[13]

In the second general interpretation of the *History*, published in 1970, Melvin E. Lyon incisively analyzes its specific themes. Although his effort to harmonize earlier deterministic interpretations with Hochfield's antiscientific reading is only partly successful, his argument that the *History*'s primary theme is the conflict between extreme democracy and extreme nationalism, with an implied compromise between the two as a necessary result, seems conclusive. Isolating the flag, the steamboat, the ocean, and the schooner as Adams' primary symbols in the work, Lyon argues that the first two symbols represent for Adams the impulse in American civilization toward unity, nationalism, and centralization, while the latter two represent its drive toward individualism, democracy, and decentralization. Although the *History* as a whole, says Lyon, seems to argue that between 1800 and 1815 America became both more democratic (ocean oriented) and more nationalistic (flag oriented), it also establishes "a fundamental irreconciliability between the flag and the ocean. . . . The national and democratic movements would thus seem to be unalterably opposed."[14]

[12] Levenson has also charted this current of thought in the *History*. Adams, he says, having "had a more than casual acquaintance with the founders of pragmatism, Chauncey Wright, Charles Sanders Peirce, and James," embraced the "new, tough American empiricism," which asserted that "an idea is not of itself demonstrable, but, in the words of William James, '*becomes* true, is *made* true by events.' " *Mind and Art*, 130.

[13] *Introduction and Interpretation*, 83.

[14] Melvin E. Lyon, *Symbol and Idea in Henry Adams*, 74.

Clearly, Adams' democracy-nationalism distinction recalls Bancroft's idea that while freedom and union, when viewed as the results of the American *e pluribus unum* process, harmonize perfectly, they are nonetheless, when viewed as the extremes of anarchy and tyranny, absolutely antagonistic. So too for Adams: democracy (freedom) and nationalism (union) are agreeable in the context of the American compromise, yet for him, as for Bancroft, they also ultimately stand for extremely dangerous and mutually repugnant opposites. According to Lyon, one manifestation of this tension in the *History* is the contrast Adams sees between Jeffersonian America and Napoleonic Europe. "Adams shows how," says Lyon,

under Jefferson and Madison, the practical necessities of the "bloody arena" drew the United States "slowly toward the European standard of true political sovereignty," even forcing it into a war, but the final result, Adams believed, would be a compromise between the [democratic] dream and European practice.[15]

Lyon holds that the *History* presents the Jeffersonian-Madisonian era as a conflict between the centrifugal drive toward decentralization and individual liberty and the centripetal drive toward national sovereignty and union, with the centralizing demands of the War of 1812 eventually ensuring national survival. He discusses, in addition to the meaning of the *History*'s major symbols, the polarities, or, as he calls them, dualities, that run throughout the work—man *versus* nature, theory *versus* energy, Federalist *versus* Republican, New Englander *versus* Virginian, America *versus* Europe, states' rights *versus* union, and so on—and suggests some of the compromises they produce. His study corroborates the argument that the theme of the *History* is at core the same as the one we have already seen controlling Bancroft's and Parkman's histories and that even in his subtle preference for nationalism over democracy, expressed at various levels of the

[15] *Symbol and Idea,* 72 f.

work's meaning, Adams shares their aversion to anarchy or, as he consistently terms it, chaos.

Other of Adams' themes, not discussed by Hochfield or Lyon, also resemble those found in Bancroft's *History* and Parkman's *France and England*. In the first place, Adams expresses an almost Bancroftian faith that American democracy is man's best hope. Though he tends with Parkman to doubt whether man in the mass is capable of high civilization, he is with Bancroft firmly committed to the ideal. According to Adams, men may in time move beyond the competitive nationalism characteristic of his own as well as of Jefferson's day to an Atlantic community, or perhaps even a system of world government which may resemble, on a larger scale, the federative democracy developed in America in 1815. The American system enjoys its greatest advantage over Old World forms of government in that it involves the mass of men in the activities of the state through a representative form of government and at the same time allows them considerable personal freedom. Convinced that a republican government, like any other sovereign power, must centralize its authority in order to use it effectively, Adams never tires of condemning Jefferson's decentralized agrarianism and approving America's tendency to centralize between 1800 and 1815. When he asserts that by 1800 the United States had made "a single great step in advance of the Old World,—they had agreed to try the experiment of embracing half a continent in one republican system,"[16] he suggests a hope that the experiment may prove successful on an even larger scale.

He does not seem to see this as an inevitable or even very likely development. Repeatedly he raises the doubt whether men in general have the ability or the inclination to cooperate on an international level, and he is thoroughly aware, as he also indicates at many points, that merely to reach the level

[16] *History of the United States During the Administrations of Jefferson and Madison*, I, 72 f.

of civilization represented by nationalism has taken man thousands of years and has cost him countless wars and unimaginable suffering. The ambiguous series of questions that concludes the *History* reflects this awareness:

[Americans] were mild, but what corruptions would their relaxations bring? They were peaceful, but what machinery were their corruptions to be purged? What interests were to vivify a society so vast and uniform? What ideals were to ennoble it? What object, besides physical content, must a democratic continent aspire to attain?[17]

As the passage suggests, Adams feels that even if American democracy were to succeed materially, it might become the nightmare of selfish and barbaric egalitarianism Parkman so often warns us against. Human selfishness, narrow-mindedness, and inertia stand, in Adams' eyes, in the way of a worthy, international, democratic civilization, as does the hard fact of nationalism itself. Yet the *History* assumes that such a goal deserves to be pursued.

Adams does not reject Jefferson's ideals. He rejects instead Jefferson's notion that he could achieve those ideals in the actual state of the world in 1800 by simply bypassing Old World nationalism altogether. His sympathy with Jefferson's ultimate goals seems unmistakable in the following passage:

Jefferson aspired beyond the ambition of a nationality, and embraced in his view the whole future of man. That the United States should become a nation like France, England, or Russia, should conquer the world like Rome, or develop a typical race like the Chinese, was no part of his scheme. He wished to begin a new era. Hoping for a time when the world's ruling interests should cease to be local and should become universal; when questions of boundary and nationality should become insignificant; when armies and navies should be reduced to the work of police, and politics should

17 *Ibid.*, IX, 242.

consist only in non-intervention,—he set himself to the task of governing, with this golden age in view.[18]

Adams' quarrel with this vision, as the passage implies and the entire *History* argues, is not that it is in itself false or unworthy but that Jefferson hoped to achieve it at once by stepping outside the parameters of history and disavowing the stage of political development which his world had actually reached. The high point of Jefferson's administration came in 1805, when in his second inaugural, says Adams, he "proved the liberality and elevation of his mind"[19] by throwing aside his earlier agrarian dogmas and proposing in their place an elaborate system of federally sponsored public works. In concluding his analysis of the second inaugural, Adams typically half-mocks and half-applauds Jefferson's conception of himself as mankind's benefactor: "Who had proposed to himself a loftier ideal? Among all the kings and statesmen who swayed the power of empire, where could one be found who had looked so far into the future, and had so boldly grappled with its hopes?"[20] The questions are by no means scornful.

But Jefferson ignored the fact of "democratic nationality."[21] Democratic nationalism emerges from the *History* not as an end in itself but as a necessary phase in any movement toward an international polity the structure of which Adams only dimly perceives and the possibility of achieving which he always questions. Democratic nationalism may move men closer to the ideal than can other kinds because, says Adams, in "[r]eversing the old-world system," it "increased in energy as it reached the lowest and most ignorant class, dragging and whirling them upward as in the blast of a furnace."[22] It might, in other words, produce "a higher variety of the human race":

18 *Ibid.*, I, 146.
19 *Ibid.*, III, 19.
20 *Ibid.*, 21.
21 *Ibid.*, 20.
22 *Ibid.*, I, 160.

"Nothing less than this was necessary for its complete success."[23] New World nationalism offered more chance for such racial improvement than Old because instead of suppressing individual initiative and hope, it encouraged men not only to work hard and to amass personal wealth but to look to the day when all Americans would share a nation bursting with riches and glowing with "youth, health, and love."[24] In other words, the vision promises more than material wealth. Men may find in it motivation for self-improvement, refinement, and cooperation as yet unknown among the world's masses. It unmistakably recalls Bancroft's vision of American progress.

As fundamental in Adams' as in Bancroft's eyes to the success of the American experiment is the *laissez-faire* economic system. Submerging his own point of view, as is his habit, in that of what he presumes was the average American's of the early nineteenth century, he comes as close in the following passage as he does anywhere in the *History* to spelling out a connection between future political possibilities and the present reality of American democracy:

The success of the American system was, from this point of view, a question of economy. If they could relieve themselves from debts, taxes, armies, and government interference with industry, they must succeed in outstripping Europe in economy of production; and Americans were even then partly aware that if their machine were not so weakened by these economies as to break down in the working, it must of necessity break down every rival. If their theory was sound, when the day of competition should arrive, Europe must choose between American and Chinese institutions, but there would be no middle path; she might become a confederated democracy, or a wreck.[25]

The passage implies that if political confederation does occur

23 *Ibid.*, 184.
24 *Ibid.*, 173.
25 *Ibid.*, 162 f.

in Europe, it will probably follow a period of brutal economic competition. The economy of the American system may in time so wear down other nations that it will force them to adopt its political means. What is certain is that there will be political and economic conflict for a long time to come.

In its insistence on conflict the *History* seems more to echo the Parkmanian than the Bancroftian ethos. Existence is a struggle in which the fittest survive. Nations must be strong or be destroyed. Yet at the center of Adams' argument, as has already been suggested, is an idea of America and America's role that embodies as much of Bancroft's world view as Parkman's. Philosophically, Adams could be said to stand between the two earlier historians. On the one hand he tends to agree with Bancroft that America has an important role to play in future world history, though for Adams there seems to be nothing inevitable about what it will be or how it will be played. On the other, he shares Parkman's doubts about the mass of men's capacity for high civilization. It might be argued that whatever Darwinism the *History* contains serves as a substitute dynamism for that of Bancroft's providential theory: although Adams' universe is no longer guided by a benevolent intelligence, it has nevertheless regained the teleological momentum that Parkman denied it. However that may be, Adams establishes a mission for American democracy less promising than Bancroft's but more promising than Parkman's. He compromises, as it were, between them.

Then, too, like Bancroft and Parkman, Adams attacks the decadence and corruption of European society, contrasting it openly or by implication with the moral health and vigor of America. Early in the *History* he opposes his well-known image of the American, "[s]tripped for the hardest work, every muscle firm and elastic, every ounce of brain ready for use, and not a trace of superfluous flesh on his nervous and supple body,"[26] with priest-ridden, war-wracked Europe,

[26] *Ibid.*, 159.

154

whose aristocracies survived by "sucking their nourishment from industry, producing nothing themselves, employing little or no active capital or intelligent labor, but pressing on the energies and ambition of society with the weight of an incubus."[27] Although the rich Europeans who scorned the American dream as a delusion "for a long time stood aloof,—they were timid and narrow-minded," says Adams, the "poor came, and from them were seldom heard complaints of deception or delusion. Within a moment, by the mere contact of a moral atmosphere, they saw the gold and jewels, the summer cornfields and the glowing continent."[28] Defending America against the attacks of English poets, Adams asserts that "between the morals of politics and society in America and those then prevailing in Europe, there was no room for comparison, —there was room only for contrast."[29] At times Adams' indignation at the immorality of European rulers resembles Bancroft's, as when he remarks that "[m]ost of the stories told about the Queen would not bear repeating, and, whether true or false, reflected the rottenness of a society which could invent or believe them."[30] His touch is lighter than Bancroft's or Parkman's but no less damning.[31]

Moreover, Adams shares Bancroft's and Parkman's opinion that energy and vigor are good and inertia and torpor are bad. At the heart of his criticism of Jefferson's political theory is his distaste for its tendency to inaction. Dozens of comments like the following dot the *History*: "Such progress toward energy was more rapid than could have been expected from a party like that which Jefferson had educated and

[27] *Ibid.*, 161.
[28] *Ibid.*, 174.
[29] *Ibid.*, 167.
[30] *Ibid.*, 347.
[31] Levenson, *Mind and Art*, 183, remarks of the *History* as a whole that "Adams' American won as signal a triumph on the international scene as any hero of a James novel." Or, it might be added, of a Bancroft or Parkman history.

which he still controlled."[32] At one point he associates torpor with inferiority of race, much in the manner of Bancroft and Parkman: "Jackson's difficulties were very great, and were overcome only by the desperate energy which he infused even into the volatile creoles and sluggish negroes."[33] Although the countless metaphors in the *History* which oppose inertia or static mass to activity, motion, and efficiency have sometimes been explained in terms of Adams' commitment to science, it seems more likely that they were inspired by the same kind of activism that is obvious in the writings of the New England historians who preceded Adams. These and many other metaphors with a scientific ring are no more prevalent in the *History* as a whole than those taken from other areas of human experience—for example, the many figures based on breaking waves or blowing winds, on military combat, on biblical or classical mythology, or on the drama and especially on Shakespeare. Adams seems to show no special preference for scientific imagery. Like all the other kinds in the *History*, it serves a largely illustrative, rather than thematic, function. Adams seems to wish not to state but to clarify his argument with his figures. Metaphors of energy and inertia, derived from an area of learning interesting and familiar to the educated nineteenth-century reader, had the further virtue of communicating Adams' own New England partiality for constant, productive work. It seems questionable to read them as evidence of a positivist or mechanistic theory of history.

There are hints throughout the *History* of sympathy with the ideal of heroism that governs Parkman's *France and Eng-*

[32] *History*, IV, 224.
[33] *Ibid.*, VIII, 354. For a full discussion of the racial attitudes underlying the vigor-torpor theme in the works of Bancroft and Parkman, see Levin, *History as Romantic Art*, 126–59. Though Adams rarely expresses the racism that permeates Parkman's *France and England*, his sympathy with it is indicated in his comment that a half blood named Weatherford was "as nearly civilized as Indian blood permitted" (*History*, VII, 229).

land. Adams tends to see war as engendering certain heroic virtues unobtainable by other means, and it is within a military context that he defines what he means by heroism.

> If war made men brutal, at least it made them strong; it called out the qualities best fitted to survive in the struggle for existence. To risk life for one's country was no mean act even when done for selfish motives; and to die that others might more happily live was the highest act of self-sacrifice to be reached by man. War, with all its horrors, could purify as well as debase; it dealt with high motives and vast interests; taught courage, discipline, and stern sense of duty. Jefferson must have asked himself in vain what lessons of heroism or duty were taught by his system of peaceable coercion, which turned every citizen into an enemy of the laws,—preaching the fear of war and self-sacrifice, making many smugglers and traitors, but not a single hero.[34]

The figure with which Adams opens the passage deserves some comment. It is an excellent example of his method of illustrating or clarifying his ideas by means of metaphor. With it and the many Darwinian images like it in the *History* he tries to suggest chiefly the solid and often bitter realism of historical experience: it does not, in other words, indicate that Adams espoused Darwinism in a more radical or systematic way than did the majority of educated men of his time. Far from asserting the iron laws of natural selection, the figure is used here merely to suggest the difficulties of life and to qualify the enthusiasm for war that the rest of the passage expresses. Seeking out whatever good there is in an imperfect world, he finds in one of its most unlovely aspects —war—the redeeming virtue of heroism.

Though more muted than Parkman's, Adams' heroic ideal resembles his in praising the courageous, disciplined, and self-sacrificing man of duty. The respect Adams feels for military virtue is indicated in his comment that Englishmen "had won

[34] *History*, IV, 277.

whatever was theirs by creating a national character in which personal courage was as marked a quality as selfishness; for in their situation no other than a somewhat brutal energy could have secured success."[35] The persistence of Jefferson and his party in avoiding war provokes caustic comments: "War, which every other nation in history had looked upon as the first duty of a State, was in America a subject for dread, not so much because of possible defeat as of probable success."[36] In retelling the *Chesapeake-Leopard* incident of 1807, Adams favorably compares the reaction of Gallatin, who having "hitherto thrown all his influence on the side of peace, was then devoting all his energies to provision for war,"[37] with that of Jefferson, who "followed without protest the impulse toward war; but his leading thought was to avoid it."[38] And at one point he says openly that much of what is best in civilization has been the product of war:

[Taylor's] denunciation of war expressed party doctrine, and he harmed no one by repeating the time-worn moral drawn from Greece and Rome, the Persian millions, Philip of Macedon, Syracuse and Carthage,—as though the fate of warlike nations proved that they should have submitted to foreign outrage, or as though the world could show either arts or liberty except such as sprung from the cradle of war.[39]

A final congruity between his volumes and Bancroft's and Parkman's is the interest his also reveal in national character. His attempt in the opening and closing sections of the *History* to define an American national character has its roots in their tradition. He asserts at the beginning of the work that the

growth of character, social and national,—the formation of men's

---

[35] *Ibid.*, III, 395.
[36] *Ibid.*, IV, 211.
[37] *Ibid.*, 32.
[38] *Ibid.*, 33.
[39] *Ibid.*, V, 196.

minds,—more interesting than any territorial or industrial growth, defied the tests of censuses and surveys. . . . A few customs, more or less local; a few prejudices, more or less popular; a few traits of thought, suggesting habits of mind,—must form the entire material for a study more important than that of politics or economics[40]

—more important, presumably, because the success of democracy depends on whether or not it can improve the character of a people as a whole. Then, four thousand pages and a million words later, he concludes the *History* with a chapter titled "American Character," in which he claims that in the course of work he has discovered that the

traits of intelligence, rapidity, and mildness seemed fixed in the national character as early as 1817, and were likely to become more marked as time should pass. A vast amount of conservatism still lingered among the people; but the future spirit of society could hardly fail to be intelligent, rapid in movement, and mild in method.[41]

In all but the prologue and epilogue of the *History*, however, he reverses the technique and, instead of trying to extract a national character from a welter of individual cases, uses an individual to suggest the traits more or less common to a group. With this device he is able to draw portraits of individual men even as he suggests attitudes held by the communities to which they belong. Timothy Pickering was a leader of the extreme New England Federalists, and his provincialism, unreasonableness, and hatred of democracy are persuasively presented by Adams as part of the man. Yet happily for Adams' purpose these traits were characteristic of many other extreme Federalists. Similarly, Harrison Gray Otis embodies the caution of moderate Federalists, Albert Gallatin the solid democratic virtues of Pennsylvania, John Armstrong the wily unscrupulousness of New York politics,

---

[40] *Ibid.*, I, 41 f.
[41] *Ibid.*, IX, 240 f.

Alexander Baring the honor and talent of enlightened British merchants, James Wilkinson the corruption and incompetence of the pre-1812 American army, Henry Clay the patriotic energy of the western states, and so on. Asserting the Bancroftian postulate that "individuals were important chiefly as types,"[42] Adams follows it throughout the work.

His treatment of Jefferson and Napoleon in this regard is the most ambitious and interesting in the work. They constitute antipodes that define and control the *History*'s centrifugal-centripetal theme from beginning to end.[43] Jefferson is Adams' quintessential early-nineteenth-century New World democrat, Napoleon his Old World autocrat. At the beginning of the *History*'s narrative proper he introduces the polar contrast between them in a passage that occurs midway through the famous paragraph in which he first describes Jefferson:

This sandy face, with hazel eyes and sunny aspect; this loose, shackling person; this rambling and often brilliant conversation, belonged to the controlling influences of American history, more necessary to the story than three-fourths of the official papers, which only hid the truth. Jefferson's personality during these eight years appeared to be the government, and impressed itself, like that of Bonaparte, although by a different process, on the mind of the nation.[44]

In succeeding volumes, Adams subtly distinguishes between the genial, rambling, unmilitaristic, centrifugal style of American democracy as it was shaped by or reflected in Jefferson, and the ruthless, selfish, centripetal militarism of Europe as it was shaped by or reflected in Napoleon.

[42] *Ibid.*, 222.

[43] Though Levenson has partially explored the parallels Adams establishes between Jefferson and Napoleon, *Mind and Art*, 156–62, he has, in concentrating on the increasing similarity between the two men's means, tended to overlook the more important contrast Adams establishes between their characters. Lyon, *Symbol and Idea*, 71f., defines some aspects of the contrast.

[44] *History*, I, 187.

This is not to say that in the *History* Jefferson equals America and Napoleon equals Europe but only that in some ways Adams makes their characters resonate with the political spheres of influence they dominated. The strategy is more obvious in Jefferson's case because Adams gives it away in his concluding chapter on American character. That Jefferson was "sensitive, affectionate, and, in his own eyes, heroic" and "yearned for love and praise as no other great American ever did"[45] suggests an image of American society which Adams fills out in his final chapter when he defines one trait of the American character as mildness. Again, Adams' portrayal of Jefferson as an incurable optimist who repeatedly shuts his eyes to unpleasant realities[46] is subsumed in the concluding chapter in the "optimism"[47] that Adams attributes to American religion and politics. Finally, Jefferson's incompetence as an administrator finds its counterpart in the "incapacity in national politics" that Adams claims was "a leading trait in American character."[48]

The same kind of suggestiveness suffuses his portrait of Bonaparte. In introducing the satanic dictator, "unapproachable on his bad eminence," Adams wryly contrasts him with his benign and befreckled opponent:

Ambition that ground its heel into every obstacle; restlessness that often defied common-sense; selfishness that eat like a cancer into his reasoning faculties; energy such as had never before been combined with equal genius and resources; ignorance that would have amused a school-boy; and a moral sense which regarded truth and falsehood as equally useful modes of expression,—an unprovoked war or secret assassination as equally natural forms of activity,—such a combination of qualities as Europe had forgotten

---

45 *Ibid.*, 324.
46 See *ibid.*, III, 96 and 329, and IV, 6, for three passages in which Adams repeats the words "shut his eyes" in describing Jefferson's response to practical difficulties.
47 *Ibid.*, IX, 240.
48 *Ibid.*, 227.

since the Middle Ages, and could realize only by reviving the Eccelinos and Alberics of the thirteenth century, had to be faced and overawed by the gentle optimism of President Jefferson and his Secretary of State.[49]

While Jefferson emerges as a temporizer unwilling to act on pressing matters and a panderer to rather than a leader of public opinion, Napoleon is a veritable demon of energy and self-will: "Bonaparte told no one his plans; but he was not a man to hesitate when decision was needed."[50] Again and again Adams shows him giving lightning orders that overturned nations. The sale of Louisiana here, the invasion of Russia there, thousands of troops being sent everywhere on brutal errands—this in contrast to the Sage of Monticello, whose passion was peace. Unfortunately, when Jefferson leaves the presidency in 1809, Adams is prevented from sustaining the dramatic, comic, quasi-symbolic interest generated by the clash between the two antagonists. Although Madison is treated as merely extending Jefferson's policies to their breaking point in the War of 1812, he is a far less interesting and suggestive figure than Jefferson, and Adams does not force the anti-Napoleonic representative mantle upon him. The conflict between Jefferson and Napoleon is at bottom a clash between two individual men, of course. Yet through it Adams is able to suggest the poles of political diffusion and centralism and the desirability of a middle course between them.

The consonance of Adams' *History* with the histories of both Bancroft and Parkman seems thus in many ways clear. Yet Adams significantly extends the pragmatic, relativistic tone introduced by Bancroft and developed more fully by Parkman. His argument rests entirely on a tough, pragmatic rationality that makes its main appeal to the reader's intellect rather than to his emotion. He makes us more keenly aware than either Bancroft or Parkman of the contingent, unpredic-

[49] *Ibid.*, I, 334 f.
[50] *Ibid.*, II, 16.

table quality of history. And, unlike them, he judges human behavior against almost wholly relativistic, humanistic criteria. He assumes that because there is no higher intelligence than man's at work on his behalf in the universe, man can improve the quality of his terrestrial existence only through his own efforts. History, he says, is the record of human attempts like those made in practical politics, which he asserts is "commonly an affair of compromise and relative truth," to "modify the severity of Nature's processes";[51] and while it often reveals simply the "lack of motive, intelligence, and morality, the helplessness characteristic of many long periods in the face of crushing problems, and the futility of human efforts to escape from difficulties religious, political, and social,"[52] it also reveals many instances of human intelligence having been successfully applied to the problems of life. "Character" is a term that Adams seems to use to signify all that is peculiarly human in history.

His fascination with character led him not only to give it a commanding position in the opening and closing sections of the *History* but to make the judgment of character the burden of the entire narrative. At bottom, the nine volumes are an analysis and evaluation of the character of the hundreds of historical personages who between 1800 and 1815 governed American and western European society. To Adams, character is the key to politics:

To impose on hostile forces and interests the compulsion of a single will was the task and triumph of the true politician, which had been accomplished, under difficult conditions, by men of opposite characters. A political leader might be combative and despotic, or pliant and conciliatory. The method mattered little, provided it obtained success,—but success depended more on character than on manoeuvres.[53]

[51] *Ibid.*, VIII, 20.
[52] *Ibid.*, IX, 223.
[53] *Ibid.*, III, 123.

Although political success must finally be measured in pragmatic terms, Adams argues, its sources lie in the personal strength and ability of individual men. And, as we have seen, he claims that the study of American character is more important than a study of American politics or economics and that knowing the impact of Jefferson's personality on those around him would be more valuable historical information than all the official documents written during his presidency.

It is in the criteria Adams uses to judge character that we find the clearest evidence of the *History*'s pragmatic, relativistic thrust. The moral *sine qua non* of the *History* is loyalty to one's country. Above all else, a man must be faithful to the duly authorized sovereign power of which he is a member. Timothy Dwight may not have been a gifted poet, says Adams, yet one quality "gave respectability to his writing apart from genius. He loved and believed in his country."[54] Pennsylvania, despite its mediocrity, was the "ideal American State, easy, tolerant, and contented. If its soil bred little genius, it bred still less treason."[55] It is not enough for a citizen merely to acquiesce in the law of the land. Adams demands an aggressive, almost Bancroftian patriotism. The tone of the following passage is audible throughout the *History*:

No more was done for national defence by land than by water, although the echo of Nelson's guns at Trafalgar was as loud as the complaints of plundered American merchants, and of native American seamen condemned to the tyranny and the lash of the British boatswains.[56]

In measuring the effects of Jefferson's embargo he laments the fact that so "deeply diseased was American opinion that patriotism vanished, and the best men in the Union took active

54 *Ibid.*, I, 98.
55 *Ibid.*, 115.
56 *Ibid.*, III, 181.

part with Lord Castlereagh and George Canning in lowering and degrading their own government."[57] Treason like that of Burr in 1806, the New England Federalists in 1814, or Napoleon during his entire career as dictator of France is the Unpardonable Sin.

Adams gives this heavy weight to patriotism because he views society as being only as stable as the laws it can enforce. In his eyes, the contractual obligation between a sovereign power and its subjects is the key to all civilization, with the rule of law resting on the ability of the sovereign to enforce it. The responsibility of individual citizens to uphold the rule of law in a democracy, where the citizens are the sovereign, is especially heavy. Adams sees the cement for the sovereign-subject contract as a patriotism so vital as to move a man to defend his country with his life's blood, if need be. Furthermore, if any subject breaks the contract by contesting the sovereign extralegally, he must be ready to suffer the consequences, as Aaron Burr discovers: "Like many another man in American history, Burr felt at last the physical strength of the patient and long-suffering government which he had so persistently insulted, outraged, and betrayed."[58]

Like most of the *History*'s major ideas, Adams' concept of social contract is revealed obliquely, in discussions of the difference between national and international law. The essence of all law, as Adams hints in his analysis of John Marshall's decision in the Marbury-Madison case,

was to maintain the sanctity of pledged word. In [Marshall's] youth society had suffered severely from want of will to enforce a contract. The national government, and especially the judiciary, had been created to supply this want by compelling men to perform their contracts.[59]

The most potent of all contracts is that which binds a subject

57 *Ibid.*, IV, 350.
58 *Ibid.*, III, 328.
59 *Ibid.*, II, 146.

to his nation. So powerful is it that it can never be broken, in theory or in practice, by the subject; both in England and America, Adams points out, "no citizen could dissolve the compact of protection and defence between himself and society without the consent or default of the community."[60] Over the majority of citizens, who never enter into it formally, the contract operates with full force. But its claims on anyone who, in taking public office, openly pledges allegiance to the state are especially potent. In order to survive, men must cooperate; in order to cooperate, they must agree to abide by laws; laws are effective only to the degree they are enforceable; enforcement is possible only in a political society whose sovereignty is clearly acknowledged; sovereignty depends on and demands the loyalty of its subjects; the more intense the subjects' loyalty, especially in a democracy, the greater their mutual peace and safety. It is from a line of reasoning such as this that Adams' patriotic ardor stems. In his mind, allegiance to country rests on stern, rational necessity. Like Bancroft and Parkman, he subtly favors the central authority of the sovereign over the individual freedom of the subject. But unlike them, he rationalizes his preference on almost wholly empirical, pragmatic grounds.

The *History* acknowledges the possibility and desirability of a future political order, probably democratic in form, in which the rule of law will be enforced internationally. Yet in the actual conditions of the nineteenth century, international law is meaningless. "A right which depended only on so-called international law," says Adams, "was worthless unless supported by the stronger force."[61] He asks: "[W]hen was international law itself anything more than a law of force? The moment a nation found itself unable to show some kind of physical defence for its protection, the wisdom of Grotius and

60 *Ibid.*, 338.
61 *Ibid.*, 327.

Bynkershoek could not prevent it from being plundered."[62] Although individuals within a nation are compelled to obey its laws, individual nations find themselves at liberty in the international jungle to take whatever they can, and they are restrained only by the limits of their military and economic power or whatever sense of fair play they may have. The fact that Adams values patriotism above all other virtues suggests that he hoped it might serve at last as the basis for broader, international loyalties. Because it was grounded in respect for law, it might be transferable to a social contract more comprehensive than the nineteenth-century nation-state.

If patriotism is the prime criterion against which Adams judges character, only just below it in importance is empirical, pragmatic reasonableness as opposed to abstract theory or dogma at one extreme and blind instinct or prejudice at the other. The type of reason that Adams praises in others and tries himself to follow in the *History* seeks compromise among men and between men and a pitiless natural environment. In general, he defines it by showing what it is not. It is not, in the first place, what "[c]enturies of study at Oxford and Edinburgh, and generations devoted to the logic or rhetoric of Aristotle, Cicero, and Quintilian" had produced in nineteenth-century England—"the stage of culture," jibes Adams, "where reasoning, in order to convince, must cease to be reasonable."[63] Nor is it the intellectual hair splitting that underlay the states' rights theory of Virginia in 1800 and New England in 1813:

No foreigner, not even Gallatin, could master the theory of Virginia and New England, or distinguish between the nation of States in union which granted certain powers, and the creature at Washington to which these powers were granted, and which might be strengthened, weakened, or abolished without necessarily affecting the nation. Whether the inability to grasp this distinction was a re-

[62] *Ibid.*, 329 f.
[63] *Ibid.*, VI, 12.

167

sult of clearer insight or of coarser intelligence, the fact was the same.[64]

Nor is it the fanatical adherence to theory which in 1808 drove Jefferson to enforce his embargo so harshly that he nearly destroyed the nation he was sworn to protect. In stubbornly maintaining the embargo, Jefferson imposed on reality a thesis it could not support and thereby reversed what Adams holds to be the proper tie between thought and action.

Yet to make no effort to shape the course of events on the basis of rational plans is to Adams as culpable as to make too much. His scorn for men in positions of public responsibility, particularly military leaders, who fail to establish firm and thoughtful policy is withering. William Hull, having shut himself in his fort at Detroit and surrendered without firing a shot, is dismissed as a "general-in-chief whose mind was paralyzed."[65] William Winder, entrusted with the defense of Washington in 1814, "whether scouting, retreating, or fighting, . . . never betrayed an idea."[66] Equally inexcusable is the abdication of reason in face of prejudice or blind instinct. Adams' prime examples of men who allowed themselves to drift according to their passions are the British Tories and the New England Federalists. The Tory ministers who came to power in 1807, representing "everything in English society that was most impervious to reason," were controlled by "prejudices . . . such as modern society could scarcely understand."[67] Similarly the Federalists: "Incredible as the folly of a political party was apt to be, the folly of the Federalists in taking up Jackson's quarrel passed the limits of understanding."[68] Congress is also often described as succumbing to an animal-like unreason. Though Adams' view of the rule of the

[64] *Ibid.*, II, 80.
[65] *Ibid.*, VI, 327.
[66] *Ibid.*, VIII, 153.
[67] *Ibid.*, IV, 55.
[68] *Ibid.*, V, 158.

previous question, adopted by the House in 1811 to limit debate, is not completely hostile, he questions whether such an act was intelligent or necessary at the time and concludes it was not. "As far as human intelligence could be called blind," he says, "the intelligence which guided the House was the blind instinct of power."[69] Its blindness lay in the fact that it had no "sufficient motive," he says: "The Republican majority in the Eleventh Congress neither needed power nor meant to use it."[70]

Adams' suggestion here that an act needs "sufficient motive" tends throughout the *History* to complement his more pragmatic argument that practical results alone justify the ideas which motivate them. He maintains a subtle balance between his judgments of reasoned means and achieved ends. The ends realized by the House in the rule of the previous question seem to Adams to be justifiable, but the means used —irrational, brutal, and unnecessary force—do not. The motivation that interests him most in the *History* is the reasonableness, or lack of it, of his characters. Because for Adams reasonableness implies sensitivity to the demands of justice, decency, and honor, as well as ability to achieve practical ends, he never separates from its human source an event that has issued in some way from human intelligence. Thus the intention, or motive, of a plan is as important to him as its results and no less subject to judgment.

At one point he reveals this interest openly. Despite his qualifying phrase "in such matters," his practice throughout the *History* supports his claim in the following paragraph that "intent" is "everything":

The project of a New England convention was well understood to violate the Constitution, and for that reason alone the cautious Federalists disliked and opposed it. Doubtless a mere violence done

69 *Ibid.*, 355 f.
70 *Ibid.*, 355.

to the law did not necessarily imply a wish for disunion. The Constitution was violated more frequently by its friends than by its enemies, and often the extent of such violations measured the increasing strength of the Union. In such matters intent was everything; and the intent of the proposed New England convention was made evident by the reluctance with which the leaders slowly yielded to the popular demand.[71]

Though Adams often contrasts real with professed intention, normally on the assumption that in the real world both the patriot and the traitor will keep their aims hidden if for expediency's sake they have to, he always tries to define the real intention and then measure it against the yardstick of loyalty to the state. It is, for example, important to see that however harshly he condemns Jefferson's embargo in terms of its final results, he never questions Jefferson's patriotism in imposing it. The reverse is true of his judgment of the extreme Federalists in 1814. Their intention was to sever the Union, and the fact that they failed in no way releases them in Adams' eyes from the onus of having tried.[72]

Joining patriotism and reasonableness as the final member of Adams' ethical trinity is the ability to translate one's patriotism and reasonableness into effective action. Although the *History* dramatizes many kinds of political effectiveness, there is only one which for Adams fully reflects reasoned implementation of the patriotic ideal. This is, without exception, the effectiveness that springs from professional competence. Professionalism has for Adams an importance comparable to that which Bancroft assigns moral intuition and Parkman self-discipline. It governs the tone of every page of the *History*. Whatever area of affairs Adams discusses—economics,

---

[71] *Ibid.*, VIII, 7.

[72] Jordy, *Scientific Historian*, 64, seems to me somewhat to oversimplify Adams' argument in saying that in Adams' "appraisal of statesmanship, then, the touchstones were two: first, the morality of the end; second, the efficiency of the means." Adams is concerned with the "morality" and "efficiency" of both means and ends.

war, law, party politics, diplomacy, art, religion, science, and so forth—he approaches it from the viewpoint of an expert in that field. Often using the specialized, professional jargon of these fields, he forces the reader into viewing problems from the inside, the way men expert in dealing with the problems see them. Whenever Adams judges a man's effectiveness, he does so on the basis of the professional criteria he feels someone in the man's field ought to meet. Accordingly, his criteria vary. He judges diplomats against the professional standards he sees as leading to effectiveness in diplomacy, military officers against those leading to effectiveness in war, congressmen against those leading to effectiveness in parliamentary politics, and so on. But the criteria remain constant in basic ways, and of all the characters in the *History*, none so closely approximates Adams' ideal as Albert Gallatin.

Gallatin, secretary of the treasury from 1801 to 1813 and joint envoy to the negotiations at Ghent in 1814, stands alone in the *History* in his excellence as a public servant. In him Adams finds a man who fulfills every criterion of character: his is "one of the loftiest characters and most loyal natures ever seen in American politics"; [73] he possesses "extraordinary abilities." [74] In a passage summing up Gallatin's administration of the treasury, Adams outlines his ideal of professional conduct by distinguishing between the responsible man of affairs like Gallatin and the "charlatan"—the adventurer or demagogue whose loyalty is ultimately not to country but to self:

If this was different finance from that which Gallatin had taught in other days, and by which he had risen to popularity and power, it was at least as simple as all that Gallatin did; but the simplicity of his methods, which was their chief professional merit, caused also their chief reproach. History showed the financial charlatan to be popular, not so much because he was dishonest as because he grati-

[73] *History*, IX, 15.
[74] *Ibid.*, VII, 46.

fied an instinct for gambling as deep as the instinct of selfishness; and a common notion of a financier was that of a man whose merit lay in the discovery of new sources of wealth, or in inventing means of borrowing without repayment. Gallatin professed to do neither. . . . If money was needed he would borrow it, and would pay whatever it was worth; but he would not suggest that any device could relieve the public from taxing itself to pay whatever the public chose to spend.[75]

The paragraph pinpoints hardheaded assessment of context and subsequent simplicity and directness of plan as the key to professionalism. Moreover, it demands that the professional be expert enough in his field to see not merely the most efficient means open to him in a given situation for achieving a given end but, equally important, their moral as well as material cost. He must, like Gallatin, bear in mind the public good even when the public itself cannot find it. He alone knows his field well enough to understand the consequences of a mistake made within it and to foresee strengths and weaknesses of proposed schemes. Always, he must resist the temptation to prostitute his experience to a lust for power or popularity. At the same time, Adams has no patience with the man who confuses the theories of his discipline with the grinding necessities of life. The financier who seeks to create wealth from nothing ignores reality; and awareness of the limitations the world imposes on human effort, an awareness that results from practical experience with the real world, is always implied in Adams' definition of expertise. It is just this consciousness that Adams believes Jefferson lacked. Although he does not accuse Jefferson of being a charlatan, he nevertheless suggests that one of his chief defects was his amateurishness as an administrator, upbraiding him, for example, for his interference in the negotiations with England in 1808. "Amateur diplomacy," he says, "never showed its evils more plainly."[76]

[75] *Ibid.*, VI, 127.
[76] *Ibid.*, IV, 190.

Thus while Adams admires men who are expert professionals, he does not seem to claim for them or their expertise the ability to achieve an ideal society. In fact, the best ones, men like Gallatin, seem to be admirable chiefly in that they themselves face, and force other men to face, the difficulties and costs of life squarely. According to Adams, the professional's professionalism lies in the fact that he knows there are no easy answers, that the price of success may well be, as in Gallatin's case, personal anguish and defeat, and that unforeseeable, catastrophic accidents may in an instant undo the efforts of a lifetime. In short, there appears to be little in Adams' concept of professionalism that echoes the positivist faith in the ability of an intellectual elite to guide men to earthly paradise. The Adamsian professional of course plans ahead, but his plans are rooted in the realities of historical experience, and to Adams their chief virtue is that they deny the ignorant the luxury of their illusions. Adams mocks theorists like John Taylor who believe they have found the cure to society's ills:

Political philosophers of all ages were fond of devising systems for imaginary Republics, Utopias, and Oceanas, where practical difficulties could not stand in their way. Taylor was a political philosopher of the same school, and his Oceana on the banks of the Rappahannock was a reflection of his own virtues.[77]

The awareness of man's capacity for self-delusion implied in such a remark prevents Adams from sympathizing with the positivist faith in sociological expertise. The positivists believed that experts could control history; Adams seems to say they should accept it.

The heavy responsibility that Adams ultimately places on the professional American politician is not a Comtian one. Behind virtually all of the *History*'s narrative lies the assumption that "simplicity, economy, and purity"[78] of means and

[77] *Ibid.*, IX, 197.
[78] *Ibid.*, VII, 40.

ends alone prevent a nation from developing tyrannical habits. When on the last page of the work Adams wonders about the future corruptions Americans may fall prey to, he is among other things restating the suspicion he expresses throughout that centralization of power, necessary though it may prove to be to achieving an international rule of law, may also encourage the selfish and ruthless despotism of a Napoleon. Only in the disinterested, peculiarly American nobility of character of a Gallatin, he seems to say, can one glimpse a proper middle course. Especially revealing in this regard is the contrast Adams draws between Gallatin and John Armstrong, the only other American in the work whose abilities are depicted as rivaling Gallatin's. The flaw in Armstrong's character which disqualifies him professionally is that he relied not on directness, simplicity, and probity but on intrigue, maneuver, and patronage—on the classic instruments, in other words, of Old World politics: "Armstrong represented everything antagonistic to Gallatin; his methods were arbitrary and underhand; his political training was that of the New York school, tempered by personal contact with the court of Napoleon; from him economy could hardly be expected."[79] Armstrong's is merely a spark when compared with Napoleon's inferno of selfishness and unscrupulosity; but Armstrong represents for Adams the Napoleonic infection that may in time, if not cauterized, destroy the American experiment. If his and not Gallatin's should become the professional norm for American politics, America might in time resemble Napoleonic France.

Thus the *History* challenges the American politician to navigate a narrow and tricky course between the Scylla of Napoleonic concentration of power and the Charybdis of Jeffersonian decentralization of power. If the American politician must on the one hand accept France and all it represents as the actual political condition of the world in the nineteenth

[79] *Ibid.,* 41.

century (and probably for many centuries to come) and work accordingly to centralize and make efficient the American nation so that it can survive the international struggle for existence, he must on the other strive to preserve for the "new variety of man"[80] that has come into existence in America the freedom from governmental oppression which Jefferson so highly prized and which formed the basis of his agrarian politics.

Building thus upon Bancroft's and Parkman's foundations, Adams applies their centrifugal-centripetal theme to a period of American history neither of them treats. Above all, it is the reality faced by real men governing vast concentrations of power which fascinates Adams and which he tries to capture in the nine volumes. The work conveys a worldliness which assumes that, except through extraordinary luck, nothing comes easily or freely, especially to those who, as leaders of nations, find themselves in the company of clever and ambitious men. Assuming that men must understand reality before they can influence it, the *History* recommends a pragmatic, flexible, relativistic approach to life which does not presume to establish values beyond those authorized by historical experience and at the heart of which lies the ideal of compromise. The nine volumes expand the earlier historians' theme of compromise into a pragmatic world view. Yet, within the limitation of historical experience, Adams agrees with Bancroft and Parkman that moral ideals do have force. To some extent, he suggests, men can control their destinies. If modern democracy can succeed in producing a patriotic, reasonable, and professionally oriented race of men, or if some fortunate historical accident brings it about, men may in time overcome nationalism and live in some such world of peace and justice as Jefferson—and Bancroft—imagined. Skeptical though Adams seems to be concerning its chances of being realized,

[80] *Ibid.*, IX, 221.

the Jeffersonian-Bancroftian vision nevertheless informs the *History.*

A similar indebtedness to and development from Bancroft's and Parkman's histories is also visible in Adams' treatment of his sources.

★ ★ ★ ★ ★ ★

CHAPTER SEVEN

Signaled and Unsignaled Paraphrase

Conceived, written, and published as a unit, Adams' *History* reveals almost none of the volume-by-volume organizational pattern found in Bancroft's and Parkman's works. The nine volumes treat only four presidential terms—roughly sixteen years—and events overlap each other from book to book in such a way that they make the division of the work into separate volumes seem purely arbitrary. Unlike Bancroft and Parkman, Adams does not maintain tight chronological sequence. He follows an idea or subject to its conclusion and then returns to deal with others that were developing simultaneously. He may, for example, trace a diplomatic negotiation from beginning to end over a course of months or years, go back to the beginning of the period and narrate events in Congress for a session or two, and once again return for military matters. The effect is to heighten the complexity and interconnectedness of the events and to obscure their chronology. There is a tidelike quality in the *History* resulting from the fact that while individual sections of the work, like breakers, repeatedly narrate a span of time from different vantage points, the movement of the whole gradually advances.

It is the *ensemble* of the entire nine volumes that we are meant to grasp. Their organizational fulcrum is a point in

time that occurs neither at the midpoint of the sixteen years
nor halfway through the *History*. The first two-thirds of the
work traces the gradual weakening of America's national
sovereignty during the first decade of the nineteenth century.
Then, at the beginning of the seventeenth chapter of Volume
V, Adams finally brings us to the nadir of this subtle downward movement: "The government of the United States
reached, March 4, 1811, the lowest point of its long decline."[1]
Two pages later he amplifies the idea by remarking that "none
but persons hostile to all central government could look toward the future without alarm; for if the system continued in
the future to lose energy as in the ten years past, the time was
not far distant when the country must revert to the old Confederation, or to ties equally weak." There follows almost
at once, however, an upsurge of national assertiveness in the
form of Pinkney's breaking off of diplomatic relations with
England and Rodgers' defeat of the British sloop-of-war
Little Belt, which occupy the first and second chapters of
Volume VI. When, midway through the sixth volume, Adams
narrates America's declaration of war, he has already reversed
the *History*'s downward movement and begun to chart the
erratic upward course of America's nationhood; and by Volume VII he is able to point out that "[n]ot so much the glories
as the disgraces of the war roused public sympathy; not so
much the love of victory as the ignominy of defeat, and the
grinding necessity of supporting government at any cost of
private judgment."[2] Finally, of course, the nation is saved
by its more or less successful prosecution of the war in 1813
and 1814, narrated in Volumes VII and VIII, and by the successful negotiations at Ghent, which introduce Volume IX
and conclude the main action. Constructed around a narrative
line that descends, reaches a low point, and then ascends to
roughly the point at which it began and which not only lies

[1] *History*, V, 359.
[2] *Ibid.*, VII, 70.

askew of the work's center but is hardly obvious on a first or even second reading, the *History* requires us to pay careful attention not only to the details of the narrative blocks from which it is built but to its overall movement. It offers practically no volume-by-volume organizational guideposts that might distract attention from the parts or the whole. Accordingly, the intellectual burdens it puts on the reader are heavy. It assumes a harder-working audience than Bancroft's and Parkman's histories do.

Adams' narrator is also more demanding. Though Adams' wit, irony, and general perspicuousness in the *History* have often been discussed, his almost Jamesian fascination with and manipulation of point of view in the work has not. In instance after instance he gives to a generalized, fictitious viewer or group of viewers contemporary with the *History*'s action attitudes that are in most cases his own. With the device, which resembles Henry James's lodgment of narrative point of view in the consciousness of the characters of his novels, he succeeds in communicating his own ideas without seeming to do so. For example, he often credits to a generalized audience of contemporary Federalists the criticisms of Jefferson's literary style he himself is making. "The Federalists," he says, "found much material for ridicule in these expressions, which were certainly open to criticism";[3] or, "The Federalist wits made fun of the moral which the President added to soften the announcement of such an event";[4] or, "If the New England Calvinists ever laughed, one might suppose that they could have found in this letter . . . material for laughter as sardonic as the letter itself."[5] Often he sets the mood that he feels is appropriate to an event not simply by describing it, as Bancroft does, or by submerging it in a description of the natural setting, as does Parkman, but by

[3] *Ibid.*, I, 227.
[4] *Ibid.*, 249.
[5] *Ibid.*, 313.

locating it in a contemporary viewpoint, as when he remarks
concerning France's threat to close the Mississippi in 1802
that the "people of the United States expected day by day
to hear of some sudden attack, from which the dexterity of
Godoy and the disasters of LeClerc had saved them."[6] Or he
may increase dramatic interest by telling the story from the
point of view of a political faction of the time. The politics
of Virginia, for instance, are explained from a "Virginia stand-
point"[7] which, along with those of New York, New England,
and other regions, he then uses to dramatize regional conflicts
of interest. On almost every page of the *History* one can find
some variation of the technique.

One of its effects is subtly to reinforce the *History*'s tone
of detachment. By allowing Adams to express his own views
without really seeming to do so and to ease the reader through
transitions in the narrative, it gives the impression that the
History is narrating itself. Adams seems to have removed
himself from the story, leaving a bland and innocuous speaker
merely to link statements and viewpoints of the period together in a sort of documentary pastiche. Although, as we have
seen, Adams' detachment is more apparent than real, it is convincing enough to make him appear to be speaking from an
Olympian height from which he only occasionally condescends
to praise or ridicule the actors below. Yet in nine cases out of
ten, this Jamesian, impressionistic device is used for purely
technical purposes, somewhat in the manner of the *History*'s
imagery. Although Adams seems not to be judging the story,
he is, in fact, judging it continually.

A similar purpose probably governs his quoting of source
materials. As Ernest Samuels remarks, quotation is "in
[Adams'] hands an extraordinarily supple instrument."
"Nothing," says Samuels, "could surpass [his] method of in-
terweaving conemporary accounts to give the illusion that nei-

[6] *Ibid.*, 418.
[7] *Ibid.*, II, 90.

ther the wear of time nor the preconceptions of the historian stand between historical reality and the reader."[8] Though somewhat similar in aim to the increased use of quotation we find in the volumes Bancroft published after 1850, Adams' quotations are more frequent and more carefully woven into the narrative than either Bancroft's or Parkman's. They are not, however, letter perfect. Practically none reproduces the exact punctuation of the original. Furthermore, Adams sometimes changes wording, though usually without significantly changing its meaning, and he almost never indicates where he has made elisions. For example, he quotes the traveler John Lambert as follows:

[T]he few solitary merchants, clerks, porters, and laborers that were to be seen were walking about with their hands in their pockets. The coffee-houses were almost empty; the streets, near the waterside, were almost deserted; the grass had begun to grow upon the wharves.[9]

Lambert, however, says:

[T]he few solitary merchants, clerks, porters, and laborers, that were to be seen, were walking about with their hands in their pockets.... [Here follow fifty-nine words.] The coffee-house was almost empty....[Here follow sixty-two words.] The streets near the water-side were almost deserted, the *grass* has begun to grow upon the wharfs, and the ... [etc.].[10]

The quotation indicates Adams' normal practice as far as changing punctuation and wording ("coffee-house was" becomes "coffee-houses were") and not signaling elisions are concerned. Like Parkman and Bancroft, he treats quotation marks not as guaranteeing absolute accuracy but as indicating that whatever has been quoted, though close to the original,

---

8 *The Middle Years*, 395f. See also Jordy, *Scientific Historian*, 56.
9 *History*, IV, 278.
10 John Lambert, *Travels through Canada and the United States*, II, 64f.

may have been slightly altered. His quoting habits differ from theirs more in degree than kind.

His purpose, though, is different from Bancroft's. Throughout the *History*, quotation gives Adams' characters rope to hang or save themselves and so allows Adams to seem to remain detached and impartial. The reader feels he is getting the past exactly as it happened, without being guided by an officious narrator. Bancroft's aim is in effect the reverse of Adams' in that whenever he quotes he tends to conform the original to his own tone and style, thereby making utterances from the past sound more or less Bancroftian. Adams tends to minimize his own presence in quoted material and to draw attention to the historical uniqueness and realism of the actors' remarks. The result is a historical verisimilitude and richness that complements the impressionism of his narrating stance well.

Yet behind the pose of Olympian detachment he maintains throughout the *History*, Adams is always striving to bring the sources into line with his own interpretations and point of view. His major weapon is the technique we have already seen Bancroft and Parkman use so often, the paraphrase. Similar to his quoting in aim, Adams' paraphrasing allows him more artistic freedom. With it, he can shape sources to his own argument even while he fulfills the Rankean dictum of describing the past *wie es eigentlich gewesen ist*. As in quotations, he lets the documents speak for themselves when he paraphrases, but he can better control them. Probably the most important difference between Adams' attitude toward source material and Bancroft's and Parkman's is that Adams seems to feel a more pressing sense of obligation than they to the documents as historical evidence. His apparent wish to be faithful to the sources as authorities is reminiscent of the scissors-and-paste dogma against which Bancroft rebelled. Though the grounds of his commitment to the sources are altogether different from those of the earlier annalist-plagiarist school—Adams, following the lead of Ranke and other German "scientific" historians,[11] is reacting against Bancroft's radically philosophical, "original" method—the effect is somewhat similar. He tries to stay as close as possible to the wording of the originals when he paraphrases, not simply because it is artistically convenient, as it is for Bancroft and to a lesser extent Parkman, but because he seems to feel that in doing so he will write "truer," more valid history. Methodologically, the tradition in this sense returns with Adams to a point near where it started.

Adams' new Rankean-scientific approach, however, renounces the use of secondary sources basic to the old scissors-and-paste method and visible, as we have seen, in a vestigial way in the histories of Bancroft and Parkman. Adams almost never paraphrases secondary sources. When he does, they are either unusually trustworthy and professional in tone or are the only sources available. His justification for using two of them, *The Life of Albert Gallatin* and *John Randolph*, is that he himself wrote them. In addition, he once or twice paraphrases Charles Gayarré's *History of Louisiana*, the anonymous *Life of the Late Gen. William Eaton*, William James's *Military Occurrences* and *Naval Occurrences*, Thomas Tooke's *A History of Prices from 1793 to 1837*, Moses Dawson's *William H. Harrison*, Robert B. McAffee's *History of the Late War in the Western Country*, Isaac Brock's *Life of Major-General Brock*, James Parton's *Life of Andrew Jackson*, Charles J. Ingersoll's *Historical Sketch of the 2nd War*, A. LaCarrière Latour's *War in West Florida and Louisiana*, and several other less important works. Most of these are military narratives, and though Adams follows

---

[11] Adams urged his students at Harvard to "appreciate and to use the German historical method" (Henry Adams to H. C. Lodge, June 2, 1872, in *Letters of Henry Adams 1858–1891* [ed. by Worthington C. Ford], 228.) In his celebrated seminar he closely followed the form and content of the *Seminar* Ranke himself originated in Berlin in 1834.

the language of these writers at a few points in his chapters on the war, he puts to heavier use the appendices of primary documents that many, most notably James and Latour, include in their books. His constant aim, even when he is paraphrasing secondary material, is to recapture the language of the men who in some sense stood closest to the actual historical experience.

Hence his heavy use of paraphrased primary material, by means of which he saturates the *History* with the language of his major characters without having to follow, as he does when he quotes, their tone. He always tries to be as faithful as he can to their verbalizations of their experience, since he seems to assume no other wording can so intimately or accurately express it, yet at the same time he frees himself to judge what they say against his own values. Almost all his paraphrasing contributes to his chief goal in the nine volumes: to reveal and judge character. Whether he is reconstructing one of Jefferson's letters, a debate in Congress, a military report, or any other kind of document, he uses it to shed light either on the man who wrote it or on those it describes.

The *History* contains basically two types of paraphrase. The first includes those that Adams sets off from his own narrative or exposition by means of explicit signal words. He will, for example, point out that the contents of a bill were this and that, that in a speech a congressman put forth this or that argument, or that a diplomat's instructions were such and such. The signal in all such cases is a word like "said," "argued," "reported," "called for," "claimed," "stated," or "explained," with which Adams attributes the paraphrase that follows to a specific source. Without checking, having been given warning by the signal word, we know that he is paraphrasing a specific document. The second type of paraphrase offers no such signal. Here Adams blends the language of the source into his own narrating voice, as do Bancroft and Parkman. We discover his debt, often unacknowledged by footnote, only by comparing his text with the original.

Signaled paraphrases, the majority of those used in the *History*, tend to occur most often in expository sections, such as the chapters devoted to background material, to Congress, to foreign relations, and to the development of key political ideas. Unsignaled paraphrases, on the other hand, tend to be found in more obviously narrative sections—in the chapters, for example, that recount the specific exploits of individual politicians, diplomats, and soldiers. Most of the *History*'s critics have commented on the difference between the largely expository, intellectual quality of the first five and the ninth volumes and the narrative, storytelling quality of those devoted to the war. The narration of Volumes I–V and IX consists not so much of physical action, with the exception of episodes like Burr's conspiracy in Volume III, as of an unfolding of the ideas implicit in quietly made legislation or administrative decisions or of a tracing of the chesslike moves and countermoves of diplomacy. The excitement of these volumes lies in the clash of ideas and of the personalities behind them. When Adams turns to war in Volume VI, his narrative style becomes noticeably more detailed and storylike, though it is never so vivid or psychologically intense as Parkman's. Thus a narrative chiefly of ideas gives way at approximately the point of reversal of Adams' national theme to a narrative chiefly of action, and unsignaled begin to outnumber signaled paraphrases.

Adams shifts continually between the two modes in all his volumes, of course, and when he does, he tends to change his narrating point of view. In episodes concerned more with ideas his narrator stands outside the *History*'s action, while in episodes recounting action he moves to a position somewhere within it, often inside the range of vision of an actor whose character he wants to judge. When Adams begins more to describe than to analyze the action, he also begins to mix his own voice with those of his documents and to use more unsignaled than signaled paraphrases. The reverse is generally true when he moves from the narrative to the expository mode. Nothing really comparable to his signaled paraphrasing can be found in Bancroft and Parkman. It broadens his strategy of sprinkling his pages with quoted material to include paraphrasing and permits him to deploy large numbers of primary documents gracefully. An excellent solution to the problem of incorporating diffuse primaries which perplexed Bancroft in his later volumes, it is perhaps Adams' major methodological contribution to the tradition.

First, then, this new, signaled-paraphrase technique. Almost all of Adams' signaled paraphrases serve to show strength or weakness of character. Assuming that what men say is often as revealing a key to their characters as what they do, Adams sets forth scores of statements by the *History*'s actors in this form. In most of these statements, he makes the actor's language square with his own judgment of the actor himself, though normally the adjustments are so subtle as to suggest that Adams assumed considerable literary sophistication on the part of the reader. Early in the *History*, he makes it clear he expects us to be sensitive throughout to the way the characters talk and write. Chapter VII of the first volume, which begins the narrative proper, offers a devastating analysis of the style of Jefferson's first inaugural address. Adams mocks not only Jefferson's "ideality calculated to please the ear of later generations forced to task their utmost powers in order to carry the complex trains of their thought"[12] but also his mixed metaphors, in which "the government, the world's best hope, had hitherto kept the country free and firm, in the full tide of successful experiment"[13] and Jefferson's "principles appeared as a constellation, a creed, a text, a touchstone, and

[12] *History*, I, 199.
[13] *Ibid.*, 201.

a road."[14] He creates an indelible image of Jefferson as a literary sloven.

Normally, Adams relies more heavily on our ability to distinguish good from poor literary style when he is attacking than when he is approving someone in a signaled paraphrase. Often his disapproval is wholly implicit in the paraphrase, making explicit comment on his part unnecessary. The following paraphrase, which he signals with the phrase "began a speech, December 4, by declaring" is a case in point.

Source:	History:
I tremble for the consequences which will follow its adoption. It will shake the party with which I am connected from either extreme of the continent to its centre. . . . Gentlemen must pardon me when I say we are *prone* to acts which 'make the angels weep.'[15]	Langdon Cheves . . . began a speech, December 4, by declaring that he trembled for the consequences of the measure; it would shake the party to pieces; it would make angels weep.[16]

The measure Cheves deplores—Gallatin's proposal to tax war profiteers—is one Adams supports. Although he makes no other comment on the speech, Adams conveys his opinion of it clearly in the paraphrase, which implies that because Cheves speaks bombastically, his objections are trivial. By saying that in his speech Cheves declared the act would make angels weep and by putting that statement at the end of a series of increasingly hyperbolic but syntactically similar clauses, Adams reduces speech and speaker to absurdity. It is not Cheves' patriotism but perhaps his reasonableness and certainly his professionalism—even congressional oratory should not, implies Adams, be so fatuous as this—that he calls into question.

---

[14] *Ibid.*, 204.
[15] *Annals of the Congress of the United States*, 12th Cong., 2nd sess., 242.
[16] *History*, VI, 441.

In other paraphrases, Adams conveys his criticism of a man's argument more through the signaling word itself than through revisions of his language. In the following example, the only unmistakably slanted word in the paraphrase proper is the signaling verb "complained."

Source:	History:
I think you have misconceived the nature of the treaty I thought we should propose to England. . . . England should stipulate not to make peace without our obtaining the objects for which we go to war, to wit, the acknowledgment by Spain of the rightful boundaries of Louisiana . . . and 2, indemnifications for spoliations. . . . Our co-operation in the war . . . would be sufficient consideration for Great Britain to engage for its object.[17]	Upon a treaty of alliance with England the President was for the moment bent, and he met Madison's objections by arguments that showed lively traits of the writer's sanguine temper. He complained that Madison had misconceived the nature of the proposed British treaty. England should stipulate not to make peace without securing West Florida and the spoliation claims to America, while American co-operation in the war would be sufficient inducement to her for making this contract.*[18]

Adams here openly states his wish to expose character by means of paraphrase—he says Jefferson's letter "showed lively traits of the writer's sanguine temper." Normally he reserves this kind of explicitness for the statements of men, like Jefferson, who are important enough to justify his developing their characters in depth, while for minor actors like Cheves he does not go beyond a trenchant paraphrase or two. Jefferson's sanguinity is allowed to speak almost entirely for itself. Most of Adams' version presents, verbatim, key phrases snipped from the letter, and in the phrases he has revised his method is neutral and detached, unlike that of the Cheves example. The only wording that carries a hint of mockery

[17] Jefferson to Madison, 27 August 1805, in *The Writings of Thomas Jefferson* (ed. by H. A. Washington), IV, 585 f.
[18] *History*, III, 63.

may be the last, "for making this contract," which contains a touch of the incredulous skepticism toward Jefferson's plans that Adams invites us in his opening sentence to share. Aside from that possibility, the paraphrase itself is tonally bland— except, of course, for the mocking signal word "complained," which serves to color everything that follows with the nagging, somewhat feminine stubbornness that Adams attributes to Jefferson throughout the *History*.

Yet the *History* contains as many favorable as unfavorable signaled paraphrases. Adams communicates his positive judgments much as he does his negative: detaching his own speaking voice from that of the source by means of a signal word, he seems to allow the source to speak for itself. Yet these too are often supported by subtle revisions within the paraphrase. For a man like Don Pedro Cevallos, the Spanish minister for foreign affairs who managed by brilliant diplomatic maneuvering to keep the Americans out of Florida for some time after the Louisiana Purchase, Adams conveys a respect that is clear whenever he reconstructs one of his diplomatic notes:

Source:	History:
For this end nothing appears better adapted than the mode proposed by your excellencies in the first part of your note:	To this note and *projet* Don Pedro Cevallos quickly replied.* Availing himself of an inadvertent sentence in Monroe's opening paragraph, to the effect that it was necessary to examine impartially the several points at issue in each case, Cevallos informed the Americans that in accordance with their wish he would first examine each point separately, and then proceed to negotiation.[20]
'It is proper to examine impartially the several points which are depending between our Governments. . . . '	
According to this principle, proposed by your excellencies, . . . we should first examine each point separately, and in this form determine the respective rights of each country; and then proceed to such negotiations as the interest of each country may require.[19]	

[19] Cevallos to Monroe and Pinkney, 31 January 1805, in *American State Papers, Foreign Relations*, II, 639.

[20] *History*, III, 24.

With the skill that marks all his work with diplomatic sources, Adams burrows beneath the ponderous, gravely proper surface of Cevallos' letter and reveals its inner, professional meaning to the lay reader. In the exchange between Monroe and Cevallos to which this note belongs, devoted to settling the boundaries of the Louisiana territory America had just bought from Napoleon, Adams argues that Monroe's posture was weak not only because the demands he made were unreasonable but because he presented them to Cevallos with a clumsiness that Adams renders particularly noticeable by contrasting it with Cevallos' steady skill. Seeing that Cevallos' attention to one of Monroe's opening sentences had special significance, Adams points out that it was a move on Cevallos' part to "avail himself" of an "inadvertent" error. By then isolating from Cevallos' letter the phrases that prove Cevallos was trying to trap Monroe in the error and by following their wording closely, he is able to define Cevallos' overall strategy of procrastination and delay as well as to reinforce his image of him as a master diplomat. As Adams at once explains, Monroe's sentence allowed Cevallos to begin an endless series of proposals and counterproposals by giving him room to "discuss indefinitely claims which the United States had again and again asserted to be too plain for discussion."[21] Behind the letter and the strategy, Adams implies, stands the man. From signaled paraphrases of other diplomats he admires, we gather the same sense of professional *eclat*.

One of the most effective occurs at the end of the first chapter of Volume VI. Adams' subject is William Pinkney, whom he regards as the best American diplomat of his generation and one of the best in the history of the American foreign service. Openly praising Pinkney's "extraordinary abilities and character,"[22] Adams narrates his breaking of relations with England in 1811 with obvious pride and respect. On

21 *State Papers, Foreign Relations*, II, 639.
22 *Ibid.*, VI, 20.

his own authority, without precise instructions from Washington, Pinkney had to decide whether to ask for a formal audience of leave—a responsibility, explains Adams, "more serious than had ever before, or has ever since, fallen to the share of a minister of the United States in England."[23] Pinkney's terse, unpretentious courage in meeting the challenge is what most impresses Adams and what he tries to convey in the chapter as a whole. He bases his climactic paragraph, in which Pinkney requests the audience, on three brief diplomatic notes that stand without gloss in the *State Papers*:

Source:	History:
I can have no inducement to trouble your lordship any further upon the subjects to which it relates. I have the honor, [etc.].[24] His Royal Highness the Prince Regent will receive the foreign ministers at his levee . . . the 19th instant.[25] I beg to be informed by your lordship at which time His Royal Highness the Prince Regent will do me the honor to give the audience of leave. I have the honor, [etc.].[26]	In a note of two lines, Pinkney replied* that he had no inducement to trouble his lordship further on the subject. The same day he received a notice that the Prince Regent would hold his first diplomatic levee February 19; but instead of accepting the invitation, Pinkney wrote with the same brevity to ask at what time the Prince Regent would do him the honor to give his audience of leave.[27]

By this "abrupt course," Adams continues, Pinkney "brought the Government partially to reason." It is certainly abruptness, or measured flouting of diplomatic convention, that Adams captures in his paraphrase. Stressing that Pinkney's first note was "of two lines" and his second of "the same

---

[23] *Ibid.*, 16.

[24] Pinkney to Wellesley, 13 February 1811, *State Papers, Foreign Relations*, III, 412.

[25] Wellesley to Pinkney, 12 February 1811, *ibid.*, 413.

[26] Pinkney to Wellesley, 13 February 1811, *ibid.*, III, 413.

[27] *History*, VI, 15.

brevity," Adams plays the apparent triviality of the documents off against their global meaning, thus heightening the tension of the moment by confining it within tight formal bounds and emphasizing Pinkney's strength of will by understatement. It is hard to imagine how he could have narrated the event better. The briefness of the documents supports his tone; his narrative builds to tremendous pressure; and he reveals the salient points of Pinkney's character.

Though Adams commends many men, such as Cevallos and Pinkney, in signaled paraphrases, he lavishes on none the number he gives Albert Gallatin, his model statesman. For instance, his version of the treasury report Gallatin sent to Congress November 7, 1807, is a veritable hymn of praise:

Source:	History:
[246] It is ascertained that the nett revenue, which has accrued during the three first quarters of the year 1807, exceeds that of the corresponding quarters of the year 1806; and [customs] may, exclusively of the duty on salt, and of the Mediterranean fund, both of which expire on the first day of January next, be safely estimated . . . [at] fourteen millions of dollars. . . . [247] [T]he sales of the public lands . . . exceeded 284,000 acres. . . . [T]he receipts . . . from that source, may . . . be estimated . . . at five hundred thousand dollars. . . . [Projected expenses for the fourth quarter] will leave in the Treasury, at the close of the year, a balance of about seven millions six hundred thousand dollars. . . . [T]he payments on account of the principal of the public debt, have [in 1807] . . . exceeded four millions six hun-	Gallatin never failed to cover every weak spot in the Administration, and in October, 1807, the Treasury was profuse of prosperity. Congress might abolish the salt tax and Mediterranean Fund alike, and still the customs would yield fourteen millions a year; while the sales of public lands exceeded 284,000 acres and brought another half million into the Treasury. December 31, after providing for all payments of public debt, Gallatin had a balance of seven millions six hundred thousand dollars on hand. During the Presidency of Jefferson, twenty-five and a half millions had been paid to redeem the principal of the public debt, and only the restraints imposed by the law prevented more rapid redemption. Even in case of war, Gallatin offered to sustain it for a year without borrowing money or increasing taxes.[29]

[28] Gallatin, "State of the Finances," *State Papers, Finance*, II, 246 ff. I have bracketed page numbers in *State Papers* for the reader's convenience.

[29] *History*, IV, 148.

dred thousand dollars; making the total public debt reimbursed from the 1st of April, 1801, to the 1st of October, 1807, about twenty-five millions eight hundred and eighty thousand dollars.

[248] [T]he specie in the Treasury, at the end of this year [plus the projected surplus for 1808 will be] . . . a sum probably adequate to meet the extraordinary expenses of a war for that year.[28]

Adams' enthusiasm for Gallatin and his report results in enthusiastic revision. After the somewhat hazy signal "Gallatin never failed to cover," Adams proceeds to blend his own voice with Gallatin's with typical sympathy. There is a jaunty tone in such remarks as "the Treasury was profuse of prosperity," "Congress might abolish," and "Gallatin offered to sustain" which is more Adams' than Gallatin's, yet Adams' version seems on the whole to be spoken by Gallatin. All but one of its statements, the one pointing out the obstacles to more rapid redemption, are based on Gallatin's own wording. Adams' strategy of condensing the report, retaining enough of its jargon to give it a professional flavor, weaving it into his own narrative, and, most important, showing with it how accomplished an administrator Gallatin was supports the almost boasting tone. The paraphrase is especially effective when seen in context. In the two or three pages before, Adams explains Jefferson's popularity in 1807 as almost entirely the result of Gallatin's management of the finances. Just before the paraphrase, he questions the professional competence of every leading member of Jefferson's administration, including Jefferson himself. Against the efforts of these men he sets Gallatin's treasury, which immediately after the paraphrase he describes as "the secret of Jefferson's strength, of his vast popularity, and of the fate which, without direct act of his, never had failed to overwhelm his enemies." The paraphrase

193

testifies as warmly as Adams can make it to the influence of a single outstanding man's character on the nation.

Signaled paraphrasing is one of the two basic types found in the *History*. The other, unsignaled type is virtually the same as that found in Bancroft's *History* and Parkman's *Montcalm and Wolfe*, except that Adams rarely follows secondary sources. Like Bancroft and Parkman, he imposes his own tone and narrating point of view without warning on language edited from the sources, so that no storyteller but he can be heard, even though a given paragraph of the *History* may consist of a dozen scraps of phrasing borrowed from several different writers. Adams, too, creates narrative unity with this kind of paraphrasing out of a jumble of documentary fragments. From the many, he, too, makes one. Also like Bancroft and Parkman, he sometimes follows single sources exclusively. At several points, for example, he virtually copies the tone and language of the diary of his grandfather, John Quincy Adams.[30] But the diary is a special case, and as a rule Adams blends relatively short passages from a number of documents into a running narrative. Of key importance to him always is the goal of revealing or judging character.

As has already been pointed out, unsignaled paraphrasing tends to occur more often in the military, storytelling chapters than in other parts of the *History*. In the military paraphrases, Adams' strategy often is to view the action through the eyes of an officer he is judging. Two examples, one negative and one positive, will suggest how the technique works. In the

[30] Compare, for example, *History*, II, 117 f., with *Memoirs of John Quincy Adams* (ed. by Charles Francis Adams), I, 267 f.; *History*, III, 139 f. and 152, with *Memoirs*, I, 383, 403–406 and 420; *History*, VII, 27 ff., with *Memoirs*, II, 401 ff., 414 ff., and 433; and *History*, IX, 17 f., with *Memoirs*, III, 4 ff. Although the argument that the *History* shows signs of family prejudice is hardly weakened by such evidence, the consensus of scholarly opinion against the argument nevertheless seems to me to be correct. Efforts like that of Peter Shaw, "Blood is Thicker than Irony: Henry Adams's History," *New England Quarterly*, Vol. XL (1967), 163–87, to prove otherwise remain unconvincing.

first, found in his account of William Henry Harrison's battle with the Indians at Tippecanoe in 1811, he argues that Harrison's behavior was self-serving and fruitless. In the second, found in his account of the battle between the American frigate *President* and the British corvette *Little Belt*, he argues that the fight was in every way creditable to the *President*'s commander, John Rodgers.

Adams devotes the whole chapter in Volume VI titled "Tippecanoe" to attacking Harrison's character. Opening with six pages justifying the Indians, he then begins his account of Harrison's invasion of Indian territory, and, having advanced Harrison and his army to within eleven miles of the Indian village Tippecanoe, he initiates a series of unsignaled paraphrases that sets the tone for the battle itself. The first in the series hints that Harrison himself had doubts about the campaign:

Source:	*History:*
Within about two miles of the town, the path descended a steep hill. . . . Before the crossing of the creek, the woods were very thick and intersected by deep ravines. . . . Being now arrived within a mile and a half of the town, and the situation being favorable for an encampment, the governor determined to remain there and fortify his camp. . . .[M]ajor Daveiss and several other field officers approached him, and urged the propriety of immediately marching upon the town. The governor answered that his instructions would not justify his attacking the Indians, as long as there was a probability of their complying with the demands of the govern-	Two miles from the town the army unexpectedly entered a difficult country, thick with wood and cut by deep ravines, where Harrison was greatly alarmed, seeing himself at the mercy of an attack; but no attack was made. When clear of the woods, within a mile and a half of the town, he halted his troops and declared his intention to encamp. Daveiss and all the other officers urged him to attack the town at once; but he replied that his instructions would not justify his attacking the Indians unless they refused his demands, and he still hoped to hear something in the course of the evening from the friendly Indians sent from Fort Harrison.[32]

[32] *History*, VI, 98.

ment, and that he still hoped to
hear something in the course of
the evening from the friendly Indians, whom he had dispatched
from Fort Harrison.[31]

Adams follows the source closely except in saying that Harrison was alarmed. The deviation seems to stem from a wish to show that Harrison, whom he has described earlier as an intelligent though selfish and untrained soldier, sensed the danger of his position, situated as he was with short supplies and a handful of men more than fifty miles inside Indian territory. Furthermore, Adams suggests in the latter part of the paraphrase that Harrison, in refusing what Adams believes was the sound military advice of his men to attack at once, merely proved he was aware of the wrongness of what he was doing.

In view of his tactic of moving inside Harrison's mind, Adams' reliance here and throughout the episode on sources not written by Harrison himself is intriguing. Only once or twice does he paraphrase Harrison's official report, which even then he treats very coolly. The most plausible explanation for the tactic may be that he wants to deny Harrison the compliment of paraphrase altogether, an explanation supported by the fact that Harrison's account, though sometimes less full, is neither less factual nor less professional in tone than those Adams does use heavily. Moreover, the few accounts of the invasion that were available to him are, like the one by McAffee just quoted, sympathetic to Harrison. In fact, Harrison's is the only significant eyewitness report. Apparently unwilling to give it the honor of being his model, Adams ignores it in favor of semisecondary works like McAffee's. There is something characteristically wry in Adams' use of sources other than Harrison's as the vehicle of entry into Harrison's mind.

[31] Robert B. McAffee, *History of the Late War in the Western Country*, March of America Facsimile Series, 23 f.

Paraphrasing McAffee again a page later, Adams fills in the portrait of Harrison that dominates the whole episode: that of a man caught between wanting to make a name for himself and knowing an attack would be unwise and unjust. The difference in tone between the first part of Adams' and McAffee's versions shows how keenly Adams wants to impress this image on us. Writes McAffee: "Governor Harrison during this last effort to open a negotiation, which was sufficient to shew his wish for an accomodation, resolved no longer to hesitate in treating the Indians as enemies. He therefore... moved on with a determination to attack them."[33] Writes Adams: "Daveiss and the other officers, looking at the matter only as soldiers, became more urgent, until Harrison at last yielded, and resolving no longer to hesitate in treating the Indians as enemies,* ordered an advance, with the determination to attack."[34] McAffee pictures Harrison as firm and resolved. Adams has him vacillate.

Adams at once reinforces this hint of Harrison's vacillation with a paraphrase that shows him again changing his mind. "They advanced about four hundred yards," says Adams, "when three Indians sent by the Prophet came to meet them, bringing a pacific message, and urging that hostilities should if possible be avoided. Harrison's conscience, already heavy-ladened, again gave way at this entreaty.*"[35] The first part of the paraphrase, taken from Harrison's report, is one of Adams' rare utilizations of that source. Says Harrison: "We had not advanced above four hundred yards when I was informed that three Indians had approached the advanced guard, and had expressed a wish to speak to me."[36] Then Adams drops Harrison in favor of McAffee, who says: "[The

---

[33] *History of the Late War*, 25.
[34] *History*, VI, 99.
[35] *Ibid.*, 99 f.
[36] Harrison to Eustis, 18 November 1811, in *State Papers, Indian Affairs*, I, 776.

Indians said that] the Prophet wished, if possible, to avoid hostilities; that he had sent a pacific message by the Miami and Potawatamie chiefs."[37] For his second sentence Adams leaves the sources altogether. Entirely his own, it sums up his argument by moving inside Harrison's mind and tracing its presumably snarled purposes.

Next, Harrison is shown as carrying on an internal debate at the end of which he decides not to attack. One of the arguments in this invented self-debate is paraphrased by Adams from a remark made not by Harrison but by Harrison's biographer, Moses Dawson:

Source:	History:
However, it is certain that no victory was ever obtained over the northern Indians, where the numbers were anything like equal.[38]	He knew that no victory over the Northern Indians had ever been won where the numbers were anything like equal.[39]

Adams' "He knew" is a clever device for giving thoughts to Harrison that were originally Dawson's. Although technically it claims only that on the basis of what Dawson says Harrison could hardly have helped knowing about the northern Indians' prowess, its practical effect is to make the reader see Harrison as fretting over his troubles.

For his account of the battle itself, a night raid by the Indians on Harrison's camp, Adams views the action through Harrison's range of vision but completely avoids entering his mind or feelings. He does not once paraphrase Harrison's report. Although he views the action as it might have appeared to Harrison, his main purpose seems to be to point out the slackness of Harrison's defensive precautions in the different sections of the camp. He moves inside Harrison's mind only

[37] *History of the Late War*, 26.
[38] Dawson, *A Historical Narrative of the Civil and Military Service of Major-General William H. Harrison*, 216.
[39] *History*, VI, 100.

once more in the episode, not to Harrison's advantage: "Harrison was naturally a cautious man; he felt strongly the dangers that surrounded him, and his army felt them not less.*"[40] And he concludes with the biting remark that "Harrison's ablest military manoeuver had been the availing himself of Tecumthe's over-confidence in quitting the country at so critical a moment."[41]

In contrast, he warmly applauds John Rodgers' behavior in the battle between the *President* and the *Little Belt* on May 16, 1811. British contempt for the American navy had gone unchallenged since the *Chesapeake-Leopard* incident in 1807, and it is with obvious satisfaction that Adams recounts the next duel between an American and a British warship. Throughout his narrative he compliments Rodgers not only by paraphrasing his reports closely but by assessing the action from his point of view.

His organization of the episode is a *tour de force.* He gives it one of the most minute and careful analyses of documentary evidence in the *History*—after, however, devoting six pages to a narrative of the battle itself. When he makes his transition between the two sections, he apologizes for interrupting with such heavy scholarship: "Some little effort to form an opinion on [the reliability of the evidence] deserves to be made, even at the risk of diffuseness."[42] His reason for analyzing the documents in such detail is that the American reports of the action completely disagree with the British, the British insisting the Americans fired the first shot, the Americans insisting they did not. Contrary to Rodgers' claim that he did not know until the morning after the battle that the *Little Belt* was less than half as powerfully armed as the *President*, the British maintained that Rodgers, knowing full well what the *Little Belt* was, brutally ran her down and

[40] *Ibid.*, 105.
[41] *Ibid.*
[42] *Ibid.*, 33.

199

opened fire. At the end of seven pages of analysis, Adams concludes the Americans were telling the truth. Buttressed by the testimony of every officer and seaman on board the *President* and by Adams' demonstration of error and contradiction in the British reports, the conclusion seems persuasive. But the artfulness of what Adams has done lies in his having narrated the battle solely from American documents *before* pointing out that the British and American documents conflict. His strategy, of course, is double pronged: he tells a lively story before asking us to wade into the "diffuseness" of his source analysis, and he primes us to accept the American version in advance. Moreover, in following Rodgers' view of the battle he is able not only to develop the action from a single point of vantage but to vindicate Rodgers' character.

In the first three paragraphs of the chapter, Adams sets Rodgers to sea with pugnacious orders from Navy Secretary Paul Hamilton in hand. Then, in his fourth paragraph, he begins his account of the battle proper with a paraphrase of a letter that Rodgers submitted to the American court-martial held three months after the battle. In the letter Rodgers explains why he chased the *Little Belt*.

Source:	History:
At this time, I discovered by the newspapers that a British frigate, supposed to be the Guerriere, had, in the vicinity of Sandy Hook, . . . impressed out of the American brig Spitfire . . . a young man by the name of Diggio. . . . On the 16th of May, at a little past meridian, being at the time . . . about fourteen or fifteen leagues to the northward and eastward of Cape Henry, and about six leagues from the land to the southward of Chingoteague, a sail was discovered to the eastward, standing towards us under a press of canvass,	Rodgers was bound for New York, but on the morning of May 16 was still about thirty miles from Cape Charles and eighteen miles from the coast, when toward noon he saw a ship to the eastward standing toward him under a press of canvas. As the vessel came near, he could make her out from the shape of her upper sails to be a man-of-war; he knew of no man-of-war except the 'Guerriere' on the coast; the newcomer appeared from the quarter where that frigate would be looked for, and Rodgers reasoned that in all

which I soon made out, by the shape of her upper sails, . . . to be a man-of-war. Not having heard of any other ship of war than the before-mentioned frigate being on our coast, I concluded (and more particularly from the direction in which she was discovered) that it was her, and accordingly determined to speak her. . . . These, gentlemen, were my motives for having chased the ship.[43]

probability she was the 'Guerriere.' He decided to approach her, with the object of ascertaining whether a man named Diggio, said to have been impressed a few days before by Captain Dacres from an American brig, was on board. The spirit of this inquiry was new.[44]

Adams transforms Rodgers' stiffly formal reasoning, written three months after the battle for purposes of the court-martial, into Rodgers' experience as he stood on deck watching the ship approach. Polishing the style of Rodgers' letter throughout, he heightens tension by reserving Rodgers' bellicosity over Diggio till the end. Because he wants to convince us that Rodgers was justified in mistaking an eighteen-gun sloop for a forty-gun frigate, he adds the comment that "Rodgers reasoned that in all probability she was the 'Guerriere,' " which invites us to accept Rodgers' estimate of the vessel two pages before Adams admits there was a hot dispute between the two countries on just that point. Gleaning from the letter every piece of information that led Rodgers to view the *Little Belt* as he says he did, Adams sets it forth in a paragraph whose conclusion implies that Rodgers' "spirit" was not only "new" but healthy and forthright.

For his next paragraph Adams paraphrases what in his eyes was the most important document to emerge from the battle, Rodgers' first official report to the Navy Department, written during the voyage home and dated May 23, 1811. Trimming and refining Rodgers' language, Adams works into the para-

[43] Rodgers to the American Court-Martial, 12 September 1811, in *State Papers, Foreign Relations*, III, 496.

[44] *History*, VI, 26 f.

phrase every piece of extenuating evidence that Rodgers offers
and some he does not:

Source:	History:
At forty-five minutes past one, P.M., hoisted our ensign and pendant, when, finding her signals not answered, she wore and stood to the southward. Being desirous of speaking her, and of ascertaining what she was, I now made sail in chase, and by half-past three, P.M. found we were coming up with her, as, by this time, the upper part of her stern began to show itself above the horizon from our deck. The wind began and continued gradually to decrease, so as to prevent my being able to approach her sufficiently before sunset, to discover her actual force . . . or to judge even to what nation she belonged, as she appeared studiously to decline showing her colors. At fifteen or twenty minutes past seven, P.M., the chase . . . hauled by the wind on the starboard tack; she, at the same time, hoisted an ensign or flag at her mizzen peak, but it was too dark for me to discover what nation it represented; now, for the first time, her broadside was presented to our view; but night had so far progressed, that although her appearance indicated she was a frigate, I was unable to determine her actual force.[45]	Until quarter before two o'clock in the afternoon the ships stood toward each other. The stranger showed no colors, but made signals, until finding them unanswered, she changed her course and stood to the southward. Rodgers then made sail in chase, his colors and pennant flying. At half-past three, the stranger's hull began to be visible from the 'President's' deck, but as the wind failed the American frigate gained less rapidly. In latitude 37° the sun, May 16, sets at seven o'clock, and dusk comes quickly on. At quarter-past seven the unknown ship again changed her course, and lay to, presenting her broadside to the 'President,' and showing colors, which in the gathering twilight were not clearly seen. The ship had the look of a frigate.[46]

Most of what Adams isolates from and adds to Rodgers' report is aimed at proving that Rodgers could not identify the

[45] Rodgers to the Secretary of the Navy, 23 May 1811, in *State Papers,
Foreign Relations*, III, 497.
[46] *History*, VI, 27.

Little Belt or judge her strength. His deliberate contrasting of the fact that the "stranger showed no colors" with the fact that Rodgers' "colors and pennant" were "flying," his evidence for the earliness of dusk at that date and latitude, his labeling the *Little Belt* the "stranger" and "unknown ship," and his somewhat melodramatic conclusion that the "ship had the look of a frigate"—interestingly enough the first technical label he gives her—all force us to view the *Little Belt* exactly as Rodgers says he viewed her.

Adams narrates the battle itself in his next three paragraphs by piecing together, in a series of brief paraphrases and summaries, the testimony of the American crew and phrases and clauses from Rodgers' report. He views the action, as in his account of the Tippecanoe battle, through the eyes of the character he holds responsible, Rodgers, again without entering his thoughts. He uses no British documents. It is in this section that Adams first admits the British and American reports disagree; yet even as he makes the confession he implies that the narrative he has already set forth, despite its subtle slant in Rodgers' favor, is simple fact. "To this point," he says, "the reports showed no great disagreement; but in regard to what followed, one story was told by Rodgers and all his ship's company, while a wholly different story was told by the British captain and his officers."[47] Though what Adams says is true as far as the time and place of the preliminary maneuvers are concerned, the British documents all scoff at Rodgers' claim he could not judge the *Little Belt*'s strength. Two months after the battle the British ambassador in Washington still professed puzzlement. "That [Rodgers] could not discover at the distance of seventy or one hundred yards that the ship was a flush-deck sloop," he says, "though it was but a little after enght o'clock, on the 16th of May, . . . must appear unaccountable to the comprehension of every unprejudiced per-

47 *Ibid.*, VI, 28.

son."[48] This is the main point at issue in the documents. Adams eases us past it by confining our view of the action within Rodgers'.

After the three paragraphs in which he gives the American version of the battle, he returns to Rodgers' letter of May 23 with a striking paraphrase that serves as a denouement to the action and a summary of the argument. The *Little Belt* has been silenced in less than five minutes, and Rodgers, having stood by during the rest of the night, has sent a boat the following morning to find out what kind of ship he has fought.

Source:	History:
P.S. The Little Belt is a corvette, about the size of the John Adams, but, owing to her great length, her having a poop and top-gallants, forecastle, and room to mount three more guns of a side than she actually carries, her deep bulwark, and the manner of stowing her hammocks, she has the appearance of a frigate, and would always be taken for such from the view we had of her during the chase, as we never had a sight of her broadside until it was too dark to ascertain that she only carried one tier of guns.[49]	Then at last Rodgers learned, certainly to his great disappointment, that he had been fighting a single-decked vessel of less than half his force. His mistake was not so surprising as it seemed. The British cruiser might easily at a distance, or in the dark, be taken for a frigate. Her great length; her poop, top-gallants, forecastle; her deep bulwarks; the manner of stowing her hammocks; and room on each side to mount three more guns than she actually carried,— were decisive to any one who could see that she carried but one tier of guns.*[50]

Adams' use of Rodgers' postscript is an excellent example of his method in unsignaled paraphrases throughout the *History*. Letting the passage take the tone of his own detached and presumably omniscient judgment, he blends it smoothly into the *History*, thereby completing his account of the battle even as he sets in place the keystone of his argument. Because

[48] Foster to Monroe, 3 July 1811, in *State Papers, Foreign Relations*, III, 471.
[49] Rodgers to the Secretary of the Navy, 23 May 1811, *ibid.*, 498.
[50] *History*, VI, 30.

Rodgers did not discover the *Little Belt*'s real strength until the morning after the battle, or so goes the argument Adams has imbedded in his narrative, he was justified in demolishing her the night before. The whole episode funnels down to the type of specific detail Adams here borrows from Rodgers: the argument, organized to exculpate Rodgers, reaches its climax; and the narrative, organized to reveal gradually the *Little Belt*'s strength, comes to a close. Furthermore, Adams readies us to discredit the British captain's report before we see it and to dismiss it with the contempt he himself voices when he brings it forward. "The rest of his story," says Adams, "is to be told in his own words."[51] Most important, the whole series of paraphrases passes favorable judgment on Rodgers' character.

In conclusion, Adams' method of moving inside the point of view of men like Harrison and Rodgers seems to recall Parkman's method in *La Salle*. There, it will be remembered, Parkman tries to re-create the psychological experience of characters like La Salle, Tonty, Joutel, and Hennepin as vividly as possible. Yet Adams' aim is not so much to bring the experience of his characters to life as to judge their conduct. He remains basically detached from them as individuals, no matter how warmly he praises or blames them. Parkman, on the other hand, wants us to become personally involved with his heroes, since in that way he can better inspire us with their heroism. Adams' tone is cool, intellectual, professional; Parkman's warm, emotional, heroic. Overall, Adams' method of unsignaled paraphrasing less resembles Parkman's paraphrasing in *La Salle* than in *Montcalm and Wolfe*, which in turn resembles that found throughout Bancroft's *History*.

Yet with his signaled paraphrases Adams made an original contribution to the tradition. Like his quotations, they reflect a reawakened interest on his part, inspired by Ranke and Ranke's followers in the German historical school, in primary

[51] *Ibid.*

documents as the stuff of narrative history. When, more than a decade after finishing the *History*, he told Sarah Hewitt that the historian's task was "only to give a running commentary on the documents in order to explain their relation,"[52] he hinted at what seems to have been his major purpose in developing the technique of the signaled paraphrase. It was, like quotation, a way of letting the documents speak for themselves, though of course, as we have seen, the kind of detachment this implies remains in the *History* more an illusion than a reality. In Adams' *History*, documents are not simply clay to be manipulated for argumentative or literary effect, as they are in Bancroft's and Parkman's histories. They are instead almost synonymous with history itself.

Yet Adams' *History of the United States During the Administrations of Jefferson and Madison* is finally no less than Bancroft's *History* or Parkman's *France and England* a compromise between the historian's own style, point of view, and argument and those of the authors of his evidence. Like Bancroft and Parkman, Adams pulls together masses of individual documents into a unified narrative even as he echoes their wording. His method, despite its Rankean bias, is as free as theirs from the scissors-and-paste, plagiarist techniques of the eighteenth and early nineteenth centuries, and his determination to hammer stylistic and argumentative unity out of his sources is just as strong. Original though his signaled paraphrasing was, it called for the same kind of compromise between fidelity to and revision of source material as did unsignaled paraphrasing, whether Bancroftian, Parkmanian, or Adamsian in kind. Representing no radical break from the methods of Bancroft and Parkman, it does suggest the special kinds of flowering to which Adams' nine volumes brought their tradition.

[52] Henry Adams to Sarah Hewitt, 7 January 1904, in *Henry Adams and His Friends* (ed. by Harold D. Cater), 548.

★ ★ ★ ★ ★ ★

CHAPTER EIGHT

Conclusion

S OME sixty years after Bancroft published his first volume
in 1834, the tradition came to an end. Having hammered
out the publishing details of the *History* and seen the first few
of the nine volumes into print, Adams left for the South Seas
in the summer of 1890, never to return, figuratively speaking,
to the kind of conventional narrative history he had just completed. Six months later, Bancroft died. Parkman died on
November 8, 1893.

Many Americans since have written narrative histories
about their country, but none of them, it is probably safe to
say, has achieved the permanence of the works of these three
dedicated amateurs. The combination of factors which produced their books will almost surely never be duplicated in
this country. A popular interest in patriotic narrative history
—stimulated by intense regional and national self-conscious-
ness and by the historical prose and fiction of such writers as
Irving and Cooper—created for the three historians' works
an American audience which by the time Adams published
his *History* had largely disappeared, making him ruefully
aware of the difference between the sale of his books and those
of Bancroft and Parkman. The academization of serious history was only beginning by 1890, and the monographic, pro-

fessional historiography written mostly from within university departments of history which the twentieth century has produced lay in the future. Moreover, few serious historians since have enjoyed the kind of leisure, whether made possible by political preferment, as in Bancroft's case, or by independent incomes like Adams' and Parkman's, which allowed the three historians to work at their own pace, for their own reasons, on historical projects of entirely their own choosing. Most important, perhaps, each of the historians at the time he was writing had his field virtually to himself. Dozens of investigators had not gone through the published and unpublished materials they grandly paid thousands of their own dollars to collect. Colonial and revolutionary history "belonged" to Bancroft, Canadian history to Parkman, and the Jefferson-Madison era to Adams in a way that no period of American history ever again will belong to a single historian.

It is perhaps the very uniqueness of their artistic achievement and that of other nineteenth-century historians like them which explains why in recent years a number of American historians have urged their colleagues to open the windows of their profession and once again breathe the air of the morally engaged, consciously artful narrative history produced during the nineteenth century. Writes Arthur M. Schlesinger, Jr.: "Let historians recover their grand tradition —the tradition of history as art—and historians will once again speak with force and cogency to their societies and their times."[1] Equally insistent is Page Smith, who argues that "great history, the history that has commanded men's minds and hearts, has always been narrative history, history with a story to tell that illuminates the truth of the human situation, that lifts spirits and projects new potentialities."[2] To these and other calls like them for fresh attention to the kind of history Bancroft, Parkman, and Adams wrote, a number of

[1] "The Historian as Artist," *The Atlantic*, Vol. CCXXII (July, 1963), 41.
[2] *The Historian and History*, 142.

philosophers have added persuasive voices.[3] To call a history a work of literary art is still for some historians to damn it, yet the tide seems to have started running the other way. Bancroft, Parkman, and Adams are, it seems to me, the three greatest literary artists American historiography has produced, and it is inevitable that as American historians continue to rediscover the literary aspects of their craft, they will also rediscover these three giants.

Further, the basic moral theme Bancroft, Parkman, and Adams express—that extremes are dangerous and that social and political well-being lies in the center—remains the basic moral theme of American civilization. Through their volumes runs the belief that American democracy rests on a compromise between anarchy, which Bancroft associates chiefly with skepticism, materialism, and sensualism, Parkman with the wilderness, and Adams with radical Jeffersonian democracy, and despotism, for which the three find equivalents in the pre- and post-Renaissance forms of European autocracy. The extreme all see as most threatening to America is anarchy, and their works narrate three historical periods at the end of which the forces of unity and centralization defeat external challenges to the colonies or nation and serious internal threats of social and political fragmentation. Bancroft's *History*, Parkman's *France and England*, and Adams' *History* are constructed with major wars at their climax not simply because such an arrangement is artistically effective but because through war they can best dramatize the successful efforts of Americans to unify in a common cause.

Yet despite their bias in favor of centralization, they are

[3] The best of these recent philosophical studies are W. B. Gallie's *Philosophy and the Historical Understanding*, Morton White's *Foundations of Historical Knowledge*, Arthur C. Danto's *Analytical Philosophy of History*, and Haskell Fain's *Between Philosophy and History*. All four argue, in different ways, that history is not a science, as the twentieth-century logical positivists have claimed, but an art, to which telling a story well and judging its moral import responsibly are essential.

in agreement that America's tradition of individual freedom must not be sacrificed to the central power of the state. It is the spirit of compromise between extremes that they all imply is the chief strength of American civilization. Moderation, balance, a sense of what is practicable as well as honorable are qualities they look for in Americans and applaud whenever they find them. Yet they also imply that these qualities are desirable not only in Americans but in all men, and in this sense their histories unmistakably hint that the American compromise deserves to be imitated throughout the world. Individual men everywhere should learn to walk the narrow path between self-assertiveness and self-sacrifice which American democracy demands. To be independent, self-reliant, and self-motivating is admirable, yet one must not carry this personal liberty to the point of injuring others or oneself. Conversely, to be public spirited, cooperative, and willing to commit oneself to national rather than private ends is equally admirable, yet one must not fall prey to demagogues or those who challenge the freedom of the individual citizen. One must always obey the law yet be ready to reform its inequities.

Most Americans, I think, continue to share these moral assumptions. Though Bancroft, Parkman, and Adams did not, of course, invent them, in giving them potent expression they did what few artists in America have done better: to capture, in artistic form, the moral spirit of American life. To discover the inner springs of this life, one can hardly do better than to read their narratives.

Yet in addition to this consistency of theme, their works also reveal much of the intellectual history of nineteenth-century America. They not only reflect major changes in the religious, philosophical, and political thought of the century but probably helped bring these changes about. Religiously, they reveal a shift from the optimistic millennialism of the 1830's and 1840's to the secular agnosticism of the 1880's and 1890's. Philosophically, they move from Bancroft's intuitionalistic idealism to Adams' rationalistic pragmatism. Politically, they begin with a Jacksonian confidence in the democratic masses and end by expressing doubts about whether the masses will be able to fulfill the American dream. As we read from Bancroft to Adams we find, it seems to me, a maturing and toughening of intellectual fiber that parallels the intellectual coming of age of America during the course of the century.

This is not to suggest that I see Bancroft's religio-philosophical theories as being totally without merit. Far from it. Reflecting the tangle of pious and patriotic ideas of most Americans in the mid-nineteenth century, they evoked an astoundingly positive response from his readers, one far more flattering than that evoked by either Parkman or Adams. Yet while not without merit, Bancroft's metaphysics does seem to be naïve in many ways. Though hinting from time to time in the *History* that his faith in human nature has limits, Bancroft argues on the whole that because Americans are fundamentally idealistic and religious, they will continue to be leaders in fulfilling God's plan of a worldwide democratic brotherhood of man. Whatever his reservations as far as individuals are concerned, he argues as resolutely in his tenth as in his first volume that men in the mass infallibly express God's will. He presents the experience of English-speaking America between the founding of the colonies and the end of the War of Independence as proof of these axioms, and he sees in the Declaration of Independence and the other great documents of the newborn United States clear expression of the moral laws that govern the universe. Perception of these laws, he argues, depends not on reason but on religious intuition, and his only real fear for the future is that Americans may abandon the religiousness and idealism which ensures their success in favor of the empty materialism, skepticism, and rationalism of the Enlightenment. So long as the individual puts his faith in God and God's higher law, he need have no fear

211

of the political anarchy or tyranny that result from secularism, whether that of the medieval church or that of Locke. Though the impulses toward anarchy and tyranny are basic ingredients in man's nature, they will be reconciled in God's democratic plan for America and all mankind.

I find Parkman's rejection of most of Bancroft's philosophy refreshing, a sign that by the 1860's there had developed in the United States an audience for historical literature which no longer needed or wanted Bancroft's vast generalizations and oversimplifications. Much more a social environmentalist than Bancroft, Parkman argues that men are the product of unique cultures. Between the Indian and the white man, for instance, lies an impassable chasm of centuries of totally different social, religious, and political training. In Parkman's view, moreover, the forces controlling the universe are inscrutable and probably indifferent to man. They are the forces that produced the physical universe before man existed, and they seem for Parkman to be best represented in the aimless fecundity and destructiveness of the wilderness. He does not deny the possibility that a god exists; but he implies that we have no real knowledge of what the god is. Civilization, he argues, is man's effort to control nature externally in the physical world and internally in himself. It is not, as Bancroft claims, progress toward fulfillment of a divine plan, nor is it the result of a capacity for moral intuition shared by all. Mastery of external nature and mastery of self are the virtues Parkman celebrates in hero after hero in *France and England*. Moral excellence to him is not, as it is to Bancroft, inherent in all men but is instead won by individuals, often at great cost. If American democracy consistently encourages and produces this kind of excellence, he is for it; otherwise, he is not. Although he often expresses pessimism and doubt about America's future, he seems to find in the Anglo-American tradition of regulated liberty grounds for hope. Resting ultimately on

212

moderation, compromise, an almost classical sense of proportion and balance, his conception of excellence is consistent with what he sees as the basic morale of Anglo-American civilization. Though on the whole suspicious of its impulse toward acquisitiveness and democratic leveling, he applauds its impulse toward self-reliance, self-discipline, and self-sacrifice.

Though most will probably agree that the thrust of Parkman's thought is more sophisticated than Bancroft's, they may also find, as I do, that his peculiar ambivalence toward modern civilization and his uncompromising racial attitudes echo some of the most confused and debatable aspects of later nineteenth-century thought. Like Mark Twain, Parkman at once champions and deplores modern technological society, never establishing a tenable stand on this slippery issue. To conquer Nature, as La Salle did, is good, yet to create factories and urban populations is bad. To fly on the wings of "modern self-reliant enterprise" is good, yet to scar the wilderness with clearings for farms is bad. Nowhere does Parkman synthesize these attitudes or even seem conscious of the inconsistencies they produce in his work from time to time. The result is a subtle atmosphere of moral evasion, heightened occasionally by hints of almost adolescent escapism, of fantasizing about physical toughness and masculine prowess, that weakens all his books. In his harsh treatment of the Indian we see, I think, the clearest example of the dogmatic inflexibility such unresolved tensions in his thought and personality seem to have encouraged in him. His attack on the Indian is so obsessive as to suggest unacknowledged feelings of guilt or doubt about him. Similarly, his withering scorn for physical or moral weakness of any kind in his characters suggests he fears he himself is capable of physical or moral direlection. Parkman seems, like many Victorian writers, not always fully honest with himself intellectually or emotionally,

213

preferring to hide his doubts or confusions behind a mask of unshakable self-confidence even when, as in his response to modern civilization, he clearly contradicts himself.

In my judgment, Adams is the most profound and mature thinker of the three. In combining Bancroft's sense of a special mission for America and Parkman's environmentalistic agnosticism with a patriotism, pragmatic rationalism, and professionalism uniquely his own, he manages to blend what is most enduring in their thought into his own great achievement. Though he shares their anti-European, pro-American tone, their distaste for torpor and inactivity, and their interest in national character, he follows criteria for judging individual character that are more secular than Bancroft's and more relativistic than Parkman's. To him the rationale for patriotism rests not on divine providence or on a quasi-metaphysical ideal of heroism but on the hard realities of historical experience. In order to survive collectively as nations or singly as individuals, men must support the most comprehensive sovereignty which can enforce the rule of law among them. In a democracy this support is more voluntary than in autocratic, centralized forms of government, making the well-being and security of the state more dependent on the goodwill—and the political wisdom—of its individual members. Since a democracy, Adams argues, can only be as strong and stable as its parts, it requires the flexibility, reasonableness, and respect for expertise and professional competence among its masses which oligarchies and aristocracies develop only among an elite. Thus Adams' interest in character is different from Bancroft's or Parkman's. To Adams, character, individual or national, is not to be measured primarily in absolute terms of good and evil, right and wrong. It is rather to be measured in terms of ability to survive in the context of historical reality. Though he by no means completely abandons Bancroft's and Parkman's tendency to measure men against nonhistorical, universal moral standards, he puts far greater weight than they on the idea that what works and succeeds is good. In stressing pragmatic, relativistic moral standards, he gives the compromising, middle-of-the-road spirit implicit in Bancroft's *History* and Parkman's *France and England* its fullest expression. He also, it seems to me, leads us to the heart of the secular, relativistic world we inhabit today, without, however, indulging in the cynicism, despair, indifference, or escapism that have been such common responses in our own century to the state of affairs he predicts. Men can live without absolute knowledge, he says, yet still maintain dignity, courage, and purpose in the midst of a technological civilization. The fact that he published these ideas ten years before the twentieth century began further testifies to their extraordinary depth and prescience.

However illuminating the three historians' works are as far as the general spirit of American civilization and the particular history of its ideas in the nineteenth century are concerned, it is their methodology that may offer the most surprises to the modern reader. Reflecting the influence of the earlier annal-chronicle concept of historical writing as facts set in chronological order, they also to some extent embody the eighteenth-century concept of history as philosophy and the nineteenth-century idea that history should be not only dramatic and entertaining but scientifically accurate. Following the techniques but not the intention of the scissors-and-paste school of American historians who preceded them, Bancroft, Parkman, and Adams saturate their own prose with the language of source documents without sacrificing the consistency of their own tone or style. Out of the mass of fragmentary, often conflicting and poorly written documents before them, they create powerfully unified narratives. Thus their method also reflects compromise, in this case compromise between the point of view and phrasing of their sources and the intellectual and emotional unity they themselves impose on those sources. The compromise is evident on virtually every one of their pages: we can measure with a fair degree of precision, as has been indicated in the sampling of representative passages in the previous chapters of this study, its line-by-line working out in their prose. In effect, the method reverses the slavish plagiarism of scissors-and-paste editing, stressing instead the literary goals of imaginativeness and originality.

We can best understand and appreciate their strategy in all this, I think, if we picture all historians as being in a sense editors. As Haskell Fain has recently remarked,

the historian can be compared with an editor who must try to preserve an original story while seeking at the same time to increase its intelligibility. Unlike the editor who deals with a single author, however, the historian is confronted with a tale produced by many authors, often working at cross-purposes, each busy with his own activities.[4]

The writing of history is neither purely scientific nor purely artistic, to borrow the terms most often used in twentieth-century debate on the issue. It is rather, I think, a compromise between art and science that is editorial in nature. While it is true that in this editorial sense the historian certainly does not enjoy the artistic freedom of the poet, novelist, or playwright, it is also true that he enjoys much more freedom than the so-called scientific historians are normally willing to grant him. He is free to run virtually any kind of order he wants through the sources, so long as they support it, and to shape and arrange them in almost any way he wants. His only check —and here we come to the crux of the matter—is that his version, or edition, must be judged against the evidence itself. The question is always, "Do the sources justify the edition?" and never, "Does the edition justify the sources?" The sources are always self-justifying. They need no historian, in this sense, to approve them. Yet within this framework his freedom is complete. He may work inductively or deductively,

4 *Between Philosophy and History*, 261 f.

follow up hunches or intuitions of any kind, freely use his own values and beliefs in his account. If his version is a sound edition of the evidence he has studied and if the evidence itself is comprehensive enough for the purposes of his work, then he has surely written a valid—that is, truthful—history. Moreover, the artistic effectiveness of his work cannot be finally separated from its validity. Both validity and effectiveness must ultimately be judged in terms of the value of the work as an edition of the sources.

At their best, Bancroft, Parkman, and Adams wove key sources together in what they took to be the most accurate and meaningful edition of all the evidence they had studied. Though their method of adhering very closely to the actual language of the documents is merely one of many possible ways to edit narrative history, it reveals unusually well the editorial impulse that seems to me to be the distinguishing mark of all historiographical art. Achievement of a successful and enduring edition of the past implies that the historian has met his historical and literary obligations well. Furthermore, a successful history retains permanent historical as well as artistic interest. It offers us an edition, or version, of its sources that will stand the test of time. Though the discovery of new evidence has sometimes undercut the validity of classic narrative histories like those written by the three historians, normally such evidence has served not so much to challenge the integrity of existing narratives as to suggest new versions of the past that have a validity different from and not in competition with theirs. History is like a geological formation that can be mined on many levels. The strata mined by Bancroft, Parkman, and Adams were as productive as those now being and yet to be mined. The notion that new histories ought to supersede previous histories on the same subject seems to me to be unreasonable. Insofar as the three historians offer sound editions· of reasonably comprehensive bodies of evidence, their works should continue to command respect as history as well as art. Indeed, as this study has implied throughout, their art is at bottom indistinguishable from their truth.

Accordingly, I find the first volume of Bancroft's *History* more artful than those which followed, not in spite of but because of the fact it is more restrained, thematically and methodologically, than they. Its treatment of the evidence is more workmanlike and responsible, and it is just this sobriety of editorial method that gives it its strength. When in the later volumes Bancroft allows his striving for philosophical originality to overpower his sources, he seems to me to forfeit much of his art. His first volume is, of course, only one of the versions of American history before 1660 that might be written and is sometimes a questionable version at that; yet on the whole it is an admirable piece of work. The same is true of Parkman's best work in *France and England*. *La Salle* gives us a solid, often brilliant version of the evidence which, however incomplete it may seem if measured against theories about what it should have done, remains valuable, even definitive, for what it actually does do. There seems to be little need for another historian ever to narrate the wilderness experience of La Salle and his companions: Parkman has done it already, sensitively and thoroughly. Although other valuable narratives about La Salle have been and will be written, they will not be likely to diminish Parkman's achievement. Perhaps less successful, methodologically speaking, than *La Salle* is his *Montcalm and Wolfe*, based as it is on techniques of source assimilation that were not as congenial to him as the one-to-one reconstruction of eyewitness reports that he uses throughout the earlier work. But it, too, like Bancroft's first volume, offers much that will endure.

Yet neither Bancroft's *History* nor Parkman's *France and England* is as successful, I think, on methodological grounds, as Adams' *History*. Plainly, Adams was more sensitive than they to the pitfalls surrounding him as he transformed source documents into narrative history. His invention of the technique of signaled paraphrasing and his greater awareness of the relation between his own and the sources' voices in unsignaled paraphrases represents a significant methodological advance in the tradition. Yet Adams' superiority to Bancroft and Parkman as a historian cannot finally be accounted for so much by the methods he used as by his greater depth as a man. That he was generally more critical than they in using sources was because he was a more penetrating thinker and a more gifted artist. The superiority of his work, of course, is by no means total. Compared with the emotional sweep of Bancroft's narrative, his sometimes seems dry and over-sculpted, and neither he nor Bancroft ever achieved the psychological intensity of Parkman's voyages into the wilderness. While on balance I see Adams' history as the greatest and Bancroft's as the least of the three, I also think each historian achieved at least one kind of artistic success neither of the others can claim. Adams' was that his nine volumes communicate the richness, complexity, and maturity of thought and feeling that characterizes all great art and that is too often missing from even the best of Bancroft's and Parkman's books.

Yet Adams' masterpiece rests squarely on the foundations laid by Bancroft and Parkman. Without their volumes, his never could have been written. Each writer made his unique contribution to the tradition they together formed, a tradition cemented finally by their unanimous respect for what they saw as a unique spirit of compromise in America. In a broad thematic sense their works argue that at its best American civilization is a delicate balance between anarchy and tyranny, license and constraint, selfishness and selflessness. In a narrower, methodological sense they represent a fascinating attempt to apply this spirit to the writing of history—to arbitrate, that is, between the particularity of the source documents of early American history and the interpretive unity each writer tried to impose on that history. Their theme might be said to be *the* American compromise, their method *an* American compromise. In both respects, the thirty volumes stand at the heart of American historical literature and of American civilization.

★ ★ ★ ★ ★ ★

List of Works Cited

Manuscripts and Government Documents

American State Papers: Documents, Legislative and Executive, of the Congress of the United States. 38 vols. Washington, Gales & Seaton, 1832–61.

Annals of the Congress of the United States. 42 vols. Washington, Gales & Seaton, 1834–56.

The Documentary History of the State of New York. Ed. by E. B. O'Callaghan. 4 vols. Albany, Weed, Parsons, 1849–51.

Oard, R. J. "Bancroft and Hildreth: A Critical Evaluation." Ph.D. dissertation, St. Louis University, 1961.

Books and Pamphlets

Adams, Henry. *Essays in Anglo-Saxon Law.* Boston, Little, Brown, 1876.

———. *The Life of Albert Gallatin.* Philadelphia, Lippincott, 1880.

———. *John Randolph.* Boston, Houghton Mifflin, 1882.

———. *Mont-Saint-Michel and Chartres.* Boston, Houghton Mifflin, 1905.

———. *The Education of Henry Adams.* Boston, Houghton Mifflin, 1918.

———. *Letters of Henry Adams 1858–1891.* Ed. by Worthington C. Ford. Boston, Houghton Mifflin, 1930.

————. *Henry Adams and His Friends: A Collection of His Unpublished Letters.* Ed. by Harold D. Cater. Boston, Houghton Mifflin, 1947.

————. *History of the United States During the Administrations of Jefferson and Madison.* 9 vols. New York, Antiquarian Press, 1962.

————, ed. *Documents Relating to New England Federalism.* Boston, Little, Brown, 1877.

————. *The Writings of Albert Gallatin.* 3 vols. Philadelphia, Lippincott, 1879.

Adams, John Quincy. *Memoirs of John Quincy Adams.* Ed. by Charles Francis Adams. 12 vols. Philadelphia, Lippincott, 1874–77.

Bancroft, George. *History of the United States from the Discovery of the American Continent.* 10 vols. Boston, Little, Brown, 1834–75.

————. *Literary and Historical Miscellanies.* New York, Harper & Bros., 1855.

Bassett, John Spencer. *The Middle Group of American Historians.* Freeport, Books for Libraries Press, 1966.

Baym, Max I. *The French Education of Henry Adams.* New York, Columbia University Press, 1951.

Belknap, Jeremy. *American Biography.* 2 vols. Boston, I. Thomas & E. T. Andrews, 1794.

————. *The History of New Hampshire.* Ed. by James Farmer. Dover, Steven, Ela, & Wadleigh, 1831.

Brock, Isaac. *The Life and Correspondence of Major-General Sir Isaac Brock.* Ed. by F. B. Tupper. London, Simpkin, Marshall, 1847.

Callcott, George H. *History in the United States 1800–1860.* Baltimore, Johns Hopkins Press, 1970.

Chalmers, George. *Political Annals of the Present United Colonies.* London, printed for the author, 1780.

Collingwood, R. G. *The Idea of History.* New York, Oxford University Press, 1956.

Cunliffe, Marcus, and Robin W. Winks, eds. *Pastmasters: Some Essays on American Historians.* New York, Harper & Row, 1969.

List of Works Cited

Danto, Arthur C. *Analytical Philosophy of History*. London, Cambridge University Press, 1965.

Dawson, Moses. *A Historical Narrative of the Civil and Military Services of Major-General William H. Harrison*. Cincinnati, M. Dawson, 1824.

Delanglez, Jean. *Some La Salle Journeys*. Chicago, Institute of Jesuit History, 1938.

Donovan, Timothy P. *Henry Adams and Brooks Adams: The Education of Two American Historians*. Norman, University of Oklahoma Press, 1961.

Doughty, Howard. *Francis Parkman*. New York, Macmillan, 1962.

Fain, Haskell. *Between Philosophy and History: The Resurrection of Speculative Philosophy of History Within the Analytic Tradition*. Princeton, Princeton University Press, 1970.

Farnham, Charles H. *A Life of Francis Parkman*. Boston, Little, Brown, 1901.

Gallie, W. B. *Philosophy and the Historical Understanding*. New York, Schocken Books, 1964.

Gayarré, Charles. *History of Louisiana*. 4 vols. New York, Widdleton, 1866–67.

Gohdes, Clarence, ed. *Essays on American Literature in Honor of Jay B. Hubbell*. Durham, Duke University Press, 1967.

Grenville, George. *The Grenville Papers*. Ed. by William J. Smith. 4 vols. London, John Murray, 1852–53.

Haliburton, Thomas C. *An Historical and Statistical Account of Nova Scotia*. 2 vols. Halifax, Joseph Howe, 1829.

Hennepin, Louis. *A Description of Louisiana*. Tr. by John G. Shea. 2 vols. New York, J. G. Shea, 1881.

Hildreth, Richard. *The History of the United States*. 3 vols. New York, Harper & Bros., 1849.

Hochfield, George. *Henry Adams: An Introduction and Interpretation*. New York, Holt, Rinehart & Winston, 1962.

Hofstadter, Richard. *The Progressive Historians: Turner, Beard, Parrington*. New York, Knopf, 1968.

Holmes, Abiel. *The Annals of America*. 2 vols. Cambridge, Hilliard & Brown, 1829.

Hutchinson, Thomas. *The History of the Colony of Massachusetts Bay*. 3 vols. London, M. Richardson, 1765–1828.

Ingersoll, Charles J. *Historical Sketch of the 2nd War*. 2 vols. Philadelphia, Lea & Blanchard, 1845–49.

James, William. *A Full and Correct Account of the Chief Naval Occurrences of the Late War*. London, Egerton, 1817.

———. *A Full and Correct Account of the Military Occurrences of the Late War*. 2 vols. London, printed for the author, 1818.

Jefferson, Thomas. *The Writings of Thomas Jefferson*. Ed. by H. A. Washington. 9 vols. New York, H. W. Derby, 1861.

Jordy, William H. *Henry Adams: Scientific Historian*. New Haven, Yale University Press, 1952.

Lambert, John. *Travels through Canada and the United States*. 2 vols. London, Cradock & Joy, 1813.

Latour, A. LaCarrière. *Historical Memoir of the War in West Florida and Louisiana in 1814–15*. Philadelphia, John Conrad, 1816.

Lettres Édifiantes et Curieuses, Écrites des Missions Étrangères de la Compagnie de Jésus. Ed. by Y. M. M. T. de Querbeuf. 26 vols. Paris, Chez J. P. Merigot, 1780–83.

Levenson, J. C. *The Mind and Art of Henry Adams*. Boston, Houghton Mifflin, 1957.

Levin, David. *History as Romantic Art*. Stanford, Stanford University Press, 1959.

Lewis, Richard W. B. *The American Adam: Innocence, Tragedy, and Tradition in the Nineteenth Century*. Chicago, University of Chicago Press, 1955.

The Life of the Late Gen. William Eaton. Brookfield, E. Merriam, 1813.

Lyon, Melvin E. *Symbol and Idea in Henry Adams*. Lincoln, University of Nebraska Press, 1970.

McAffee, Robert B. *History of the Late War in the Western Country*. Ann Arbor, March of America Facsimile Series, 1966.

Marcus W. Jernegan Essays in American Historiography. Ed. by William T. Hutchinson. New York, Russell & Russell, 1958.

Margry, Pierre, ed. *Découvertes et Établissements des Français dans l'Ouest et dans le Sud de l'Amérique Septentrionale (1614–1754)*. 6 vols. Paris, D. Jouaust, 1876–86.

Martin, François-Xavier. *The History of North Carolina*. 2 vols. New Orleans, A. T. Penniman, 1829.

Mather, Cotton. *Magnalia Christi Americana: or, The Ecclesiastical History of New England.* 2 vols. Hartford, Silas Andrus, 1820.

Nash, Roderick. *Wilderness and the American Mind.* New Haven, Yale University Press, 1967.

Noble, David W. *Historians Against History: The Frontier Thesis and the National Covenant in American Historical Writing Since 1830.* Minneapolis, University of Minnesota Press, 1965.

Nye, Russell B. *George Bancroft: Brahmin Rebel.* New York, Knopf, 1944.

———. *George Bancroft.* Great American Thinkers Series. New York, Washington Square Press, 1964.

Parkman, Francis. *The Conspiracy of Pontiac and the Indian War after the Conquest of Canada.* 2 vols. Boston, Little, Brown, 1870.

———. *The Oregon Trail.* Boston, Little, Brown, 1892.

———. *Letters of Francis Parkman.* Ed. by Wilbur R. Jacobs. 2 vols. Norman, University of Oklahoma Press, 1960.

———. *France and England in North America.* Ed. by Allan Nevins. 9 vols. New York, Frederick Ungar, 1965.

Parton, James. *Life of Andrew Jackson.* 3 vols. Boston, Houghton Mifflin, 1887.

Pease, Otis. *Parkman's History: The Historian as Literary Artist.* New Haven, Yale University Press, 1953.

Pochmann, Henry A. *German Culture in America: Philosophical and Literary Influences, 1600–1900.* Madison, University of Wisconsin Press, 1957.

Pomeroy, Seth. *The Journals and Papers of Seth Pomeroy.* Ed. by Louis E. DeForest. New York, New York Society of Colonial Wars, 1926.

Prince, Thomas. *A Chronological History of New England.* Boston, Cummings, Hilliard, 1826.

Purchas, Samuel. *Purchas His Pilgrimes.* 4 vols. London, Henrie Fetherstone, 1625.

Samuels, Ernest. *Henry Adams: The Middle Years.* Cambridge, Harvard University Press, 1958.

Sargent, Winthrop. *The History of an Expedition Against Fort Duquesne in 1755.* Philadelphia, Historical Society of Pennsylvania, 1855.

Sedgwick, Henry D. *Francis Parkman*. Boston, Houghton Mifflin, 1904.

Shea, John G. *The Bursting of Pierre Margry's La Salle Bubble*. New York, T. B. Sidebotham, 1879.

Smith, Page. *The Historian and History*. New York, Knopf, 1964.

Smollett, Tobias. *The History of England*. 4 vols. London, Longman, Brown, Green & Longmans, 1848.

Somkin, Fred. *Unquiet Eagle: Memory and Desire in the Idea of American Freedom, 1815–1860*. Ithaca, Cornell University Press, 1967.

Sparks, Jared. *The Life of George Washington*. Boston, F. Andrews, 1839.

Tooke, Thomas. *A History of Prices from 1793 to 1837*. 2 vols. London, Longman, 1838.

Trumbull, Benjamin. *A Complete History of Connecticut*. 2 vols. New Haven, Maltby, Goldsmith, 1818.

Tuveson, Ernest. *Redeemer Nation: The Idea of America's Millennial Role*. Chicago, University of Chicago Press, 1968.

Washington, George. *The Journal of Major George Washington*. London, T. Jefferys, 1754.

Wasser, Henry. *The Scientific Thought of Henry Adams*. Thessaloniki, 1956.

White, Morton. *Foundations of Historical Knowledge*. New York, Harper & Row, 1965.

Williamson, Hugh. *The History of North Carolina*. 2 vols. Philadelphia, Thomas Dobson, 1812.

Williamson, William D. *The History of the State of Maine*. 2 vols. Hallowell, Glazier & Masters, 1832.

Winters, Yvor. *In Defense of Reason*. Denver, University of Denver Press, 1947.

Winthrop, John. *The History of New England from 1630 to 1649*. Ed. by James Savage. 2 vols. Boston, Phelps & Farnham, 1825.

Wright, Robert. *The Life of Major-General James Wolfe*. London, Chapman & Hall, 1864.

ARTICLES

"Bancroft's *History of the United States*," *North American Review*, Vol. LII (January–June, 1841), 75–103.

List of Works Cited

Burwick, F. L. "The Göttingen Influence on George Bancroft's Idea of Humanity," *Jahrbuch für Amerikastudien*, Vol. XI (1966), 194–212.

"Continuation of Bancroft's History," *North American Review*, Vol. LXXIV (1852), 507–15.

Eccles, W. J. "The History of New France According to Francis Parkman," *William and Mary Quarterly*, Vol. XVIII (1961), 163–75.

Everett, Edward. "Bancroft's History of the United States," *North American Review*, Vol. XL (January–April, 1835), 19–22.

Griffin, David E. " 'The Man for the Hour': A Defense of Francis Parkman's *Frontenac*," *New England Quarterly*, Vol. XLIII (1970), 605–20.

Jacobs, Wilbur R. "Some of Parkman's Literary Devices," *New England Quarterly*, Vol. XXXI (1958), 244–52.

Jennings, Francis P. "A Vanishing Indian: Parkman Versus His Sources," *Pennsylvania Magazine of History and Biography*, Vol. LXXXVII (1963), 306–23.

Lewis, Merrill. "Organic Metaphor and Edenic Myth in George Bancroft's History of the United States," *Journal of the History of Ideas*, Vol. XXVI (1965), 587–92.

Peterson, Merrill D. "Henry Adams on Jefferson the President," *Virginia Quarterly Review*, Vol. XXXIX (1963), 187–201.

Rathbun, J. W. "George Bancroft on Man and History," *Transactions of the Wisconsin Academy of Sciences, Arts, and Letters*, Vol. XLIII (1954), 49–72.

Ripley, George. "Bancroft," *Putnam's Monthly Magazine*, Vol. I (1853), 300–308.

Schlesinger, Arthur M., Jr. "The Historian as Artist," *The Atlantic*, Vol. CCXXII (July, 1963), 35–41.

Shaw, Peter. "Blood is Thicker than Irony: Henry Adams's History," *New England Quarterly*, Vol. XL (1967), 163–87.

Taylor, William R. "A Journey into the Human Mind: Motivation in Francis Parkman's *La Salle*," *William and Mary Quarterly*, Vol. XIX (1962), 220–37.

Index

Index

Index

The paper on which this book is printed bears the watermark of the University of Oklahoma Press and has an effective life of at least three hundred years.